Sport Marketing:
Managing the Exchange Process

SPORT MARKETING:
MANAGING THE EXCHANGE PROCESS

George R. Milne, Ph.D.
Associate Professor
University of Massachusetts
Amherst, Massachusetts

Mark A. McDonald, Ph.D.
Assistant Professor
University of Massachusetts
Amherst, Massachusetts

JONES AND BARTLETT PUBLISHERS
Sudbury, Massachusetts
BOSTON   TORONTO   LONDON   SINGAPORE

World Headquarters
Jones and Bartlett Publishers
40 Tall Pine Drive
Sudbury, MA 01776
978-443-5000
info@jbpub.com
www.jbpub.com

Jones and Bartlett Publishers Canada
P.O. Box 19020
Toronto, ON M5S 1X1
CANADA

Jones and Bartlett Publishers International
Barb House, Barb Mews
London W6 7PA
UK

Acquisitions Editor: Paul Shepardson
Production Editor: Lianne B. Ames
Manufacturing Buyer: Therese Bräuer
Design: Modern Graphics
Editorial Production Service: Modern Graphics
Typesetting: Modern Graphics
Cover Design: Dick Hannus
Printing and Binding: Courier
Cover Printing: Courier

Library of Congress Cataloging-in-Publication Data

Milne, George R.
    Sport marketing : managing the exchange process / by George R. Milne and Mark A. McDonald.
        p.   cm.
    Includes bibliographical references (p.).
    ISBN 0–7637–0873–9
    1. Sports--United States--Marketing.   2. Sports--United States--Management.   3. Sports--Economic aspects--United States.
I. McDonald, Mark A.   II. title.
GV716.M55   1998
796'.06'98--dc21   98–40345
                                                                        CIP

Cover Image   © Bob Daemmrich/Stock Boston Inc./PNI

Printed in the United States
05 04 03   10 9 8 7 6 5 4 3 2

While most of this book represents original unpublished research, portions of some chapters have been adapted from research appearing in academic journals. Much of the second half of Chapter 2 on fan identification was previously published by the *Sport Marketing Quarterly*. The conceptual framework of Chapter 4, "Evaluating the Impact of Winning and Brand Management," was published in 1998 by the *Journal of Sport Management*. Portions of Chapter 6, "Managing Niche Markets," were also previously published in the *Sport Marketing Quarterly* and the *Journal of Sport Management*. Research presented in Chapter 8, "Measuring Service Quality," was part of Mark McDonald's dissertation, "Service Quality and Customer Lifetime Value in Professional Sport Franchises."

To Susan, Patrick, and Courtney
for your generosity, love, and understanding during the incredible summer of 1997.
I look forward to supporting each of you as you embark on your adventures.

—George Milne

To my beautiful wife Sharon
and two wonderful children, Benjamin and Kelsey.

—Mark McDonald

Contents

Preface

Sport is a growing and rapidly evolving industry. As such, managers need increasingly sophisticated approaches to evaluate and serve their markets. *Sport Marketing: Managing the Exchange Process* presents cutting edge conceptual and empirical approaches for managers to manage relationships with consumers. The central theme of the book is the sport marketing exchange process. We have chosen to focus on exchange since this process is fundamental to marketing and can be used to highlight the challenges and opportunities faced by the sport marketer.

Our reason for writing this book was to challenge students, researchers, and managers in sport marketing to embrace current marketing tools that are being employed by marketers in other industry sectors. In this book we discuss and illustrate several recent marketing techniques within the sport con-

text. We contribute to the knowledge of sport marketing by developing numerous conceptual frameworks and models that tap into the unique aspects of sport. The empirical results demonstrate how to conduct these types of studies. In addition, the empirical studies present informative, generalizable findings about sport consumers.

This book is unique because of the collection of topics on the discipline of sport marketing. These topics include fan identification, measuring participant and spectator motivations, brand equity, databases, niche marketing, four new segmentation approaches, service quality, sport sponsorship personality matching, and Internet marketing. In each of the book's ten chapters, we illustrate how these approaches can help sport marketers be more effective in managing their relationships with consumers.

Acknowledgments

The two authors would like to acknowledge the following people and organizations who have been instrumental in the completion of this book. To Bill Sutton for his encouragement. Thanks to Mike Musante for coauthoring Chapter 9 on sport sponsorship personality matching. Also we thank Jay Gladden, Andrew Rohm, Mark Samperi, Sara Gooding-Williams, Susan Milne, Greg Putnam, Karen Parker, and Sharon McDonald for their advice and research assistance on different aspects of this book. In addition, we thank the four reviewers for their helpful suggestions for improving the manuscript.

James M. Gladden, Ph.D.
Assistant Professor of Sport Management
University of Massachusetts
Amherst, MA

Brenda G. Pitts, Ph.D.
Associate Professor of Physical Education
Florida State University
Tallahassee, FL

Matthew J. Robinson, Ph.D.
Assistant Professor of Sport Management
Allentown College of St. Francis de Sales
Center Valley, PA

Terese Stratta, Ph.D.
Assistant Professor of Kinesiology and Health
Georgia State University
Atlanta, GA

Several organizations helped fund or support the research for several of the chapters. First, thanks to the University of Massachusetts for a $5,000 internal faculty grant that helped support the sport consumer survey used in Chapters 2, 3, and 6. George Milne would like to acknowledge the University of Massachusetts School of Management for summer research financial support. We would like to thank Claritas, Inc., for geocoding our zipcode data in Chapter 7. Lastly, thanks goes out to the Orlando Magic for allowing us to survey season ticket holders. Two years of data from their members was essential to the completion of Chapter 8.

As with all major undertakings, many people were crucial to the publishing of this book. Without naming all who have provided assistance, we would like to say thank you.

Sport Marketing:
Managing the Exchange Process

CHAPTER 1

Reframing the Sport Marketing Exchange Process

Introduction

Today the sport industry is advancing on many fronts. The rapid adoption of technology, the creation of new consumption opportunities, the forging of innovative partnerships with corporations, the development of modern sport facilities, and the opening of new markets are all propelling this industry to new levels of popularity. Unfortunately, sport marketing practitioners and academicians are not keeping pace. While understanding "sport" is still necessary to play the game, it is no longer sufficient to guarantee victory in an increasingly competitive marketplace. Sport can no longer remain the sole domain of traditional sport researchers. What is needed is the addition of cutting-edge marketing concepts from business schools, along with a clear understanding of the uniqueness of sport from sport management. These two worlds are colliding, and it is imperative that new perspectives and tools be created to better understand this complex and rapidly changing industry.

This book attempts to blend the marketing and sport management perspectives. Throughout, we will highlight the unique aspects of the sport experience and interject advances from business literature to provide tools and frameworks with which to better understand the sport marketing exchange process. The goal is to advance both the understanding of and the ability to positively influence the sport marketing exchange process.

In Chapter 2 we will examine the relationship of sport fans to sport teams. Because sport is emotion laden, consumers have a tendency to form close, long-lasting bonds with sport organizations. A wide range of motivations determines the benefits consumers desire from the sports they participate in or watch. In Chapter 3, we will address questions such as

- What types of psychological needs are satisfied by the consumption of various sport products?
- What motivations divert individual consumers away from other entertainment options and toward sport participation and spectatorship?
- How are motivations for sport participation and sport spectatorship similar or different?

- What factors can be used to explain and predict consumption decisions and behavior?

Consumers have particular expectations that greatly influence the exchange process. For a sports team, consumers have an expectation for their team to win; at a minimum, they want their team to be competitive. For the marketer, this expectation is hard to manage, yet if victory is delivered, it pays off. In Chapter 4 we will investigate the question of what winning is worth. In that chapter we will also present evidence of how a victorious season pays off in terms of gate receipts, merchandise sales, and overall franchise value. Still, controlling the outcome of any particular athletic contest is impossible. Thus, marketers need to focus their attention on seeing that consumers' expectations are fulfilled on various service dimensions.

In Chapter 5 we will also present a methodology for measuring the relationship strength of a sport customer, as well as an approach for calculating the lifetime value or individual worth of a customer. This helps marketers deal with their heterogeneous customer base. The power of a database is in recording how customers are different. The key for a marketer is to use it to react differently to a committed fan versus a casual fan.

Although sport is pervasive, a marketer still faces the challenge of heterogeneous markets. Consumers have many different sport options. As such, it is important for sport marketers to understand which sporting options are competing for customers' attention. In Chapter 6 we will present a new methodology called *niche analysis*, which allows marketers to define their customer base and find which sports are competing for their audience. Besides dealing with internal customers and understanding competition, sport managers are always trying to understand markets and find groups of potential new customers. Chapter 7 will present four different segmentation approaches that sport managers can use for these purposes.

The most fundamental challenge facing the sport marketer is the unpredictability of the core product. Since winning and losing cannot be directly controlled, this makes controlling service quality even more important. Chapter 8 will expand upon the difficulties of measuring service quality and examine the gap between expectations and perceptions for various lifetime value segments. In Chapter 9 we will present a new methodology for linking brands and sponsorship opportunities. Through a series of studies, we document the development of a personality scale and demonstrate its usefulness in assessing the match between sporting events and sponsors.

Finally, in Chapter 10 we will look to the future of sport marketing. We see the Internet (or World Wide Web) as a key facilitator in creating communities with common interests in sport. Often web sites are maintained by external stakeholders, which helps influence a sport marketer's relationship with consumers. We will use ESPN's Sportszone, a website created by the ESPN cable television channel, as an example of one such virtual community that enables teams, leagues, and retailers to reach their target audiences.

Overview of Sport Marketing

One functional area under the sport management umbrella is sport marketing. A number of definitions of sport marketing have been developed in the literature (Mullin, Hardy, and Sutton, 1993; Parkhouse, 1996; Pitts and Stotlar, 1996). Although all of these definitions broadly describe sport marketing, the Mullin, Hardy, and Sutton definition (1993), which explicitly mentions the consumer exchange process, best reflects the focus of this book:

> [A]ll activities designed to meet the needs and wants of sport consumers through exchange processes. Sport marketing has developed two major thrusts: the marketing of sport products and services directly to consumers of sport, and the marketing of other consumer and industrial products or services through the use of sport promotions (p. 6).

Several aspects of this definition warrant elaboration. First, sport consumers can be divided into two markets—sport spectators and sport participants. Sport spectators are event attendees, television viewers, radio listeners, and press readers (Brooks, 1994). Sport participants, as the label indicates, are those who play sports. Spectator and participant markets are distinct in that different needs are being satisfied through participation and spectatorship with different delivery systems being utilized to facilitate the exchange process. Improving health and fitness, experiencing a sense of achievement, building self-esteem, developing motor skills, and managing stress are all central to sport participation. Delivery systems for participant sports include health and fitness clubs, high schools, colleges, and special events (such as road races and basketball tournaments). In contrast, some of the needs satisfied through following sport are entertainment, belonging, and sociability needs, with the latter addressed by providing opportunities to interact freely without commitment (Melnick, 1993). The options to follow sport—attendance, television, radio, and the press—give rise to a myriad of delivery systems. These range from the oldest and most traditional (stadiums and arenas) to newer delivery systems such as DirectTV and the Internet.

Another aspect of sport marketing that merits further explanation is the distinction between marketing *of* sport and marketing *through* sport. "Marketing of sport" refers to producing and marketing goods and services directly to end-users—sport spectators and participants. In contrast, marketing through sport involves corporations affiliating with spectator and participant sport to reach their own consumers (Mullin, 1985). Affiliation in this context includes advertising, sponsorship, athlete endorsements, and the use of luxury seating to entertain clients. The sport product, therefore, can either be classified as a consumer good (marketing of sport) or an industrial good (marketing through sport).

Applying the Marketing Concept

Whether sport is being marketed as a consumer good or as an industrial good, it is crucial to understand and properly apply the marketing concept. According to Kotler (1997): "The marketing concept holds that the key to achieving organizational goals consists of being more effective than competitors in integrating marketing activities toward determining and satisfying the needs and wants of target markets"

(p. 19). Marketing is focused on satisfying the needs of customers. Success in this endeavor requires developing an understanding of who sport consumers are and what factors influence their consumption behaviors.

Each sport attracts a distinct type of consumer. People who watch auto racing on television have a different profile than those who play golf. Identifying the various types of people who are attracted to certain sport products and services is referred to as *segmentation*. "Market segmentation" means creating specific groups of customers or potential customers based on similar characteristics. Four bases of segmentation have traditionally been used to segment sport consumers:

1. benefits derived,
2. product usage rate (e.g., light, medium, heavy),
3. demographics (e.g., age, income, education, gender, marital status), and,
4. psychographics (e.g., lifestyles, opinions, and interests).

Beyond segmenting customers on these characteristics and targeting specific markets, the sport marketer is concerned with the exchange process. The exchange process involves satisfying consumers' sport needs by offering valued products and services. Sport marketers need to manage the exchange process so that they add value for consumers. Unfortunately, creating value for customers within sport is easier said than done. Unique aspects of sport products and services present interesting challenges to sport marketers.

For example, sport differs from other forms of entertainment in that it evokes high levels of emotional attachment. Consumers identify closely with sport teams and even begin to define themselves via these organizations (Mael and Ashforth, 1992). Escalating player salaries, franchise relocation, and player mobility, however, threaten the special relationship between fans and sport teams by creating psychological (or real) distance. Sport marketers are challenged to better manage those elements under their direct influence, such as product extensions and customer service, in order to maintain consumer identification.

Although people are becoming disconnected as a result of changing lifestyles and technological innovations (Putnam, 1995), sport has the opposite effect. Through promoting communication and providing common symbols, sport fosters a sense of community and helps build a collective identity (Lever, 1983). Although creating and strengthening relationships with individual consumers is a key marketing challenge in most industries (Peppers and Rogers, 1993), this is compounded in sport by the need to communicate effectively with entire communities. The challenge to sport marketers is converting community relations from an add-on function to a core mission. The power of athletes, combined with the increasing power of coaches, further complicates this situation. Clearly, the high levels of fan identification and community involvement induced by sport can support the marketing function. Because these are complex issues, sport marketers need conceptual models to help them develop appropriate long-term strategies.

The nature of the sport product presents additional challenges for sport marketers. A sport product can be tangible, such as basketball or athletic apparel. It can also be intangible, such as satisfying a need for entertainment or providing an environment for socializing. Different people are looking for different things from the sport product, with purchases often based on intangibles, such as emotion and image, rather than on easily identifiable and comparable attributes like price and delivery time. For instance, athletic footwear appears to be a very tangible product. However, one person may buy athletic footwear solely for performance features, while another buys it because he identifies with the athlete who endorses the sneaker, and a third person purchases it to make a fashion statement.

Since the needs consumers are satisfying through sport are varied and often difficult to predict, the sport product is more elusive than most realize. Marketing the sport product becomes more complicated when you consider that it is marketed to two distinct markets, spectators and participants, and that sport can also be utilized by sponsoring corporations as an industrial product.

All of these factors combine to create an endless array of research questions to be studied by academicians from business schools and sport management departments. Research in sport management, however, has largely focused on physical education and athletic programs, with very few studies of support companies, multisport organizations, or firms that promote their products through sport. Additionally, this research has failed to integrate theories and concepts from management and marketing literature (Slack, 1996). Although researchers from business schools have conducted research within the sport industry, they often have been more interested in using the sport industry context to test existing theories and methodologies than in developing new theories and conceptual frameworks that address the unique aspects of the sport product.

The remainder of this chapter will introduce the sport marketing exchange-process framework we will use to organize the subsequent chapters of this text.

The Sport Marketing Exchange Process

Figure 1–1 outlines our view of the sport marketing exchange process. This conceptual framework serves as the organizing structure of this book. We have chosen to focus on exchange because this process is fundamental to marketing and can be used to highlight the challenges and opportunities faced by the sport marketer.

The focal point of the model is the exchange between consumers and the sport marketer. Consumers desire particular benefits from their consumption of sport, whether it is participant or spectator based. These desired benefits are determined by consumers' motivations and their expectations of the sport marketer. Sport marketers, in turn, create a delivery system to help satisfy consumers' needs. Depending upon the particular sport market being served (participant or spectator), the delivery systems can fluctuate widely—from large, 100,000-seat stadiums, broadcast programs, and clubs and resorts, to retail and direct mail, among others.

With the exception of the sale of sports equipment and apparel, sport marketers offer services with features that are inconsistent, intangible, perishable, and often coproduced with the consumer. This exchange process, as noted in Figure 1–1, is

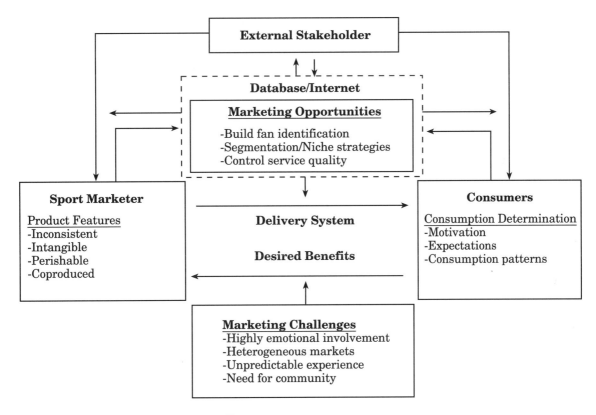

FIGURE 1–1. The Sport Exchange Process

influenced by marketing challenges that are relatively unique to the sport context. Marketers have to deliver a product (service performance) to emotional fans with numerous motivations. Furthermore, the product they offer is unpredictable. Additionally, with the particular nature of sport, the marketer has to try to promote a sense of community in which the consumer can belong.

At the same time, this model also shows that the exchange process includes marketing opportunities for the sport marketer. The marketer, using database and Internet tools, can help build fan identification, understand the various consumer segments, and control service quality. Finally, the model indicates that external stakeholders, including corporate sponsors and the media (in their attempts to use sport in their marketing and business endeavors) have a profound effect on the sport marketer–consumer exchange process.

Consumers

For all marketing organizations, the consumer is the most important element. By understanding the consumer, sport managers, merchandisers, television network producers, advertisers, and corporate sponsors can attract sport consumers and increase the consumption of sport-related products and services. Developing an understanding of who sport consumers are and what factors influence their consumption behaviors, therefore, is critical to reaching these goals.

Sport Marketers and Their Products

Many sport marketers are service providers or at least have a large service component as part of their market offering whether they run a ski resort, health club, baseball team, or sport news network. For example, when attending a sporting event, consumers usually take nothing away other than impressions and memories. This service component, coupled with an inability to directly control the core product (team performance), provides a great challenge and opportunity for sport managers to influence customer satisfaction through the provision of high-quality service. Given that service quality is important to professional sport consumers, how can it be accurately measured? The measurement of quality for services is more difficult than it is for physical goods because of the unique characteristics of the product—inconsistent, intangible, perishable, and coproduced. The primary evaluative model that has been applied in both academic research and consulting efforts is the Gap Model of Service Quality. In Chapter 8, we will demonstrate how the Gap Model of Service Quality can be applied to the sport industry.

The exchange between consumers and the sport marketer ideally results in a gain for both sides. The sport marketer gains a profit, while the consumer gains value. For the consumer, value is the difference between what the consumer perceives he/she has received from the marketer above and beyond the consumer's initial expectations. We show how the Gap Model can be used to assess the value received by various consumer groups.

Marketing Challenges and Opportunities

The sport marketing exchange process is moderated by particular challenges that are more pronounced in the sport world. Every challenge, however, is accompanied by opportunity. In this book we will present several new concepts and methodologies that can be used by sport marketers to convert challenges into opportunities.

The emerging tools of database and Internet marketing can help facilitate the development and maintenance of close relationships with consumers. Because of the importance of business trends, we will discuss database marketing and Internet marketing development in Chapters 5 and 10, respectively. The database allows the marketer to communicate on a one-to-one basis. Such communication can be useful for helping build fan identification. Similarly, league and team web sites can be instrumental in strengthening a fan's emotional bond with a team and in allowing the fan to connect with the wider sports community.

External Stakeholders

Although much of the sport marketing literature focuses on the marketing *of* sport, marketing *through* sport continues to be big business. Many corporations are sponsoring sporting events as a way to identifying with sport and improving their image through this association. Sport sponsorship has grown at a rapid pace: corporate sponsorship was reported to be $2.3 billion in 1989 and grew to $9.6 billion in 1993. As the stakes have increased, so has the need for corporations to find the correct fit with sponsors.

Summary

Sport is developing at a rapid rate and it is growing increasingly imperative that academic research strive to match this pace. The unique aspects of the sport product, coupled with changing technology and increased corporate involvement and consumption options, are creating new challenges for sport marketers. These challenges, however, can only be met through the combined resources and perspectives of sport management and business school academicians. This book, in many ways, reflects an effort to combine these perspectives to create conceptual frameworks and managerial tools to assist sport marketers in their efforts to manage the tremendous changes sweeping through this exciting industry.

References

Brooks, C. (1994). *Sports marketing: Competitive strategies for sports*. Englewood Cliffs, NJ: Prentice-Hall.
Kotler, P. (1997). *Marketing management: Analysis, planning, implementation, and control*, 9th ed. Upper Saddle River, NJ: Prentice-Hall.
Lever, J. (1983). *Soccer madness*. Chicago, IL: University of Chicago Press.

Mael, F., and B. E. Ashforth (1992). Alumni and their alma mater: A partial test of the reformulated model of organizational identification. *Journal of Organizational Behavior*, 13: 103–123.

Melnick, M. J. (1993). Searching for sociability in the stands: A theory of sports spectating. *Journal of Sport Management*, 7: 44–60.

Mullin, B. (1985). Characteristics of sport marketing. In G. Lewis and H. Appenzeller (eds.). *Successful sport management*, Charlottesville, VA: Michie. pp. 101–123.

Mullin, B., S. Hardy, and W. A. Sutton (1993). *Sport marketing*. Champaign, IL: Human Kinetics.

Parkhouse, B. (1996). *The management of sport: Its foundation and application,* 2nd ed. St. Louis, MO: Mosby-Yearbook, Inc.

Peppers, D., and M. Rogers (1993). *The one-to-one future: Building relationships one customer at a time*. New York: Doubleday/Currency.

Pitts, B. G., and D. K. Stotlar (1996). *Fundamentals of sport marketing*. Morgantown, WV: Fitness Information Technology, Inc.

Putnam, R. D. (1995). Bowling alone: America's declining social capital. *Journal of Democracy*, 6(1): 65–78.

Slack, T. (1996). From the locker room to the board room: Changing the domain of sport management. *Journal of Sport Management*, 10: 97–105.

Fan Identification

Introduction

This chapter focuses on fans and their relationships with sport teams. As discussed in Chapter 1, sport is emotion laden, and consumers have a tendency to form close, long-lasting bonds with sport organizations. Appropriately, we begin this chapter by examining the characteristics of sport fans. In doing so, we discuss the results of our national study, which defines and contrasts the background of behaviors of different levels of fans. From a sport marketing perspective, it is critical to understand how fans become and remain identified with a particular team. Thus, in the second part of this chapter, we discuss the conditions that create and foster the identification between a sport team and its fan base. Lastly, the chapter outlines specific steps a sport organization can take to nurture and develop fan identification.

Profile of the Sport Fan

Profiling the sport fan is not straightforward. "Fandom" varies by sport and, in overall intensity, by individual. Nonetheless, over the years several studies have attempted to provide a portrait of the sport fan. Simmons Market Research, for example, annu-ally offers rich demographic and media-habits pro-files of consumers in their *Sports and Leisure* report. However, most of the syndicated research like Sim-mons focuses on general sport consumer profiles and does not focus on fans per se. Perhaps the study that came closest to profiling the sport fan was the *Miller Lite Report* conducted in 1986. This report calculated a "Sportfan Index" based on frequency of watching, listening, reading, or talking about sport.

In this section, we report the results of a study we conducted in 1995 that attempted to build a sportsfan index similar to that of the 1986 Miller Lite study. Our study is based on 1367 complete responses from a national mail survey of sport enthusiasts (see Chapter 3 for more detail). As part of this survey, we asked a set of questions similar to those in the Miller Lite survey. Specifically, we included nine questions regarding the frequency with which individuals watched, listened, read, or talked about sport. Addi-tionally, we inquired about their purchases of sport products and services. Response options measured the frequency of these fan behaviors, i.e., every day or almost every day, about once or twice a week, about once or twice a month, less than once a month, and never. For each question, respondents were as-signed a score ranging from 4 to 0 based on these frequency levels. A total score, across all nine ques-tions, was calculated providing a possible range from 36 to 0. Fan segments of roughly equal size were

TABLE 2-1. Percent respondents doing following activity every day or almost every day

Activity	Fan segments			
	Total	Low	Medium	High
Watch or listen to sports news on TV or radio	72.1	42.7	76.8	94.7
Read the sports pages of your newspaper	65.3	32.9	72.6	88.2
Talk about sports with your friends	38.3	6.1	33.1	74.4
Watch sport events on television	30.2	5.6	21.1	63.5
Listen to sports on radio	10.3	0.5	4.3	26.2
Read magazines on sports and athletes	6.1	0.0	1.2	17.2
Read books on sports and athletes	3.7	0.0	0.6	10.5

TABLE 2-2. Demographic profile of fan segments

	Fan segments			
	Total	Low	Medium	High
N	1367	426	492	449
Gender (%)				
Males	75.5	61.8	78.9	85.0
Females	24.5	38.2	21.1	15.0
Highest education level (%)				
Did not graduate high school	2.7	2.8	2.1	3.4
High school graduate	21.5	23.1	22.2	19.1
Attended college	29.8	31.4	29.3	28.8
Graduated college	31.4	28.6	32.2	33.3
Graduate school	14.6	14.0	14.3	15.1
Age (%)				
18–34	27.3	24.3	28.1	29.4
35–44	19.6	18.2	17.4	23.5
45–54	19.0	18.4	19.0	19.6
55–64	16.5	17.2	18.8	13.3
65 and over	17.5	21.9	16.7	14.2
Level of athletics played (%)				
Professional	3.1	2.7	1.2	5.5
Semi-professional	11.7	6.3	8.5	18.8
Intercollegiate athletics	33.0	23.2	31.2	42.1
Intramural/recreational	62.2	67.7	59.6	60.4
High school athletics	74.5	74.6	77.4	74.1
Never played organized athletics	16.3	28.5	13.9	6.4

Note: Percentages may not add to 100% due to rounding.

then formed. *Low-level fans* were individuals who had a score of 0–17; *medium-level fans* had a score of 18–22, and *high–level fans* had a score of 23–36.

Table 2–1 shows how the resulting segments vary on seven of these activities. The table reports the percentage of the fan segment that either watched, listened to, read, or talked sport every day or almost every day. By definition, the high-level fans were more likely to do these activities than the medium- or low-level fans. Still, it is interesting to note the wide differences in activities across the fan segments. In terms of reading or watching sports news every day, high-level fans are more than twice as likely to do so compared to low-level fans. Remarkably, high-level fans are over twelve times as likely to talk sports with friends and over eleven times as likely to watch sport events on television every day than are low-level fans. Interestingly, high-level fans are more than twice as likely as medium-level fans to talk about sports every day with their friends.

The demographic profile of the three fan segments is depicted in Table 2–2. The data show that the fan level varied by gender. Males were disproportionately more likely to be medium- and high-level fans. For example, while the total number of respondents answering these questions included 75.5%

males, 85% of the high-level fans were males. In contrast, females were disproportionately more likely to be classified as low-level fans; females represented 24.5% of total respondents, yet they comprised 38.2% of the low-level fan segment.

Interestingly, our study showed that the level of interest in sport does not vary much by educational level. Education has the potential to create highly vested fans, however, because these individuals are more likely to do more reading in general, which may translate to reading more about sport.

Other research, such as the *Miller Lite Report*, found that the sport fan level decreased with age. Our study also supports this finding. The data in Table 2–2 indicate that people over the age of 55 are less likely to be included in the high-fan level than the low and medium levels.

TABLE 2–3. Reported interest in sports by fan segments

	Fan segments		
	Low	Medium	High
Interest as a participant (1 = low, 7 = high)	2.7	3.4	3.9
Interest as a spectator (1 = low, 7 = high)	3.3	4.1	4.5

In addition to the standard demographics, Table 2–2 also reports the percentage of respondents who participated in sport at various levels. There appears to be a strong positive relationship between having played sport and being a high-level fan. Individuals who have played sport, and in particular those who played at higher levels of competition, are more likely to be high-level fans than others. For example, the one-third of respondents (33%) who played intercollegiate athletics are overrepresented in the high fan segment (42.1%).

Our sample of sport fans is diverse regarding their overall interest in sports. In general, the sample was more interested in spectating than in participation. As shown in Table 2–3, individuals in the higher fan segments were more interested in both participation and spectatorship than individuals in the low fan segment.

As part of the survey, we had respondents evaluate 40 participant sports and 25 spectator sports as to whether the sport was a favorite of theirs. A five-point scale was used, anchored by 1 = "not one of your favorites" and 5 = "one of your favorites." In addition, respondents also indicated how important it was for them to participate in and to watch sport. For both participating and spectating, respondents answered 16 questions. The objective of each question was to determine what motivates individuals to play or watch sports. Responses included such options as for the "enjoyment of the game" and "sport competition." A seven-point scale was used, anchored by 1 = "extremely unimportant" and 7 = "extremely important." The fan segments were then profiled by participation and spectatorship interests, intensity, and motivations.

Interest in and motivations for participation varied significantly across segments. Table 2–4 reveals the top five participation activities and the top five motivations for participation by fan segment. The extent to which each sport was a favorite, or each motivation was important, is indicated in the table by

TABLE 2–4. Sport participation profile by fan segment

	Fan segments		
	Low	Medium	High
Favorite Participation Activities [a]	1. Swimming (3.1) 2. Bicycle Riding (3.0) 3. Golf (2.9) 4. Fishing (2.9) 5. Basketball (2.8)	1. Golf (3.5) 2. Basketball (3.4) 3. Baseball (3.3) 4. Swimming (3.2) 5. Softball (3.2)	1. Basketball (3.7) 2. Golf (3.5) 3. Softball (3.5) 4. Football (3.4) 5. Baseball (3.4)
Motivations to Participate [b]	1. Enjoyment of game (5.5) 2. Relaxation (4.9) 3. Improved health and fitness (4.8) 4. Thrill of victory (4.8) 5. Skill mastery (4.7)	1. Enjoyment of game (5.8) 2. Thrill of victory (5.3) 3. Relaxation (5.2) 4. Improved health and fitness (5.2) 5. Sense of personal pride (5.1)	1. Enjoyment of game (6.2) 2. Thrill of victory (5.7) 3. Sense of personal pride (5.5) 4. Sport competition (5.5) 5. Relaxation (5.5)

[a] Numbers in parentheses based on a 5-point scale where 1 = not one of your favorites and 5 = one of your favorites
[b] Numbers in parentheses based on a 7-point scale where 1 = extremely not important and 7 = extremely important

TABLE 2–5. Sport spectating profile by fan segment

	Fan segments		
	Low	**Medium**	**High**
Favorite Spectating Events [a]	1. Pro football (3.8) 2. College football (3.3) 3. College basketball (2.9) 4. Pro baseball (2.9) 5. Pro basketball (2.9) 6. Golf (2.6)	1. Pro football (4.3) 2. College football (4.0) 3. College basketball (3.5) 4. Pro baseball (3.5) 5. Pro basketball (3.3) 6. Golf (3.1)	1. Pro football (4.5) 2. College football (4.2) 3. College basketball (3.9) 4. Pro baseball (3.7) 5. Pro basketball (3.6) 6. Golf (3.2)
Motivations to Spectate [b]	1. Enjoyment of game (5.8) 2. Sport competition (5.1) 3. Thrill of victory (5.0) 4. Beauty of game (4.8) 5. Relaxation (4.4)	1. Enjoyment of game (6.1) 2. Thrill of victory (5.6) 3. Sport competition (5.5) 4. Beauty of game (4.9) 5. Relaxation (4.7)	1. Enjoyment of game (6.2) 2. Thrill of victory (5.7) 3. Sport competition (5.6) 4. Beauty of game (5.1) 5. Relaxation (4.9)

[a] Numbers in parentheses based on a 5-point scale where 1 = not one of your favorites and 5 = one of your favorites

[b] Numbers in parentheses based on a 7-point scale where 1 = extremely not important and 7 = extremely important

the numbers in parentheses. In general, the absolute magnitude of rating increased with fan level. Perhaps more interesting was that the types of sport considered top favorites and the motivations for participating varied substantially by segment. High-level fans exhibited many more competitive tendencies than the low-level fans. Although all segments stated "enjoyment of the game" as the highest motivation, high-level fans also rated "sense of personal pride" and "sport competition" much higher than low-level fans. In contrast, low-level fans were more interested in "relaxation" and "improved health and fitness" as motivations for their participation.

For sport spectating, there is surprising similarity in the top six events watched by segment. Pro and college football, pro and college basketball, pro baseball, and golf were seen as favorites by each group in Table 2–5. Still, the high-level fans rated each of these sports more favorably. Curiously, the motivations for spectating are also similar across fan segments. "Enjoyment of the game," "thrill of victory," "sport competition," "beauty of the game," and "relaxation" were all seen as important motivators by all segments.

While the patterns of spectating are similar across type of fans, the intensity of consumption var-

TABLE 2–6. Spectating intensity by fan segments

	% Watch sport			% Watch 1–2 times per week in season		
	Low	**Medium**	**High**	**Low**	**Medium**	**High**
Pro football	82.5	92.4	95.4	51.6	76.2	84.3
College football	70.6	89.0	93.2	31.0	54.8	69.8
College basketball	56.6	76.2	86.0	18.6	37.5	54.8
Pro baseball	70.6	84.2	87.5	23.3	39.3	51.9
Pro basketball	64.3	81.0	88.7	19.5	33.3	51.5
Golf	46.5	66.0	67.9	14.4	24.1	29.1

ies considerably. Table 2–6 shows, for the top six spectator sports, the percentage of each fan segment that watches a sport and the percentage of each fan segment that watches the sports at least one to two times a week when the sport is in season. Large differences in spectating frequency are shown among groups.

The results of this survey show that high-level fans consume more sport than other levels of fans—whether by reading, listening, watching, or talking about sports. High-level sport fans tend to be more aggressive and prefer higher levels of participation in more rigorous sports. The high-level fan is likely to be male and young. The key differentiating variable is intensity. In terms of spectating frequency, high-level fans spend much more time watching sport than other fan segments. The question remains: How does a sport organization focus this intensity of interest on its team? We discuss this in the next section.

The Importance of Fan Identification

As shown in Table 2–6, fans, especially high-level fans, tend to follow a number of sports simultaneously. One management challenge is to make the sport fan highly identified with a particular organization. Fan identification is defined as the personal commitment and emotional involvement customers have with a sport organization. When a consumer identifies closely with an organization, a sense of connectedness ensues and he or she begins to identify with the organization (Mael and Ashforth, 1992). Sport differs from other sources of entertainment by its evocation of high levels of emotional attachment and identification.

Because the marketing and communication functions of a sports team cannot directly influence on-field success, fan identification has an important function in minimizing the effects of team performance on long-term fiscal success and position in the sport entertainment hierarchy. For example, the Boston Red Sox, have not won the World Series since

1918. Failure to win the championship, however, has not stopped fans from vigorously supporting the team by attending games and watching games on NESN, a regional sports television channel offering coverage of the Red Sox throughout New England.

Although people in the United States are becoming disconnected from a sense of community as a result of changing lifestyles, societal interests, and technological innovations (Putnam, 1995), this does not hold true for spectator sports. Spectator sports foster a sense of community by promoting communication, involving people jointly, and providing common symbols, a collective identity, and a reason for solidarity (Lever, 1983). Noting the effect that sports has upon a community, former L.A. Lakers and Hall of Fame basketball star Kareem Abdul-Jabbar stated, "Our collective success has forged some kind of unity in this huge and fragmented metropolis, and it cuts across class and cultural lines" (Fox, 1994, p. 89).

In recent years, franchise movement, or the threat of such movement, has galvanized fan identification into not only a social force but also a political and judicial force. The recent move of the NFL's Cleveland franchise to Baltimore (where they operate as the Ravens) demonstrates the depth of fan identification. At the time of the move, the Browns had ranked among the top five teams in the NFL in terms of attendance for 12 of the previous 20 years. When Art Modell, the owner of the Browns, announced he was moving the team to Baltimore, the community mobilized into a cohesive entity with a mission to retain its beloved franchise. Advertisers responded by pulling their advertising from Cleveland Stadium; the city received a preliminary injunction against the relocation; and at least nine independent lawsuits were filed by Browns' season ticket holders and fan groups against Modell and the Browns (Rushin, 1995). Fans described the Browns as part of the history of their families and referred to Modell as a murderer for killing their memories and future. Fan identification with the Browns was so established that the *Browns Backers* included over 63,000 members located in 200 chapters throughout the United States, the United Kingdom, and Japan. Despite the history, tradition, and support of the city

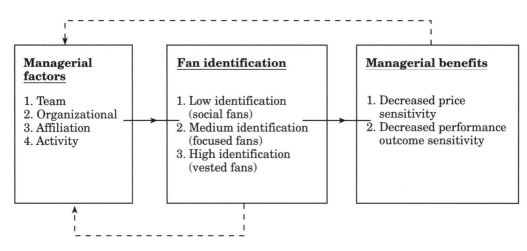

FIGURE 2-1. A Model of Fan Identification

of Cleveland, Art Modell was given permission to move his franchise to Baltimore for the 1997 season. However, in a negotiated settlement, the city of Cleveland retained the colors and nickname "Browns" and will be awarded an NFL expansion team when the city constructs a new facility (Rushin, 1995).

During the same year, the Oilers, after 35 years in Houston, announced they were planning to move to Nashville, Tennessee. Support days were planned, protests scheduled, and lawsuits contemplated in response to the potential relocation. But in contrast to the Cleveland Browns situation, fan interest and support were lacking, indicative of a lack of fan identification with the franchise. As a result, the Oilers will be moving to Nashville by the year 2000. While fan identification is clearly a powerful social and market force, there are no guarantees that it will develop for every team.

A Model for Fan Identification

What factors increase levels of fan identification? What are the benefits of having highly identified fans? Social identification researchers believe that the level of identification with an organization depends on such factors as satisfaction with the organization, the reputation of the organization, frequency of contact, and the visibility of affiliation (Bhattacharya, Rao, and Glynn, 1995). Member identification can be related to three broad factors:

1. organizational and product characteristics,
2. affiliation characteristics,
3. activity characteristics.

Organizational and product characteristics relate to members' perceptions of the focal organization and its offerings—specifically, the perceived prestige of the focal organization and satisfaction with the membership benefits. Affiliation characteristics refer to the characteristics of a person's membership, such as length of membership, visibility of membership, and the number of other similar organizations patronized. Activity characteristics refer to behavior patterns such as level of contact with the organization and donation of money to the focal organization (Bhattacharya, Rao, and Glynn, 1995).

Figure 2–1 depicts a conceptual model of fan identification in which managerial factors influence the level of fan identification, which then results in managerial benefits. This process is a closed system where managerial factors are influenced by feedback loops from fan identification and managerial benefits. The feedback loops can produce ever higher levels of fan identification. This section examines each part of the model in depth and concludes by outlining strategies for increasing fan identification and association.

As modeled in Figure 2–1, the level of fan identification with a sport organization (team) is directly impacted by four managerial factors:

1. team characteristics,
2. organizational characteristics,
3. affiliation characteristics,
4. activity characteristics.

Each of these factors contributes to the attraction and, ultimately, the identification a fan has for a sports team. Fan identification can be divided into three discernible levels:

1. low identification (social fans),
2. medium identification (focused fans),
3. high identification (vested fans).

Fan identification, in turn, leads to two notable managerial benefits:

1. decreased price sensitivity,
2. decreased performance outcome sensitivity.

Levels of Fan Identification

Fanatics, by Webster's definition, are exaggeratedly zealous for a belief or a cause. In the case of sport fans, this belief or cause is the team they support. Not all fans, however, have the same level of fervor, devotion, and commitment to their favorite team. We suggest that there are three discernible levels of fan identification, with certain key characteristics associated with each level.

Low Identification (Social Fans) have a relatively passive long-term relationship with the sport—low on emotion, low on financial commitment, low on involvement—but a definite relationship exists nonetheless. Fans characterized as low in identification may be attracted purely by the entertainment value of the product. Initially, these fans do not have an emotional attachment to a team or a particular sporting event, but rather are attracted to the sport for its pleasure and stress-relieving qualities or for

the opportunities for social interaction within the community.

Fans with this level of identification are thus followers of "sport entertainment" and not necessarily the team. For these fans, the outcome of the sporting event is less important than the overall quality of the entertainment opportunity provided. A "tailgating party," post-game concert, picnic at the ballpark, or enjoyment of social interaction with fellow attendees might be the most important aspect of the sport entertainment experience. It should also be noted that this initial attraction to a sport for its entertainment value or opportunities for social interaction can lead to greater identification with the team. It could represent the introductory phase of a relationship that could grow and lead to a higher level of involvement, including meeting players, attending a team function such as a team preview or draft party, or purchasing a season ticket plan.

Medium Identification (Focused Fans) have an association with a sport or team that is based upon some attributes or elements found to be attractive. In many cases, this level of identification may be based upon fad, social factors, team performance, or player personality. Fans attracted to the achievement-seeking aspect of sport tend to project many of the qualities of the strongly identified fan. Although the achievement-seeking fan will make significant personal and financial investments for their team, the behavior is directly correlated to team performance and therefore may only be short-term in nature.

These fans may also be attracted to the "big event." Examples of this attraction include the purchase of baseball season tickets to guarantee the right to All-Star game tickets or the purchase of football season tickets for Purdue University to ensure a ticket for the Notre Dame game. It is at the time of the big event when the greatest short-term emotional attachment to a team is displayed. A common behavior of achievement-seeking fans is the wearing of team apparel, which signifies the positive association between them and the team. These types of involvement with the team may lead to a greater level of identification or may follow the fate of fads and die out. Factors such as poor team performance and having a favorite player traded could end the relationship.

High Identification (Vested Fans) have the strongest, most loyal, and longest-term relationships a fan can have with a sport or team. This relationship is indicative of a heavy financial and emotional investment. A strongly identified fan can feel an emotional ownership in the sport team. They often refer to the entity as "we" and recruit other fans. Most importantly, according to Pooley (1978): "The intensity of these fans' interest often leads to devoting parts of each day to their team or sport in general."

The fan with a strong identification is a "team" follower. While they will be attracted to the sport itself, their loyalty to their team, just like their loyalty to their community, is unwavering and long term. Fans who view the team as an extension of their community have a strong emotional attachment to the team. The success of the team reflects personally upon individual fans, and it also reflects upon the collective identity of the community. For example, a lawsuit was filed in Cleveland, Ohio to retain ownership of the names and trademarks associated with the Cleveland Browns and Browns (Rushin, 1995).

In 1993, Wann and Branscombe found that individuals high in identification with a sports team were more involved with the team. This involvement translated into a greater number of years as a fan, greater attendance at both home and away games, and higher propensity for future attendance-related behaviors. Highly identified fans were willing to invest greater amounts of money and time in their attempts to follow their team. James Michener (1976) interviewed Russel Swanson, a Nebraska football fan, who noted:

> Fans in other states think that football fever strikes the nation from late summer to midwinter, but in Nebraska we follow it longer. We expect news coverage from August practice through the fall season, including bowl practice in December and the bowl game in January. The balance of January and February are ugh. We look at the line-ups in March, follow spring practice in April and attend the spring Red-

White squad game in May. Somehow we manage through June, but pro football with some former Big Red players starts in July, which carries us back to August practice" (p. 276).

Managerial Factors

Fan identification with sport organizations is impacted by four factors under the direct influence of managers. By manipulating these factors, managers can incrementally increase levels of fan identification with their teams.

Team Characteristics

Successful teams attract fans who desire the positive association to be reflected upon them. In many cases, this results in "jumping on the band wagon" and embracing teams such as the Atlanta Braves, San Francisco 49'ers, Chicago Bulls, and Dallas Cowboys, who have been very successful and popular. Also worth noting is that fans of a team, described as "affiliated others," can attract the achievement-seeking fan. If a team is perceived to attract a socially desirable fan base, other fans will seek to associate themselves with the team to gain stature in the eyes of their peers and to enhance their feelings of personal worth.

Team support groups such as the Baltimore *Orioles Designated Hitters*, who function as unpaid sales personnel and team ambassadors to help promote the club, are excellent examples of associations that can enhance team image and help build prestige. As noted, for many fans team affiliation may be short term and heavily dependent upon team performance. As a means of protecting their image, fans may avoid associations with a team when performance falters.

Examining professional team sports' apparel purchases reveals similar findings. The merchandise sales of championship teams consistently outrank those of the competition. Merchandise sales for the National Basketball Association's Houston Rockets, for example, increased 397% after their 1994 NBA Championship season (NBA Properties, 1995). People associate themselves in terms of interest, appearance, speech, and behavior with winning sports teams to enhance their image and inflate their self-esteem.

Organizational Characteristics

Organizational characteristics differ from team characteristics in that they encompass the "off-field" image of ownership, decision making, and tradition of the franchise. For example, recent criticism of the Browns' move to Baltimore was directed at the organization and not the team. Organizational characteristics also include the reputation and prestige of the franchise and the league/conference in which the team competes. All of these characteristics can contribute to fan identification. Teams do not exist and thrive in isolation. Fans tend to identify with teams which play in competitive divisions with well-developed rivalries.

An organization's reputation depends on a history of on-field success, constant commitment to excellence from team ownership, and a record of dealing with the surrounding community with integrity. Commitment to excellence is reflected by continuously striving to bring in top coaches/managers and a willingness to invest financial resources to acquire available free agents. Strong community relations and forthright and honest negotiations with community representatives regarding stadium leases and capital improvements (new or enhanced facilities) all reflect high levels of organizational integrity.

Affiliation Characteristics

Community affiliation is the most significant correlate of fan identification. This component is instrumental in building fan identification and consequently has the strongest long-term effects. Community affiliation is defined as the kinship, bond, or connection the fan has with a team. It is derived from common symbols, shared goals, history, and a fan's need to belong. The expression of these ties links the team to the community and provides an identity for the team that is inseparable from the community. As an embodiment of this bond, a fan's affinity for his/her community is associated and extended to the team. This association, or "BIRG" (Basking in Reflective Glory), phenomenon, was found to manifest itself in a number of ways by Cialdini et al. in their 1976 study of college students. In this study, students used the pronoun *we* to describe a team victory while using the pronoun *they* to describe a team's defeat. It was also discovered that the wearing of school-related apparel increased after team victories.

The community affiliation component is comprised of an individual's "need to belong." As friendship research suggests, individuals seek a sense of belonging and an opportunity for communication and interaction. A sports team provides the individual with an attachment to a larger community with similar interests and goals, functioning much like a fraternal organization. Proprietary research, conducted through focus groups for the Orlando Magic, reveals that ticket holders form relationships with other season ticket holders in their seating section to exchange tickets during the season and often socialize at activities after the season with their "new friends" (Audience Analysts, 1993).

Activity Characteristics

While event attendance can lead to increased involvement, so can the exposure received via electronic and print media coverage and programming. Access to tickets, combined with available broadcast coverage, provides fans exposure opportunities at varying levels of financial commitment.

As technology has evolved, particularly in the media area, fans have increased opportunities to become more identified with players and teams. National and regional twenty-four-hour sport networks, Internet home pages, radio call-in shows, pay-per-view television, and print media devoted exclusively to particular teams have all provided the fan unparalleled access to sport. For example, a cable television subscriber in Western Massachusetts has access to three twenty-four-hour sport channels (ESPN, Sport Channel America, and the New England Sports Network [NESN]) plus sports coverage through WTBS (Atlanta) as well as limited sports offerings available through USA Network, The Nashville Network, and the over-the-air networks (ABC, CBS, NBC, and FOX). In addition, the subscriber also has access to pay-per-view sporting events throughout the year.

The convenience and affordability of satellite programming now offers the fan the opportunity to follow his/her favorite team regardless of geographic location. All of the major professional leagues—the

National Football League (NFL), the National Basketball Association (NBA), the National Hockey League (NHL), and Major League Baseball (MLB)—have created DirectTV packages for this purpose.

Managerial Benefits

The four factors described in the preceding paragraphs lead to the establishment of fan identity and are essential in preserving and expanding the levels and types of expression associated with it. From a managerial perspective, fan identity produces two beneficial outcomes, decreased price sensitivity and decreased performance outcome sensitivity.

Decreased Price Sensitivity

The relative price inelasticity among sports fans is demonstrated annually for each sport franchise or organization. In spite of ever-increasing ticket prices, sport teams continue to attract fans in record numbers. Entering their respective 1994–95 seasons, the average ticket prices for the major sports in the United States were as follows:

	1994	1995	1996
National Basketball Association	$27.12	$31.56	$34.08
National Football League	$31.05	$33.52	$35.74
National Hockey League	$33.66	$34.75	$38.34
Major League Baseball	$10.45	$10.55	$11.19

(Team Marketing Report, 1994–1996)

This price insensitivity has also manifested itself in several other forms of financial commitment. Fans who are plan holders often must pay for their tickets as much as six months in advance. This willingness to pay in advance has not been lost on astute sport marketers, such as Max Muhleman of Charlotte, North Carolina-based Muhleman and Associates, who created the concept of personal seat licenses (PSL) for the Charlotte Panthers of the National Football League. Modeled after priority seating systems, which are prevalent in college sports, PSLs are advance payments by the fan merely to reserve the right to purchase a ticket. This right can be permanent or, in the case of the NFL's Oakland Raiders, can be for a fixed term, such as 20 years.

Decreased Performance Outcome Sensitivity

As fan identification and involvement increases, the less likely the fan's behaviors will be impacted by team performance. It has been over 70 years since the Red Sox won the World Series, yet attendance (percentage of capacity) consistently ranks among the highest in the league. This is largely due to "vesting," a process in which a ticket holder's seat location is improved on an annual basis to the point that it would be foolish to lose the prime location that the fan has "earned" as a result of renewing the tickets. Other sport teams are in the process of developing benefit packages, similar to frequent flyer/buyer programs, based upon the accumulation of points. This type of program essentially rewards a fan for continued involvement and investment in the team.

Strategies for Increasing Fan Identification

While sport marketers cannot control sport history and rules, nor team composition and team performance, there are a number of available strategies to increase fan identification.

Team/Player Accessibility

Fan access to the team and its players will result in greater fan identification. Player appearances, autograph sessions, and grass-roots events such as fan festivals, pep rallies, and youth clinics are all methods of increasing the team's exposure in the community. In the NBA, for example, most teams host their own "Draft Party" in conjunction with the annual NBA draft in June. These events feature current and past players as well as team personnel, who interact with the fans in attendance throughout the evening, helping build a sense of community.

Community Relations

The community relations efforts of professional sports teams and their players play a significant role in building fan identification. Adding credibility to these activities is that they usually take place on the community's own "turf." Community relations programs can include any or all of the following: fundraising events, such as social cause projects, and involvement with literacy or reading programs at elementary schools, drug education programs, and programs designed to develop youth leadership abilities.

Philanthropic efforts reinforce the team's position in the community and reflect positively on the team as well as its fans. Individual player community relations are also important. When he was with the Orlando Magic, Shaquille O'Neal sponsored a very successful annual *Shaqsgiving* celebration. It should be noted, however, that in order to maximize the impact on fan identification, proactive media campaigns are necessary to communicate the goodwill efforts of the team and its players.

Team's History and Tradition

The evocation of childhood memories can elicit positive memories, emotions, associations, and loyalties. Additionally, the reinforcement of the team's history will serve to increase the connection between the team, the community, and the fans. A team's history communicates that being a fan spans not only seasons but generations.

Common vehicles to reinforce history and tradition include "turn back the clock" games in which both competing teams wear replica uniforms of past teams to commemorate their success and history; old-timers games and events, which provide the heroes of the past with an opportunity to meet their past fans and for the current fans to meet the legends of the game; retiring uniform numbers; contests to select all-time teams; and fantasy camps, which provide active fans a chance to play with and against their heroes.

Affiliation Opportunities

Teams need to communicate that fans are "part of the team" and that this is "their team" and that "we" compete together as a unit. Establishing fan clubs, creating newsletters, and organizing trips to away games are all methods of promoting affiliation and participation. For example, the San Diego Pa-

dres have initiated *The Compadres Club*, a program that rewards fans for their attendance by use of a bar-coded membership card (Sutton and Johnson, 1997). Additionally, marketing communications can reinforce the positive attributes of the fan group. Fans want to be associated with others who share their enthusiasm, and if the followers of a team are perceived in a positive way, more fans will be attracted to the fan group and, in turn, to the team.

Challenges to Development of Fan Identification

Labor disputes in the National Hockey League and Major League Baseball have dramatically impacted fans. Franchise relocations, increasing player mobility, escalating salaries, and, in some instances, negative perceptions of athlete behavior are detrimental to the fostering of fan identification. The concepts set forth in this chapter can be part of a long-term-relationship building process that leverages the unique personal involvement characteristic of sport in order to withstand forces conspiring to damage the relationship.

References

Audience Analysts (1993). *Orlando Magic season ticket holder report. Unpublished Consulting Report.* Amherst, MA.

Bhattacharya, C. B., H. Rao, and M. A. Glynn (1995). Understanding the bond of identification: An investigation of its correlates among art museum members. *Journal of Marketing*, 59: 46–57.

Cialdini, R. B., R. J. Borden, R. J. Thorne, M. R. Walker, S. Freeman, and L. R. Sloan (1976). Basking in reflected glory: Three football field studies. *Journal of Personality and Social Psychology*, 34: 366–375.

Fox, S. (1994). *Big leagues*. New York: Morrow.

Lever, J. (1983). *Soccer Madness*. Chicago, IL: University of Chicago Press.

Mael, F., and B. E. Ashforth (1992). Alumni and their alma mater: A partial test of the reformulated model of organizational identification. *Journal of Organizational Behavior*, 13: 103–23.

Michener, J. A. (1976). *Sports in America*. New York: Random House.

Mullin, B., S. Hardy, and W. A. Sutton (1993). *Sport marketing*. Champaign, IL: Human Kinetics.

NBA Properties (1995). Personal Correspondence.

Pooley, J. C. (1978). *The sports fan: A psychology of misbehavior.* Calgary, Alberta: CAPHER Sociology of Sports Monograph Series.

Putnam, R. D. (1995). Bowling alone: America's declining social capital. *Journal of Democracy,* 6 (1): 65–78.

Rooney, J. F., Jr. (1974). *The geography of American sport.* Reading, MA: Addison-Wesley Publishers.

Rushin, S. (1995, Dec. 4). The Heart of a city: Cleveland won round 1 in what will be an agonizing battle to hold on to its beloved Browns. *Sports Illustrated,* 84 (23): 58–70.

Sutton, W. A., and D. Johnson (1997). Interview with Don Johnson, Vice President of Marketing, San Diego Padres. *Sport Marketing Quarterly,* 6 (2): 5–8. Morgantown, WV: Fitness Information Technology, Inc.

Team Marketing Report (1994–1996). Chicago, IL: TMR Publishing.

Wann, D. L., and N. R. Branscombe (1993). Sports fans: Measuring degree of identification with their team. *International Journal of Sport Psychology,* 24: 1–17.

Motivations of the Sport Consumer

Introduction

A casual survey of media outlets will show that sport pervades much of our daily lives and is firmly embedded in contemporary culture and marketing campaigns. Nike and its "Just Do It" theme, star athlete celebrity endorsers, college and professional sport advertisements, promotion of the Olympics, and the myriad of specialized sport television networks and publications are all examples of highly visible sport marketing efforts. Underlying this flurry of activity is a need for sport managers, merchandisers, television network producers, advertisers, and corporate sponsors to attract sport consumers and increase their consumption of sport-related products. Critical to reaching this goal is developing an understanding of who sport consumers are and what factors influence their consumption behaviors.

Although there has been a great deal of proprietary and unpublished market research in the sport marketing field, academic marketing research has not focused on the motivations of sport consumers. Rather, much of the extant research has addressed the issue of sport demand. The four primary categories of demand-based research include

1. Studies on the effects of economic factors such as ticket price, per capita income, substitute forms of entertainment, television, and the effects of other sport local attractions on spectator activities;

2. Studies of the relation between sociodemographic factors such as population, geography, and sport consumer activities;

3. Studies of the effects of factors such as promotions and special events, star players, team placement in the standings, and closeness of the pennant race upon the attractiveness of attending a sports event to consumers; and,

4. Residual preference studies that examine the effects of scheduling games, fan accommodation, new stadia, accessibility, and weather upon consumer behavior (Hansen and Gauthier, 1989).

Unfortunately, much of the empirical research concerning sport marketing shares the common characteristics of using secondary data, examining factors largely out of the marketer's control, and attempting to predict behavior in the aggregate rather than at the individual level (Assimakopoulos, 1993). Further, the research does not address many critical questions of interest to both market researchers and sport organizations:

- What types of psychological needs are satisfied by the consumption of sport products?

- What motivations divert individual consumers away from other entertainment options and toward sport participation and spectatorship?
- How are motivations for sport participation and sport spectatorship similar or different?
- What factors can be used to explain and predict consumption decisions and behavior? (Barrett and Zeiss, 1980)

The field of sport marketing is now at a critical point of development. More study is needed to develop a theory of sport consumption. A recent symposium at the North American Society for Sport Management (NASSM) conference stressed the need to develop better measures of sport consumption behavior (Howard, Madrigal, and Kahle, 1994). This book is an effort to answer this call for research. The goals of this chapter are to (1) start to integrate existing knowledge concerning motivational constructs used to explain sport participation and spectatorship into a unified conceptual framework; and then (2) use these theoretically based constructs to develop typologies for both spectating and participant markets.

We will begin by reviewing the relevant literature on sport motivation and by defining key constructs. Following standard scale development procedures, we will arrive at a final set of items to measure our constructs of interest. Next, based on responses from a national survey sent to sport enthusiasts, we will create sport motivation typologies for spectators and participants. The typologies show that motivations help explain the differences among sport enthusiasts in sport behavior, attitude, and background characteristics.

A Review of Sport Motivation Constructs

There are several motivational theories that are relevant to the analysis of participant and fan behavior in sport marketing. Sloan (1985) categorized these theories as follows:

- salubrious effects theories,
- stress and stimulation-seeking theories,

- catharsis and aggression theories,
- entertainment theories, and,
- achievement-seeking theories.

Salubrious effects theories suggest that involvement in sport is motivated by pleasure and increased physical and mental well-being. Stress and stimulation-seeking theories propose that when levels of risk, stress, and arousal fall below desired levels, organisms will seek opportunities to increase arousal intensity. Catharsis and aggression theories suggest that participation in, or being a spectator of, aggressive acts will result in either a reduction of aggression levels or, alternatively, increased levels of aggression. Entertainment theories are concerned with attractions to sport based on the aesthetic and moral representations derived from the meaning of the sports event. Lastly, achievement-seeking theories propose that individuals fulfill their needs for achievement through athletic competition (Sloan, 1985).

While numerous theoretical formulations concerning independent motivational factors for sport consumption exist, quantifiable research on these motivations is fragmented and inconclusive. As a result, there is little consensus on the boundaries and domains of such theories. Interestingly, most of the motivation literature has focused on sport participation. However, Sloan's (1985) review of sport motivation literature suggested that motivational factors traditionally used to explain sport participation could also be applied to sport spectatorship. Sloan (1985) also argued that motivations differ from situation to situation and from sport to sport.

Rather than focusing on a single theory based on minimal empirical support, we have chosen to focus instead on broad motivational constructs. Thus, in an effort to build a theory of sport participation and spectatorship, we will examine various constructs to enhance our understanding of these activities. To gain a broad perspective and organize the numerous constructs that have been used in sport, we have organized our literature review around Abraham Maslow's (1943,1968) human needs hierarchy. This framework proposes that there are five categories of human needs that account for much

TABLE 3–1. Sport motivation construct positions within Maslow's needs hierarchy

Sport motivation constructs	Deficiency needs				Growth needs			
	Physiological		Social		Self-Esteem		Actualized	
	Part.	Spec.	Part.	Spec.	Part.	Spec.	Part.	Spec.
Physical fitness	♦				♦			
Risk-taking	♦	♦			♦	♦		
Stress reduction	♦	♦			♦	♦		
Aggression	♦	♦						
Affiliation			♦	♦				
Social facilitation			♦	♦				
Self-esteem					♦	♦		
Competition					♦	♦		
Achievement					♦	♦		
Skill mastery					♦	♦		
Aesthetics					♦	♦	♦	♦
Value development							♦	♦
Self-actualization							♦	♦

of human behavior: (1) physiological, (2) safety, (3) social, (4) esteem, and (5) self-actualization. Maslow theorized that these needs are arranged hierarchically, with individuals working their way up through the hierarchy (from 1 to 5) as their needs are satisfied. These needs are of two kinds: deficiency needs and growth needs. Because each of these general needs (with the exception of safety needs) have been proposed in sport literature as motivating factors for sport participation and spectatorship, Maslow's hierarchy, seems an appropriate base upon which to build a theory of sport activity. From an extensive review of the literature we have distilled 13 broad types of motivation for sport participation and spectatorship. These are listed in Table 3–1. Table 3–1 depicts our conceptualization of the likely relationships between our motivation constructs and Maslow's hierarchy of needs. In the remainder of this section, we will briefly define our 13 motivational constructs and how they have been developed within the sport literature.

Physical Fitness

Perhaps one of the most obvious reasons for sport consumption is the pursuit of physical fitness. The construct of physical fitness refers to the state of

being in good physical condition and health. Several studies (Adamson and Wade, 1986; Mathes and Battista, 1995) have concluded that improving health and fitness is the prime motivator for sport participation. Research conducted on triathletes concerning the motivations for participation (Brooks, 1994) indicated that 62% of the sample mentioned security needs, in which health and fitness was a prominent response category.

Risk-Taking

Risk-taking refers to the desire to engage in thrill seeking through activities such as parachuting, hang gliding, and mountain climbing (Zuckerman, 1984). Zuckerman (1979) maintains that organisms seek a certain level of stress and that stress-seeking behavior increases when obtained levels fall below this optimal level. Sport participation provides socially acceptable opportunities for risk-taking and stress creation that may not otherwise be possible in the course of everyday life (Elias and Dunning, 1970). Clearly, as athletic risks become more extreme, stress increases, especially in sports such as sky diving, auto racing, and hang gliding. Risk taking has also become an outlet that allows individuals to feel better about themselves. The extreme games on

ESPN point to the persuasive power of risk on 18–34-year-old sport participants and spectators.

Stress Reduction

Stress reduction is defined as the process of reducing state anxiety, an emotional state characterized by apprehension, fear, and tension accompanied by physiological arousal (LeUnes and Nation, 1989). While numerous studies have explored the positive effect of exercise on physical health (Gurin and Harris, 1985; Haskell, 1987), research into the psychological changes associated with exercise is a relatively new area of inquiry. The available research, however, has reported consistent reductions in state anxiety with acute physical exercise (Dienstbier, 1984; Mihevic, 1981; Morgan, 1979), with aerobic exercises such as running, bicycling, swimming, and cross-country skiing having the most to offer in terms of psychological benefits. Additionally, other research represents evidence that sport spectating can be cathartic. For instance, Spreitzer and Snyder (1983) reported that 64% of the general population agreed that "watching an athletic contest provides me a welcome relief from the cares of life."

Aggression

Aggression is defined as "the infliction of an aversive stimulus upon one person by another, an act committed with intent to harm, one perpetrated against an unwilling victim, and done with the expectancy that the behavior will be successful" (LeUnes and Nation, 1989). Some researchers (Lorenz, 1966; Perls, 1969; Storr, 1970) subscribe to the theory that either actively participating in or vicariously watching aggressive acts reduces aggression levels. While there is little evidence to support the notion that watching aggressive acts results in catharsis (LeUnes and Nation, 1989), research has found that witnessing violence tends to increase aggressive behavior in viewers (Tannenbaum and Zillmann, 1975; Zillmann, 1983). In terms of spectatorship the entertainment value of aggression is widely known. Bryant, Comisky, and Zillman (1981) found that the ratings of enjoyment of preselected plays from National Football League (NFL) games increased as the intensity of rough play increased.

Affiliation

Affiliation is defined as connecting or associating oneself with the need to interact, socialize with others, and belong. Spectators' and participants' involvement in sport is motivated by a desire to confirm their sense of identity. In their analysis of mountain climbers and rugby players, Donnelly and Young (1988) detail a complex process of identity construction and subculture affiliation. Scholars have frequently noted that spectating at sporting events brings together disparate peoples in communal experience (Kutcher, 1983; Melnick, 1983) and can affirm class (Taylor, 1987), national unity, or a sense of community (Klein, 1984, 1991). Mullin, Hardy, and Sutton (1993) suggest that sport consumers are constantly filtering and interpreting cues about sport products relative to their self-image, and, thus, there must be a convergence between the image of the core sport product and the consumer. Members of exclusive country or sailing clubs, for example, gain much of their enjoyment from enhancements in self-esteem derived from exclusivity of membership.

Social Facilitation

Social facilitation is defined as the social gratification of being with others who enjoy the same activity. Both spectators and participants are motivated by the chance to spend more time with family members, friends, and business associates. In studies of tennis participation (Game Plan, Inc., 1987), athletic club membership (Game Plan, Inc., 1989), and fan motivations (*Team Marketing Report*, 1989; McDonald and Fay, 1993), consumers report that being with friends was one of the major reasons for their involvement in sport. Studies have found this social motivator to be particularly salient for female athletes (Ryckman and Hamel, 1992), with the importance of social facilitation increasing with advancing age (Gill and Overdorf, 1994).

Self-Esteem

In sport research, self-esteem is defined as holding oneself in high regard. A large body of research supports the contention that involvement in physical activities leads to positive attitudes about one's self (Dishman, 1982; Foon, 1989). Specifically, studies of female athletes and elementary school children (Gruber, 1986) concluded that physical activity contributed to the development of self-esteem. Sonstroem and Morgan (1989) propose that high self-esteem both leads to the adoption of physical activity and also results from sport participation. Mullin, Hardy, and Sutton (1993) indicate that understanding the impact of sport on self-concept is critical to understanding motivations for consumption, whether the product is a spectator sport or a participation sport.

Competition

Competition refers to the act of entering into a rivalry. From a participant's perspective, the primary goal of competition is to determine ability in relation to others. This purpose is met by a variety of mechanisms, the most obvious being through comparing the opposition to previously encountered competition (Roberts, 1984). The pervasiveness of this motive is indicated by one study which reported that 77% of racquetball players and 53% of the general population sampled agreed with the following statement: "I believe that one of the greatest values of physical activity is the thrill of competition" (Spreitzer and Snyder, 1983). A study of intercollegiate athletics indicated that the competitive aspects of participation are more important than social or fitness motives (Flood and Hellstedt, 1991). Competition as a value (and motive) is just as crucial for spectators. Koppett (1981), in *Sports Illusion and Sports Reality*, noted:

> The complex emotions stirred by one-to-one triumph, like one armored knight unhorsing another, can find release in sports as in no other recreational context. The enemy is present, identifiable, and given, by definition, a fair chance. When the enemy is beaten, forced to yield, brought into submission, mas-

tered, conquered, or proven inferior, deeper (and more primitive) layers of human experience are touched than when one experiences simple enjoyment of the prize won.

Achievement

Achievement is defined as accomplishing a desired result. Sport is clearly an achievement-oriented activity (Mullin, Hardy, and Sutton, 1993). The athlete strives to achieve a goal—perhaps defined in terms of winning or losing, perhaps as measured against individual standards of excellence (McClelland, Atkinson, Clark, and Lowell, 1953)—and can easily be evaluated in terms of success and failure (Roberts, 1992). It has been suggested that achievement for spectators takes the form of "basking in the reflected glory " of the victorious team (Cialdini *et al.*, 1976). Fans attempt to associate themselves with a successful athlete/team and thus appear more positive as a result. This concept parallels the "vicarious-relational" style in which individuals satisfy needs for achievement by identifying with achieving others and by sharing their successes (Lipmann-Blumen, Handley-Isaksen, and Leavitt, 1983).

Skill Mastery

Skill mastery refers to the goal of performing as well as possible, regardless of the outcome. The participant attempts to achieve mastery through improving or perfecting a skill (Roberts, 1984). Skill mastery involves being totally absorbed in a task for its own sake and is indicative of being intrinsically motivated. This motive for participation is critical in that athletes tend to evaluate their relative standing to other participants in terms of skill levels. The importance of skill mastery as a motivator increases with an athlete's self-perceptions of physical ability (Ryckman and Hamel, 1993). Skill mastery, as a spectator motive, results in attempts by the viewer to transfer the knowledge obtained through spectating to participation in the activity. Classic examples of skill transference between spectating and participating are the sports of tennis and golf.

Aesthetics

Aesthetics refers to the beauty, grace, or other artistic characteristics of sport (Willis and Campbell, 1992). Miller (1970) has stated that sport provides an opportunity for freedom of experience and creative expression. Spreitzer and Snyder (1983) report that 72% of the general population and 76% of runners sampled agreed with the following statement: "Participation in physical activities represents a type of beauty or artistic expression." Some sports, such as figure skating, synchronized swimming, and women's gymnastics, involve pure expressions of beauty, while others require flowing and visually attractive movements only at various moments during a competition (Cratty, 1983). One study found that women favored aesthetic activities such as swimming, gymnastics, and aerobic dance (Biddle and Bailey, 1985).

Value Development

Value development refers to the building of loyalty, character, and altruism. It is a widely held belief that sport is attractive because it teaches cultural values and builds character (Miller, 1970). The contribution of sport to value development, however, has not been conclusively supported (Edwards, 1973). Kleiber and Roberts (1981) examined the impact of sport on the "prosocial" behaviors of altruism and cooperation and found that the sport experience had a detrimental impact on the occurrence of prosocial behavior. Bredemeier and Shields (1983) have reported that reasoning about moral issues in everyday life is significantly higher for nonathletes than for athletes. Although the notion that sport aids in moral development and builds character has come under severe attack, one of the continuing attractions of sport may be that it purports to teach life's ideals (Sloan, 1985).

Self-Actualization

Self-actualization refers to "man's desire for self-fulfillment, namely, to the tendency for him to become actualized in what he is potentially" (Maslow, 1970). Sport would appear to be a natural realm for fulfilling self-actualization needs by providing opportunities to exceed personal expectations, to express oneself, or to transcend ordinary life. Self-actualization can occur when athletes enter into a state of "flow" (Csikszentmihalyi, 1979), where time becomes warped and complete control seems possible. Rudnicki and Wankel (1988) found self-challenge to be a predictor of long-term exercise involvement, and Johnsgard (1983) found that the main motive for running was to challenge oneself.

Measurement Development Process

We followed the paradigm outlined by Churchill (1979) to develop measures for our 13 constructs. The following section discusses our measure development process.

Item Generation

After reviewing the literature that covered the domain of motivational constructs applicable to sport participation and spectatorship, we began to generate multiple survey questions to measure each construct. For constructs that had been used in previous research, we adapted items whenever possible. However, much of the previous empirical research had focused on single sports, and item wording was not applicable to both spectator and participant situations. Thus, many of the survey questions we used were generated specifically for this study.

To create these items, we reviewed compendiums of published scales to look for related scales (Brunner and Hensel, 1992). Next, to help us evaluate word items, we held a series of focus groups with master's-degree students in a highly ranked U.S. sport management program, most of whom had extensive experience in athletics, coaching, or sport administration. The members of the focus groups were asked to discuss the usefulness and domains of each of the constructs.

As a result of focus group responses, we decided to word the motivation questions so that respondents answered with respect to their favorite sport. Prior to completing the battery of spectator and participant questions, respondents were asked to write down their favorite sports to watch and play. We felt that by basing responses on their favorite sport (which could be different for spectating and participating), the measure would best capture the overall motivation for sporting activity. We decided this would be more effective than asking respondents to answer global questions for all spectating sports or all participation sports. Our methodology avoids the danger that a respondent would answer motivational questions inconsistently due to perceptual shifting from sport to sport while responding.

Pretesting Initial Items

Two pretests of undergraduates were conducted to investigate the initial reliabilities of the participant and spectator scales, respectively. In each pretest, Chronbach's coefficient alpha was calculated for all constructs. The participant sample ($n = 68$) tested 13 constructs that ranged from 6 to 12 items each (average, 7.38 items). The average interitem reliability for each construct in the participant scale was 0.828. The spectator sample ($n = 82$) tested 12 constructs that ranged from 4 to 11 items each (average, 7.08 items). The average interitem reliability for each construct in the spectator sample was 0.730. Several items were dropped due to low item-to-total correlations. Although a large number of items can increase coefficient alphas (Peter, 1981), our goal in selectively dropping survey items was to remove questions that did not track well with others. At this point in the pretest our goal was to retain a rich and diverse set of items. When possible, we made an attempt to reword items that had low item-to-total correlations.

Next, a third pretest of an instrument containing both participant and spectator items was administered to 142 undergraduates. The number of items ranged from 6 to 10 for participant constructs and 5 to 10 for spectator constructs. We then purified the scales by examining the item–total correlations and factor structures. We were able to reduce the average number of participation items per construct from 6.69 to 3.31 while maintaining the same meaning and level of reliability (0.808 to 0.816). A similar improvement was found for spectator constructs. The average number of items per constructs was reduced from 6.33 to 3.08, while average coefficient alpha improved from 0.787 to 0.808.

Survey of Motivations of the Sport Consumer

A national sample of 5000 individuals, with gender selects of 65% male and 35% female, was randomly drawn from our sampling frame of 1.5 million men and women who had purchased mail-order sporting goods or had indicated an interest in sport. In September 1994 we mailed a prenotification postcard asking cooperation in the study. Ten days later, a cover letter, survey booklet, and metered return envelope were mailed to the sample of 5000. The cover letter appealed to the respondent's "generosity and enjoyment of sport." In addition to obtaining responses on motivations (for spectating and participation) and demographic background, the survey inquired about attitudes and rates of spectating and participation for various sports.

Survey Response Rate and Characteristics

We received 1624 completed surveys, of which 1611 were usable. Forty-eight, or 0.96%, of the surveys were returned for address problems or other reasons. This resulted in a response rate of over 32%. The sample, as expected, consisted of sport enthusiasts. Ninety-two percent reported having a high interest in sport spectatorship. Interestingly, 71% had purchased hats or shirts printed with sports logos. Seventy-two percent reported having medium to high interest in participation. Although participation rates were lower than spectating rates, 55% of respondents had played high school athletics and 83% had purchased sport equipment. The demographics revealed that 75% were male, 45.4% were college graduates, 46.5% had an annual household income over $50,000, and 45.5% were less than 45 years old.

Assessing Reliability and Validity of Scales

Reliability of the scales was assessed using Chronbach's coefficient alpha. The final scales used were the same as those developed in the pretests except for two participation constructs (aggression and risk-taking), which each had an item dropped. Thus, 22 of the scales had three items and 3 scales had four

TABLE 3–2. Reliabilities and correlations between spectating and participation constructs

Constructs	Spectating α	Participation α	Correlation
Physical fitness	—	0.94	—
Risk-taking	0.90	0.73	0.29
Stress reduction	0.88	0.91	0.35
Aggression	0.85	0.85	0.50
Affiliation	0.84	0.84	0.38
Social facilitation (s-4, p-4)	0.84	0.67	0.34
Self-esteem	0.93	0.90	0.39
Competition	0.74	0.80	0.41
Achievement	0.82	0.76	0.13
Skill mastery	0.79	0.78	0.22
Aesthetics (p-4)	0.83	0.84	0.42
Value development	0.85	0.82	0.48
Self-actualization	0.92	0.88	0.47

items. The coefficient alphas for the spectating and participation scales are shown in Table 3–2. Table 3–2 also presents the correlations between the spectating and participation scales. The pattern of correlations suggests that consumers have different motivations for playing and watching sports.

To examine the factor structure underlying the scales, we divided the data into analysis and holdout samples. With the analysis sample, we first separately examined the factor structure of the spectator and participant scales using principal factoring with a Varimax rotation. In both sets of analyses, a four-factor solution emerged that accounted for over 80% of the variation in the data. The results of the factor analyses, which are reported in Tables 3–3 and 3–4, showed that for each of our 13 constructs, all construct items loaded on the same factor. Because of the large sample sizes, loadings over 0.3 were significant (Hair *et al.*, 1995). There were 9.8% mixed loadings for participation data and 9.0% for spectator data. The pattern in which construct items loaded on each dimension corresponds to the possible relationships with Maslow's hierarchy of needs depicted in Table 3–1. However, the four motivation factors that emerged from the multivariate analysis reflect the unique features of sport.

The factor analysis revealed four factors of higher-order needs that can potentially explain spectator and participant motivations. The participation data factor structure revealed three of the four factors were growth needs. We labeled the first factor "Mental well-being needs," because these motivations help keep balance in one's life. This factor consisted of the constructs self-actualization, self-esteem, value development, aesthetics, and stress reduction. The second participation factor was labeled "Sport-based needs" because these motivations are basic to sport. The constructs comprising this factor included competition, aggression, risk-taking, and achievement. "Social needs" was the third factor, consisting of the constructs social facilitation, affiliation, and skill mastery. We labeled the last factor, a deficiency need unique to participation, "Fitness needs," which was measured by the physical fitness construct.

The factor structure for the spectator data repeated three of the four participation factors. The mental well-being, social, and sport-based factors were apparent for spectating, though for each factor there was one less construction associated with the factor. The constructs of skill mastery, aesthetics, and stress reduction migrated to form the fourth higher-order growth factor (for spectating only), which we labeled "Personal needs."

To examine the discriminate validity and unidimensionality of the constructs, we ran seven confirmatory factor-analysis models on the holdout sample of 200 observations. The purpose of the analysis was

TABLE 3–3. Factor structure for participation items

	Item	Factor 1	Factor 2	Factor 3	Factor 4
1	Helps me grow as a person	0.776			
1	Helps me accomplish things	0.727			
1	Helps me to reach my potential	0.735			
2	Makes me feel that I am a successful person	0.712			
2	Makes me feel confident about my abilities	0.695			
2	Gives me a feeling of self-assurance	0.733			
3	Has helped me understand the value of hard work and dedication	0.557	0.358		
3	Teaches me lessons that I may not learn elsewhere	0.604			
3	Has helped make me the kind of person I am	0.695			
4	Is an excellent remedy for me if I am tense, irritable, and anxious	0.498		0.361	
4	Helps me to get away from daily pressures	0.516		0.470	
4	Makes me feel less stressed than I did before I started	0.473		0.385	
5	Can be beautiful	0.435		0.429	
5	I enjoy the artistry of playing my favorite sport	0.407		0.452	
5	Is one way in which I can express myself	0.570	0.301	0.338	
5	I put a bit of my own personality into my performance of my favorite sport	0.485	0.365	0.391	
6	Can bring out my aggressive nature		0.580		
6	Much of my enjoyment from . . . comes from the aggressive aspects		0.665		
6	I feel less aggressive after participating in my favorite sport		0.483		
7	Helps me develop a competitive work ethic	0.308	0.510		
7	Competition is the best part of participating in my favorite sport		0.633	0.302	
7	The better the opposition, the more I enjoy playing my favorite sport		0.632	0.337	
8	Part of the fun of my favorite sport is the danger involved		0.386		
8	If I have to sacrifice my body when playing my favorite sport, so be it		0.586		
8	I put my entire self on the line when I play my favorite sport		0.586		
9	I have a strong desire to be a success in my favorite sport		0.322	0.314	
9	I would be willing to work all year to be successful in my favorite sport		0.487		
9	My goal is to be outstanding in my favorite sport		0.500		
10	I enjoy playing . . . because it gives me a chance to meet new people			0.423	
10	Participation in . . . with a group leads to improved social relationships			0.307	
10	Participation in . . . gives me a chance to spend time with my friends			0.606	
10	My enjoyment of . . . rests on other people to share the experience			0.515	

TABLE 3–3.   Continued

Item		Factor 1	Factor 2	Factor 3	Factor 4
11	Makes me feel like I belong to a special group	0.387		0.418	
11	There is certain camaraderie among the people who play my favorite sport			0.679	
11	I feel a bond with people who play my favorite sport	0.340		0.643	
12	I enjoy playing my favorite sport because it is difficult to master			0.309	
12	Is constantly challenging because it is a difficult sport to master			0.497	
12	It takes a high degree of skill on my part to attain the results I expect			0.547	
13	I play my favorite sport to stay physically fit				0.833
13	I play my favorite sport because I feel it keeps me healthy				0.832
13	I play my favorite sport because it develops physical fitness				0.871

Notes: Factor structure created by principal factoring and varimax rotation.

Loadings > 0.30 are reported.

Negatively worded items were reverse scored prior to analysis.

Wording of a few items was altered by table format.

1 = Self-actualization, 2 = Self-esteem, 3 = Value-development, 4 = Stress-release, 5 = Aesthetics, 6 = Aggression, 7 = Competition, 8 = Risk-taking, 9 = Achievement, 10 = Social facilitation, 11 = Affiliation, 12 = Skill mastery, 13 = Physical fitness.

Factor 1 = "Mental well-being needs"

Factor 2 = "Sport-based needs"

Factor 3 = "Social needs"

Factor 4 = "Fitness needs"

TABLE 3–4.   Factor structure for spectating items

Item		Factor 1	Factor 2	Factor 3	Factor 4
1	Helps me develop and grow as a person	0.831			
1	Helps me accomplish things I thought I never could accomplish	0.830			
1	Helps me to reach my potential as an individual	0.852			
2	Makes me feel that I am a successful person	0.816			
2	Gives me a feeling of self-assurance	0.845			
2	Gives me a feeling of personal pride	0.696			
3	Can help me develop values that will help me in life	0.580	0.310		
3	Has helped teach me the value of hard work and dedication	0.477		0.391	
3	Teaches me lessons that I may not learn anywhere else	0.624			
4	Because it gives me a chance to meet new people	0.389	0.547		
4	Watching . . . with a group leads to improved social relations		0.662		
4	Watching . . . gives me a chance to spend time with my friends		0.724		
4	Is based on having other people share the experience		0.640		

TABLE 3–4. Continued

Item	Factor 1	Factor 2	Factor 3	Factor 4
5 I feel connected to people with whom I watch my favorite sport		0.546		
5 Makes me feel like I belong to a special group	0.465	0.523		
5 There is certain camaraderie with the people I watch		0.646		
6 Is enhanced knowing the high level of skill required by the players			0.663	
6 I enjoy watching a highly skilled player perform			0.652	
6 I enjoy watching . . . because it is a difficult sport to master			0.576	
7 My favorite sport can be a beautiful sport to watch			0.611	
7 I enjoy watching the artistry of my favorite sport			0.727	
7 My favorite sport should be considered an art form	0.378		0.451	
8 Is an excellent remedy for me if I am tense, irritable, and anxious	0.341		0.441	
8 Helps me to get away from daily pressures			0.509	
8 Makes me feel less stressed than I did before I watched			0.442	
9 Because it involves a good deal of risk to the athletes				0.700
9 Is exciting because the athletes are always in danger of being injured				0.747
9 Part of the fun in watching is the danger involved to the athletes				0.689
10 Watching my favorite sport can bring out my aggressive nature				0.620
10 I enjoy watching my favorite sport when it reflects an aggressive style				0.629
10 I am free to express my aggressive feelings while watching				0.628
11 Helps me develop a competitive ethic	0.329	0.408		0.382
11 The main reason I watch my favorite sport is for the competition				0.389
11 The more intense the rivalry, the more I enjoy playing my favorite sport			0.335	0.382
12 If my favorite team/athlete plays poorly, I feel tense		0.320		0.379
12 The success of my favorite team/athlete is important to me		0.425	0.305	0.344
12 I feel elated for hours after a victory by my favorite team/athlete		0.436		0.388

Notes: Factor structure created by principal factoring and varimax rotation.

Loadings > 0.30 are reported.

Negatively worded items were reverse scored prior to analysis.

Wording of a few items was altered by table format.

1 = Self-actualization, 2 = Self-esteem, 3 = Value-development, 4 = Social-facilitation, 5 = Affiliation, 6 = Skill mastery, 7 = Aesthetics, 8 = Stress release, 9 = Risk-taking, 10 = Aggression, 11 = Competition, 12 = Achievement.

Factor 1 = "Mental well-being needs"

Factor 2 = "Social needs"

Factor 3 = "Sport-based needs"

Factor 4 = "Personal needs"

TABLE 3–5. Confirmatory factor analysis results

Participation data					
Factor	Motivational constructs	X²	RMR	AGIF	NFI
Mental well-being	Self-actualization, self-esteem, value development, stress release, aesthetics	220.9	0.049	0.80	0.92
Sport-based	Competition, aggression, risk-taking achievement	119.7	0.075	0.81	0.90
Social	Social facilitation, affiliation, skill mastery	90.9	0.059	0.83	0.89
Fitness	Physical fitness	—	—	—	—
Spectator data					
Factor	Motivational constructs				
Mental well being	Self-actualization, self-esteem, value development	98.9	0.038	0.80	0.96
Social	Social facilitation, affiliation	25.6	0.052	0.88	0.94
Personal	Skill mastery, aesthetics, stress release	93.6	0.066	0.81	0.91
Sport-based	Risk-taking, aggression, competition, achievement	199.7	0.062	0.77	0.89

to see if the related constructs (based on the exploratory factor analysis) were distinct. For each of the models, a CFA model was run for the constructs that fell in a particular EFA factor. The CFA model was then compared to the base model, which had all items loading on a single construct. Table 3–5 indicates that all the models had acceptable fit indices and the constructs were found to be unidimensional by confirmatory factor analysis.

Motivational Typologies of Sport Consumption

In this section we will report on our efforts to examine the predictive validity of the motivational scales by forming spectator and participant sport-motivation typologies. Typological methods have been recognized as a parsimonious classification of objects and as one approach to developing complex theories (Bailey, 1994). The two typologies we created highlight the ability of the constructs to describe ideal types of sport consumers that account for differences in sport consumption behaviors. Given our current level of understanding, we elected to form typologies based upon ideal types that were tied to theoretical literature, as opposed to a purely empirically based typology formed by cluster analysis, which would not

account for the relationships among the underlying constructs. In other words, we planned to use the 13 constructs and their relationships to each other to form ideal-type consumers. Next, we assigned each individual to an ideal type that closely matched the individual's consumption patterns. We believe our ideal-type-driven approach is directly traceable to the underlying motivational theory and structure in the data.

For both spectator and participant data, we formed an eight-cell classification scheme. The eight cells represented individuals who had either high or low characteristics measured along one of the four underlying motivational factors. "High" or "low" represented individuals who had characteristics that were one or more standard deviations away from the mean. The factors roughly corresponded to Maslow's hierarchy, shown in Table 3–1, and directly reflected the factor analyses shown in Tables 3–3 and 3–4. The ideal types were based on a vector of dimension scores. In this analysis, factor scores were the average of the constructs that loaded on the factor. For the social factor (spectators), the score was the average of the social facilitation and affiliation constructs. Thus, as depicted in Table 3–6, the ideal type was the mean of one factor score plus or minus the standard deviation plus the means of the remaining three factor scores.

TABLE 3–6. Typology of ideal-type characteristics

Ideal type 1: $(\mu_1 + \sigma_1)$, μ_2, μ_3, μ_4	Ideal type 2: $(\mu_1 - \sigma_1)$, μ_2, μ_3, μ_4
Ideal type 3: μ_1, $(\mu_2 + \sigma_2)$, μ_3, μ_4	Ideal type 4: μ_1, $(\mu_2 - \sigma_2)$, μ_3, μ_4
Ideal type 5: μ_1, μ_2, $(\mu_3 + \sigma_3)$, μ_4	Ideal type 6: μ_1, μ_2, $(\mu_3 - \sigma_3)$, μ_4
Ideal type 7: μ_1, μ_2, μ_3, $(\mu_4 + \sigma_4)$	Ideal type 8: μ_1, μ_2, μ_3, $(\mu_4 - \sigma_4)$

Each observation was assigned to the cell where the Euclidean distance from the ideal-type vector was the shortest. This was done for both the spectator and participant questions, and a summary of this classification is shown in Table 3–7 (for participants) and Table 3–8 (for spectators). These tables show the propensity for individuals assigned to one of the eight cells in the typology to share backgrounds (e.g., female) or attitudinal characteristics (e.g., those individuals who strongly agree they are sport participants). The classification rates are reported as indices, where 1.00 equals the propensity of the entire sample to have a particular characteristic. Cells with indices ≥ 1.25 reflect that the motivational type is more likely than average to contain this characteristic. These cells are boxed. In contrast, cells with indices ≤ 0.75 reflect that the motivational type is less likely than average to contain this characteristic. These cells are also boxed.

Participant Motivation Typology

Table 3–7 profiles individuals with especially high or low levels of mental well-being, sport-based, social, and fitness needs. The first row in the table shows the subsample size for each typology cell. Not surprisingly, the cells with the largest number of members are the fitness needs cells, with 356 having high needs and 440 having low needs.

The first block of indices are the motivations underlying the typology. As expected, the pattern of high and low motivations corresponds to the factor structure. Thus, individuals with high mental well-being participation needs were more likely to have higher motivations of self-actualization, self-esteem, value development, aesthetics, and, to some extent, stress reduction. Individuals with sport-based participation needs were more likely to have motivations of aggression, competition, risk-taking, and achievement. The high social needs group was more likely

to have higher social facilitation, affiliation, and skill mastery motivations. Finally, individuals with fitness needs were more likely to be motivated by physical fitness.

Sport-based needs appeared to be the most important predictor of high interest as a participant, followed by social and fitness needs. Individuals with high sport-based needs also were more likely to watch sports on TV, listen to sports on the radio, read books on sports, talk sports with friends, and purchase merchandise with logos and equipment. Social needs were only predictive in terms of the extent to which individuals talked about sport with friends and read the sports page (so they could talk intelligently about sport). Mental well-being needs predicted the level of reading behavior.

The typology also explains differences in demographic backgrounds. High sport-based needs individuals were less likely to be female and more likely to be aged 18–34. Individuals with high social needs were also more likely to have annual household incomes above $60,000.

Finally, the participation motivation typology also explained differences across sports. Table 3–7 profiles aerobics, distance running, freshwater fishing, golf, and rollerblading. Aerobics, distance running, and rollerblading all have high indices for the sport-based and fitness needs groups. Fishing was high for the mental well-being needs group, and golf was high for the social needs groups.

Spectator Motivation Typology

Table 3–8 profiles individuals with especially high or low mental well-being, social, personal, and sport-based needs for spectating. These eight groups of individuals are profiled by motivations, behaviors, demographics, and type of sport watched.

As with the participation data, the indices of sport spectating motivations reflect the underlying

TABLE 3–7. Participation motivation typology

Characteristic	Mental well-being needs		Sport-based needs		Social needs		Fitness needs	
	1. High	2. Low	3. High	4. Low	5. High	6. Low	7. High	8. Low
n	101	123	208	120	115	87	356	440
Self-actualization	1.40	0.58	1.16	0.86	1.05	0.92	1.13	0.86
Self-esteem	1.31	0.62	1.15	0.85	1.10	0.89	1.11	0.88
Value development	1.39	0.59	1.19	0.83	1.07	0.89	1.09	0.89
Stress release	1.17	0.70	1.06	0.97	1.08	0.95	1.09	0.93
Aesthetics	1.26	0.68	1.13	0.90	1.10	0.84	1.07	0.94
Aggression	1.14	0.78	1.37	0.58	1.09	0.83	1.05	0.91
Competition	1.09	0.86	1.39	0.57	1.11	0.83	1.07	0.86
Risk-taking	1.04	0.81	1.70	0.50	0.84	0.99	1.02	0.86
Achievement	1.13	0.84	1.39	0.56	1.14	0.80	1.05	0.91
Social facilitation	1.09	0.93	1.07	0.98	1.23	0.72	1.03	0.92
Affiliation	1.19	0.79	1.12	0.92	1.25	0.62	1.05	0.95
Skill mastery	1.10	0.91	1.15	0.90	1.28	0.66	0.94	1.00
Physical fitness	1.05	0.93	1.06	0.98	1.01	1.03	1.45	0.47
High interest as participant	1.07	0.84	1.65	0.48	1.36	0.63	1.28	0.62
Watch sports on TV	0.90	0.72	1.62	0.59	1.32	0.81	0.95	0.92
Listen to sports on radio	0.86	0.94	1.28	0.98	0.76	0.98	1.15	0.88
Read sports pages	0.98	1.08	1.06	0.89	1.10	0.84	0.98	0.99
Watch or listen to sports news	0.98	0.99	1.03	0.89	1.18	0.80	1.03	0.99
Read books on sports	1.35	0.43	1.62	0.49	1.20	0.53	1.19	0.77
Read sports magazines	1.73	0.90	1.24	0.66	1.03	0.94	1.08	0.77
Talk sports with friends	0.98	0.72	1.60	0.48	1.20	0.63	1.06	0.88
Purchase merchandise with logo	0.97	0.58	1.73	0.67	0.93	1.23	1.11	0.76
Purchase sport equipment	1.12	0.69	1.74	0.42	1.72	0.84	1.20	0.56
Female	1.06	0.94	0.66	1.74	0.78	1.13	0.99	1.02
Age 18–34	0.93	0.91	1.83	0.49	0.70	0.93	1.08	0.79
Income > $60,000	1.04	0.96	1.16	1.15	1.40	0.69	0.95	0.91
Aerobics	1.24	0.61	0.68	0.97	0.51	1.54	1.64	0.76
Distance running	0.78	0.22	1.27	0.66	0.80	0.91	2.11	0.48
Freshwater fishing	1.51	0.80	1.03	0.90	1.12	1.09	1.04	0.87
Golf	0.89	1.20	0.92	0.97	1.81	0.56	1.03	0.85
Rollerblading	0.95	0.67	1.71	0.45	0.59	0.94	1.38	0.71

dimensions upon which the groups were formed. Individuals in the high mental well-being group had high indices for self-actualization, self-esteem, and value development. The social needs group was distinguished by especially high or low indices for social facilitation and affiliation motivations. The high personal needs group had high indices for aesthetics and stress reduction. The group with low personal needs also had a low index for skill mastery. Finally, the sport-based groups had especially high or low indices for risk-taking, aggression, and competition.

For spectators, sport-based needs also appear to be important in explaining interest in spectating, media consumption, and sports watched. Individuals with high sport-based needs were more likely to read about sports. Like the sport-based needs group, the

TABLE 3–8. Spectating motivation typology

Characteristic	Mental well-being needs		Social needs		Personal needs		Sport-based needs	
	1. High	2. Low	3. High	4. Low	5. High	6. Low	7. High	8. Low
n	286	196	219	250	101	154	168	177
Self-actualization	1.81	0.45	1.12	0.65	0.95	0.81	1.04	0.80
Self-esteem	1.71	0.46	1.17	0.67	0.96	0.82	1.11	0.76
Value development	1.51	0.52	1.17	0.75	1.12	0.76	1.09	0.87
Social facilitation	1.18	0.95	1.53	0.48	0.96	0.91	1.05	0.87
Affiliation	1.24	0.88	1.48	0.48	1.13	0.82	1.12	0.84
Skill mastery	1.06	0.99	1.07	0.99	1.17	0.69	1.07	0.96
Aesthetics	1.14	0.87	1.09	0.98	1.33	0.58	1.03	0.96
Stress release	1.18	0.88	1.10	0.90	1.34	0.64	1.05	0.91
Risk-taking	1.08	0.86	1.07	0.80	0.81	1.06	1.75	0.56
Aggression	1.15	0.92	1.13	0.83	1.08	0.89	1.43	0.52
Competition	1.15	0.95	1.14	0.87	1.09	0.85	1.25	0.64
Achievement	1.11	1.00	1.12	0.89	1.05	0.90	1.25	0.62
High interest as spectators	1.24	1.08	1.27	0.84	1.22	0.94	1.26	0.85
Watch sports on TV	1.19	0.97	1.09	0.83	1.27	0.81	1.19	0.80
Listen to sports on radio	1.21	1.22	1.06	0.71	1.32	0.81	1.21	0.61
Read sports pages	1.14	1.07	0.99	0.97	1.03	0.86	0.93	0.88
Watch or listen to sports news	1.10	0.99	1.01	0.95	1.12	0.89	1.04	0.91
Read books on sports	1.25	0.79	1.22	0.60	1.32	0.79	1.32	0.74
Read sports magazines	1.37	0.98	0.94	0.52	1.20	0.69	1.42	0.94
Talk sports with friends	1.14	1.05	1.32	0.61	1.12	0.77	1.43	0.64
Purchase merchandise with logo	1.25	0.79	1.42	0.60	1.15	1.08	1.31	0.63
Purchase sport equipment	1.23	1.04	1.12	0.79	1.23	0.66	1.14	0.84
Female	0.78	1.05	1.21	0.92	0.90	0.99	0.61	1.60
Age 18–34	0.88	0.67	1.41	0.74	0.93	1.24	1.60	0.73
Income > $60,000	0.84	1.18	1.10	0.98	0.88	0.91	0.91	1.12
Sports car racing	1.18	1.19	1.33	0.61	0.94	0.69	1.38	0.60
Boxing	1.19	0.78	1.29	0.66	1.23	0.88	1.38	0.57
Ice skating	1.04	0.73	1.12	0.98	1.42	0.81	0.85	1.25
Sand volleyball	1.19	0.77	1.15	0.79	1.41	0.77	1.36	0.71
Pro wrestling	1.35	0.27	1.52	1.12	0.52	0.91	1.36	0.59

group with high social needs was more likely to talk sports with friends and purchase merchandise with printed logos. The group most likely to watch and listen to sports were the personal needs group—most likely because of aesthetic and skill mastery motivations.

Gender and age appeared to be linked to spectating needs. The group with the lowest sport-based needs had the highest concentration of females. Not surprisingly, this group was more likely to watch ice skating. In contrast, the group with high sport-based needs was most likely to be represented by 18–34 year olds.

The pattern of sport spectating can be explained in part by the typology. For example, the high social needs group was very likely to watch sports car racing, boxing, and pro wrestling. For people who fit in this motivation group, going to these events was a big occasion to be shared with friends and relatives. Those in the personal needs group were more likely to watch ice skating and beach volleyball.

Study Limitations

This study represents the first systematic attempt to measure a wide array of motivations for sport spectating and participation. In interpreting the findings, there are several limitations that should be kept in mind. First, although we employed a national sample, the sampling frame was limited by the characteristics of the mailing list. Thus, the findings do not necessarily generalize to a broader population. Second, respondents were asked to answer questions with respect to their favorite sport in an effort to make their responses consistent across scales. In subsequent analyses, we assumed that an individual's response for his or her favorite sport was indicative of an individual's general motivational patterns across all sports. Third, the constructs examined and the items used to measure the constructs could be further refined. Although we thoroughly reviewed the existing sport literature, there may be other sport motivation constructs not yet studied. Also, we had to create many of the survey items used to measure the constructs. These survey questions could benefit from additional psychometric testing and enhancements. Finally, our typologies were based upon eight ideal types that represented especially high or low levels of the dimensions in the data that were generated by exploratory factor analysis. Although these typologies simplified the classification procedure, there may be classifications that capitalize on possible interactions among data dimensions that we did not examine.

Summary

This research has addressed basic questions regarding motivations for sport consumption such as which psychological needs are satisfied through sport participation and spectatorship and which motivations divert individual consumers away from other entertainment options. Although this research does not provide definitive answers to these questions, it has provided several useful insights to guide theory development.

While Maslow's human-needs hierarchy provided the basic framework for organizing constructs related to sport consumption, the pattern of construct loadings on each dimension produced four motivational factors that reflected unique aspects of the sport consumption experience. For participation, these four factors were labeled as mental well-being, sport-based, social, and fitness needs. The four dimensions of spectatorship were referred to as mental well-being, social, sport-based, and personal needs.

Prior research studying these constructs independently has provided insights into the nature of needs being satisfied by sport; however, little information regarding the relative importance of these needs has been provided. This research has highlighted the centrality of sport-based needs such as aggression, competition, risk-taking, and achievement to both sport participation and spectatorship. While many activities outside of sport can, and do, fulfill mental well-being, social, and personal needs, sport is still a unique and valuable outlet for needs that may be unfulfilled.

In addition to motivating individuals to play and watch sports, these sport-based needs appear to be linked to indirect consumer involvement in sport. Consumers rating high in sport-based needs are also strong followers of sport through print and radio media. They also converse with friends about sport and purchase sport equipment and licensed merchandise. Clearly, these results indicate that when competing with other entertainment options for the consumer's attention, concentrating on satisfying the sport-based needs will provide sport marketers with a sustainable competitive advantage.

These findings offer new insights that should be of use to managers involved in sport participation and spectating. The study offers a set of motivational measures for examining sport consumption and developing marketing communications. The typologies formed from these measures show that needs-based segments differ in their attitudes, media consumption, and sport behaviors. For an industry that has a strong history of relying on demographics to project participation and spectating rates, this is an important improvement.

In conclusion, understanding consumers is fundamental to the marketing concept. This research suggests that motivations are an important determinant of sport consumer behavior. Future research is needed to better develop these constructs and see how sports differ in terms of motivations. Such an understanding might lend itself to predicting the likelihood of an individual engaging in various sporting activities. Finally, sport consumption is a complicated activity in which participation and spectating are often intertwined. This study examined both participation and spectating separately; future research is needed to understand the links or connections between these consumption realms.

References

Adamson, B. J., and K. J. Wade (1986). Predictors of sport and exercise participation among health science students. *Australian Journal of Science and Medicine in Sport*, 18(4): 3–10.

Assimakopoulos, A. K. (1993). Corporate sport sponsorship in Greece: Perception of knowledge, attitude and involvement of business executives, sport administrators, and advertising executives. *Unpublished Dissertation.*

Bailey, K. D. (1994). Typologies and taxonomies: An introduction to classification techniques. *Sage University Paper Series on Quantitative Applications in the Social Sciences, 07–102.* Thousand Oaks, CA: Sage.

Barrett, A. L., and C. A. Zeiss (1980). Behavioral commitment to the role of sport consumer: An exploratory analysis. *Sociology and Social Research*, 64(3): 405–419.

Biddle, S., and C. Bailey (1985). Motives for participation and attitudes towards physical activity of adult participants in fitness programs. *Perceptual and Motor Skills*, 61: 831–834.

Bredemeier, B. J., and D. L. Shields (1983). *Body and balance: Developing moral structures through physical education.* University of Oregon: Microform Publications.

Brooks, C. M. (1994). *Sports marketing: Competitive business strategies for sports.* Englewood Cliffs, NJ: Prentice-Hall.

Brunner, G., and P. Hensel (1992). *Marketing scales handbook.* Chicago: American Marketing Association.

Bryant, J., P. Comisky, and D. Zillmann (1981). The appeal of rough-and-tumble play in televised football. *Communication Quarterly*, 29: 256–262.

Burnett, J., Ajay Menon, and Denise T. Smart (1993). Sport marketing: A whole new ball game with new rules. *Journal of Advertising Research* (Sept/Oct): 21–35.

Churchill, Gilbert A., Jr. (1979). A paradigm for developing better measures for marketing constructs. *Journal of Marketing Research*, 21 (November): 360–375.

Cialdini, R. B., R. J. Borden, R. J. Thorne, M. R. Walker, S. Freeman, and L. R. Sloan (1976). Basking in reflected glory: Three football field studies. *Journal of Personality and Social Psychology*, 34: 366–375.

Cratty, B. J. (1983). *Psychology in contemporary sport: Guidelines for coaches and athletes,* 2nd ed. Englewood Cliffs, NJ: Prentice-Hall.

Csikszentmihayli, M. (1979). Concept of flow. In B. Sutton-Smith (ed.), *Play and learning.* New York: Gardner Press.

Dienstbier, R. A. (1984). The impact of exercise on personality. In M. L. Sachs and G. W. Buffone (eds.), *Running as therapy: An integrated approach.* Lincoln: University of Nebraska Press.

Dishman, R. K. (1982). Compliance/Adherence in health-related exercise. *Health Psychology*, 1: 237–267.

Donnelly, P., and K. Young (1988). The construction and confirmation of identity in sport sub cultures. *Sociology of Sport Journal*, 5: 223–240.

Edwards, H. (1973). *Sociology of sport.* Homewood, IL: Dorsey

Elias, N., and E. Dunning (1970). The quest for excitement in unexciting societies. In G. Luschen (ed.), *The cross-cultural analysis of sport and games.* Champaign, IL: Stipes.

Flood, S. E., and J. C. Hellstedt (1991). Gender differences in motivation for intercollegiate athletic participation. *Journal of Sport Behavior*, 14(3): 159–167.

Foon, A. E. (1989). Sport participation among adolescents: Sex differences and effects on academic achievement, self-esteem, affiliation patterns and locus of control. *Journal of Applied Research in Coaching and Athletics*, 4(3): 157–175.

Game Plan, Inc. (1987). *Why people play: A report on the sport of tennis.* Lexington, MA: Game Plan, Inc.

——— (1989). *Why people join: A marketing research study for racquet and fitness clubs.* Boston: IRSA.

Gill, Kathy, and Virginia Overdorf (1994). Incentives for exercise in younger and older women. *Journal of Sport Behavior*, 17(2): 87–97.

Gruber, J. J. (1986). Physical activity and self-esteem development in children: A meta-analysis. *American Academy of Physical Education Papers*, 19: 30–48.

Gurin, J., and T. G. Harris (1985). Look who's getting it together. *American Health*, March.

Hair, J., R. Anderson, R. Tatham, and W. Black (1995). *Multivariate data analysis.* New York: Macmillan.

Hansen, H., and R. Gauthier (1989). Factors affecting attendance at professional sport events. *Journal of Sport Management*, 3: 15–32.

Haskell, W. (1987). Developing a plan for improving health. *Exercise and Mental Health*.

Howard, D. R., R. Madrigal, and L. Kahle (1994). Symposium on the social psychology of fan behavior. *The North American Society for Sport Management 9th Annual Conference*, Pittsburgh, PA.

Johnsgard, K. (1983). Why do you do it? *Running Times*, 1: 38–39.

Kleiber, D. A., and G. C. Roberts (1981). The effects of sport experience in the development of social character: An exploratory investigation. *Journal of Sport Psychology*, 3: 114–122.

Klein, A. M. (1984). A review of soccer madness. *Sociology of Sport Journal*, 1(2): 195–197.

Klein, A. M. (1991). *Sugarball*. New Haven: Yale University Press.

Koppett, L. (1981). *Sports illusion, sports reality*. Boston: Houghton Mifflin.

Kutcher, L. (1983). The American sport event as carnival: An emergent norm approach to crowd behavior. *Journal of Popular Culture*, 24: 121–136.

LeUnes, A. D., and J. R. Nation (1989). *Sport psychology: An introduction*. Chicago: Nelson-Hall, Inc.

Lipmann-Blumen, J., A. Handley-Isaksen, and H. J. Leavitt (1983). Achieving styles in men and women: A model, an instrument and some findings. In J. T. Spence (ed.), *Achievement and achievement motives*. New York: Freeman.

Lorenz, K. (1966). *On aggression*. New York: Harcourt, Brace & World.

Maslow, A. H. (1943). A theory of human motivation. *Psychological Review*, July: 370–396.

—————— (1968). *Toward a psychology of being,* 2nd ed. New York: Van Nostrand.

—————— (1970). *Motivation and personality*. New York: Harper & Row.

Mathes, S. A., and R. Battista (1985). College men's and women's motives for participation in physical activity. *Perceptual and Motor Skills*, 61: 719–726.

McClelland, D. C., J. W. Atkinson, R. A. Clark, and E. L. Lowell (1953). *The achievement motive*. New York: Appleton-Century-Crofts.

McDonald, M. A., and T. G. Fay (1993). *U.S. Soccer Cup Spectator Research Report. Unpublished Paper.*

Melnick, M. (1983). Searching for sociability in the stands: A theory of sports spectating. *Journal of Sport Management*, 7: 44–60.

Mihevic, P. M. (1981). Anxiety, depression, and exercise. *Quest*, 33: 140–153.

Miller, D. L. (1970). *Gods and games: Toward a theology of play*. New York: World.

Mullin, B. J., S. Hardy, and W. A. Sutton (1993). *Sport marketing*. Champaign, IL: Human Kinetics Publishers.

Morgan, W. P. (1979). Anxiety reduction following acute exercise. *Psychiatric Annals*, 9: 113–121.

Peter, J. (1981). Construct validity: A review of basic issues and marketing practices. *Journal of Marketing Research*, 18 (May): 133–145.

Perls, F. S. (1969). *Ego, hunger, and aggression*. New York: Random House.

Roberts, G. (1984). Achievement motivation in children's sport. In J. G. Nicholls (ed.), *Advances in motivation and achievement: Vol. 3. The development of achievement and motivation*, pp. 251–281. Greenwich, CT: JAI Press.

Roberts, G. (1992). Motivation in sport and exercise: Conceptual constraints and convergence. In G. Roberts (ed.), *Motivation in sport and exercise*. Champaign, IL: Human Kinetics.

Rudnicki, J., and L. M. Wankel (1988). Employee fitness program effects upon long-term fitness involvement. *Fitness in Business*, 3: 123–129.

Rychkman, R. M., and J. Hamel (1993). Perceived physical ability differences in the sport participation motives of young athletes. *International Journal of Sport Psychology*, 24(3): 270–283.

Sallis, J. F., and R. Needle (1985). The relation of physical activity and exercise to mental health. *Public Health Reports*, 100: 195–202.

Sloan, L. R. (1985). The motives of sports fans. In J. H. Goldstein (ed.), *Sports, games, and play: Social and psychological viewpoints.*, 2nd ed. Hillsdale, N.J.: Lawrence Erlbaum Associates.

Sonstroem, R. J., and W. P. Morgan (1989). Exercise and self-esteem: Rationale and model. *Medicine and Science in Sports and Exercise*, 21: 329–337.

Spreitzer, E., and E. E. Snyder (1983). Correlates of participation in adult recreational sports. *Journal of Leisure Research*, 15: 27–38.

Storr, A. (1970). *Human aggression*. New York: Atheneum.

Tannenbaum, P. H., and L. Zillmann (1975). Emotional arousal in the facilitation of aggression through communication. In L. Berkowitz (ed.), *Advances in experimental social psychology*. New York: Academic Press.

Taylor, I. (1987). Putting the boot into a working-class sport: British soccer after Cradfor and Brussels. *Sociology of Sport Journal*, 4(2): 171–191.

Team Marketing Report (October 1989). Meeting friends, p. 5.

Willis, J. D., and L. F. Campbell (1992). *Exercise psychology*. Champaign, IL, Human Kinetics Publishers.

Zillmann, D. (1983). Arousal and aggression. In R. G. Geen and E. I. Donnerstein (eds.), *Aggression: Theoretical and empirical reviews* (Vol. I). New York: Academic Press.

Zuckerman, M. (1979). Attribution of success and failure revisited, or: The motivational bias is alive and well in attribution theory. *Journal of Personality*, 47: 245–287.

—————— (1984). Experience and desire: A new format for sensation seeking scales. *Journal of Behavioral Assessment*, 6: 101–114.

Evaluating the Impact of Winning and Brand Management

Introduction

Today's professional and collegiate sport industries appear to place the utmost importance on winning as a means of increasing revenues and stimulating marketing activities. The importance of winning is manifested in the lengths to which franchises go in order to put a winning team on the field (consider the frequent personnel changes in coaching and sport management positions). The pressure to generate revenue is increasing. New stadiums are being built and their regular, club, and luxury seats must be filled. In collegiate sport, Title IX pressures and escalating tuition are increasing pressures to bring in revenue.

Academic literature has presented a theoretical argument supporting the importance of winning. Research has suggested that winning has a positive impact on fan interest and attendance (Whitney, 1988), team revenues (Scully, 1989), and, for college teams, donations to the university's athletic department (Sigelman and Bookheimer, 1984).

Interestingly, given the importance of winning, there has been little empirical research that examines the relationship between winning and positive marketplace consequences. In addition, there is a noticeable dearth of research regarding the impact of a sport team's brand on marketplace outcomes in the absence of winning. In other words, are teams with losing records destined to have negative marketplace outcomes *or* can the team's brand be managed successfully under such conditions? The purpose of this chapter is to examine both of these issues. We begin by presenting an empirical study that examines the question of what winning is worth. This exploratory study examines the market performance of successful and unsuccessful teams. We then discuss the concept of brand equity, developing a conceptual model that can guide managers in enhancing the value of their brand even when a winning season does not occur.

The Impact of Winning

The objectives of our first study on "team winning" were to provide a descriptive update on prior research and create a starting point for understanding the predictors of positive marketplace consequences.

39

Specifically, this study collected and analyzed secondary data on the National Football League (NFL), National Basketball Association (NBA), National Hockey League (NHL), and NCAA Division I basketball and football teams that related winning to outcomes.[1] To determine the value of winning, data was collected on attendance, gate receipts, facility capacities, merchandise sales, media revenues, winning percentages, postseason participation, and television appearances.

The research methodology involved assimilating financial and performance data for the years 1990 through 1995. For each of these five years, we collected data on 28 NFL teams, 27 NBA teams, 25 NHL teams, 71 NCAA football teams, and 67 NCAA basketball teams. Data was collected from a variety of secondary and proprietary sources. Secondary sources included *Financial World* magazine, *USA Today*, *The Sporting News*, and NHL/NFL/NBA yearbooks. In order to complete the data set, proprietary information was utilized from NBA and NFL league offices, *Team Marketing Report*, and *Collegiate Licensing*. Since this information is confidential, it is reported here only on an aggregate basis. The definitions and sources of these data are summarized in Table 4–1.

For purposes of data analysis, winning was defined in two ways:

1. *Winning record* referred to teams with a winning record for a given year.
2. *Postseason participation* referred to teams reaching the playoffs/postseason for a given year.

Two time frames, the current year and the following year, were examined to analyze the impact of winning. These time frames account for the short-term as well as the long-term impact of winning on brand equity. Given that this was a descriptive study, means of the outcome variables were compared for winners versus losers and playoff teams versus non-playoff teams. In the reporting of results, we provide some illustrative top-line findings for the outcomes of merchandise revenue, attendance, media revenue, and franchise value.

[1]Major League Baseball was not included because no playoffs occurred in 1994.

TABLE 4–1. Study variable definitions and data sources

Capacity	Percentage derived by calculating average attendance divided by stadium capacity and multiplying by 100.
All-Star members	For professional sports, defined as playing in the league's all-star game. For college sports, defined as being named "Consensus All-American," as determined by the NCAA (various yearbooks, *NCAA News*, *USA Today*).
Attendance	Average attendance for the given year (various yearbooks, *NCAA News*, *USA Today*).
Championship	Defined as winning the team championship in a given year (various yearbooks and *USA Today*).
Franchise value	Approximate value of the franchise calculated based on last three years' average total revenues, venue, and lease (*Financial World*).
Gate receipts	Gross gate receipts, including club seats, but excluding sales taxes (*Financial World*).
Media revenues	Includes national television contracts, local television contracts, cable television contracts, and radio contracts (*Financial World*).
Merchandise rank	Where a team ranks with respect to merchandise sales (*Team Licensing Business*).
Merchandise sales	Annual revenues from merchandise sales (proprietary data).
Playoffs	Defined as making the playoffs (NFL, NBA, NHL) or participating in postseason play (NCAA football games and NCAA postseason tournament) (various yearbooks and *USA Today*).
Total revenues	Includes all revenues received by a club, including licensing royalties and merchandising revenues (*Financial World*).
TV appearances	Number of times a team appeared on national television (national television defined as ABC, CBS, NBC, or ESPN); regional appearances on these networks were included (*USA Today*).

TABLE 4–2. Impact of winning on NFL merchandise sales (average per team in $ millions)

	1994	1995	% Change
Winners	112.4	115.6	+2.8
Losers	40.2	32.3	−19.7
Difference	72.2	83.3	
Playoffs	121.5	133.4	+9.8
Nonplayoffs	52.0	40.9	−21.3
Difference	69.5	92.5	

Merchandise Revenue

Table 4–2 shows the impact of winning and reaching the playoffs on gross annual sales in the NFL. The data show the level of merchandise sales in 1994 compared to the sales the following year (1995). Thus, merchandise sales for those teams who had winning seasons in 1994 averaged $112.4 million. By winning, their merchandise sales rose 2.8% to $115.6 million in 1995. In contrast, merchandise sales for teams who had a losing record in 1994 averaged $40.2 million. As a result of losing, their merchandise sales fell by 19.7% to $32.3 million. The data reveal a similar pattern for teams in the playoffs versus nonplayoff teams. Merchandise sales of teams with postseason participation increased by 9.8% the following year, while merchandise sales for teams without postseason participation fell by 21.3%.

The data strongly indicate that merchandise revenues in the NFL are greatly impacted by winning. Successful NFL teams typically generate over $70 million more in annual merchandise sales than losing teams. What makes these results interesting is that the Dallas Cowboys were excluded from this analysis. If the team had been included, the results would be even more pronounced, since the Cowboys account for 25% of annual NFL merchandise sales. The old saying "everyone loves a winner" is undoubtedly at work here. Fans are more likely to seek to identify or affiliate themselves with teams or athletes that they perceive to be successful. The oft-cited article by Cialdini et al. (1976), which developed the basking-in-reflected-glory (BIRGing) theory, showed that fans tended to wear more team-related merchandise after their team's victory and less after a defeat.

Establishing and maintaining the image of a winner not only increases the amount of merchandise sold by a team locally but through national outlets as well. However, since the majority of these revenues are shared, successful teams leverage this merchandising opportunity by opening their own stores within the arena/stadium or at one or more off-site locations. These stores become profit centers for the team and can then be augmented by producing a catalog for additional telephone, direct mail, or team website sales.

Teams perceived to be successful (as well as expansion franchises where demand for licensed products is usually very high initially) can also capitalize on the recent trend of creating a third or special uniform. The Chicago Bulls and Orlando Magic have been very successful in promoting this endeavor. The Boston Red Sox, a team which has not changed its logo or uniforms for many years, unveiled two special occasion hats for the 1997 season.

Attendance

Winning resulted in higher attendance in NHL, NFL, NBA, and NCAA Division I men's basketball and football. In addition, winning had a significant impact on stadium capacity (percentage of seats filled) and gate receipts. Differences in capacities ranged from 5% to 10% depending on the league. In terms of gate receipts, winning teams averaged $2 to $5 million more per season, again depending on the league. Table 4–3 shows the impact of winning and playoff (postseason) participation on average stadium capacities for basketball and football at both the professional and collegiate levels. Winning is very important to filling up the stadium or arena. As would be expected, winning teams not only attained a higher capacity they also generated additional revenue (see Table 4–4).

Clearly, maximizing the season ticket base should be a priority for every sport organization. As team performance improves and the demand for tickets increases, the need for the organization to resort to selling partial ticket plans is reduced. The increased fan interest allows the organization to con-

TABLE 4–3. Impact of winning/playoffs on average stadium capacities (1991–1994)

	Winning record	Losing record	Playoffs (postseason)	Nonplayoffs (regular season)
NBA	94%	86%	93%	86%
NFL	91%	80%	92%	83%
NCAA basketball	86%	80%	89%	79%
NCAA football	87%	76%	90%	76%

TABLE 4–4. Additional gate receipts per team produced by winning/playoffs by league (average 1991–1994)

	Winning ($ in millions)	Playoffs ($ in millions)
NFL	$1.9	$1.6
NBA	$3.7	$3.6
NHL	$4.7	$4.9

TABLE 4–5. Percentage changes in total media revenue the year following a winning season by league (average 1991–1994)

	Winning	Losing
NFL	13.6	8.5
NBA	10.0	5.5
NHL	7.0	13.5

centrate on the sale of full-season tickets and also consider premium seating such as club seating and, in certain cases, personal seating licensing (PSLs). Additionally, winning teams are less pressured to discount their tickets in order to sell them, thus ensuring a higher return per ticket. Winning teams are usually associated with having more entertainment value, thus positively impacting the sale or rental of luxury suites, which are generally purchased by corporations for the purpose of entertaining/rewarding clients and prospective clients. Unfortunately, for nonwinning teams these opportunities are not usually available. The Orlando Magic, whose ticket demand far outstrips supply, have become creative in finding ways to further capitalize on its popularity. The Magic are constructing a practice facility that will generate revenue through having fans pay to watch exhibitions and scrimmages (and purchase merchandise at an accompanying retail outlet). This innovative strategy is one that will surely be emulated by other successful teams.

Media Revenue and Exposure

Media revenue is critical to the success of most big-time sports teams. Table 4–5 shows that successful teams have higher media revenues in the NFL and NBA the year following a winning season. In the NFL, in the years following winning seasons, teams averaged a 13.6% increase in media revenue compared to 8.5% for losing teams. Likewise, media revenue for winning NBA teams increased by 10.0% compared to 5.5% for losing teams. (Interestingly, the opposite occurred in the NHL, with losing teams' media revenue [13.5%] increasing more than winning teams' [7.0%]. This is likely a result of the growth on the numbers of expansion teams during the time period of the study.)

What specific factors contribute to increased media revenues? For professional teams, increased media dollars can be generated from the following sources:

- higher fees on local broadcasts,
- increasing the number of affiliates broadcasting the games,
- increasing the geographic scope of the radio/television network, thus increasing the number of affiliates and widening the pool of potential sponsors.

At the collegiate level, winning has a large impact on the number of scheduled television appearances. Our study found that for both NCAA basketball and football, the number of television appearances roughly doubled the year following postseason play. Basketball teams competing in the postseason increased the number of television appearances from 3.1 to 6. Football teams with postseason play increased the number of appearances from an average of 1.9 to 4.1.

Although winning teams receive more exposure on national telecasts, in the majority of cases such revenue is pooled and shared with other league or conference members. Given this arrangement, some of the more successful programs have adopted a more aggressive approach towards boosting income from this source. A number of winning teams have opted to move their local/regional television and/or radio packages in-house as a means of increasing media revenue. Instead of selling the rights to television and radio stations in exchange for a fee, the university buys the time for the broadcasts from the station and then sells the advertising itself. At the collegiate level, the benefits of increased television exposure are tremendous. Television broadcasts function as advertising and promotional tools for not only the school itself but the sport program as well. Previous studies have shown that winning teams attract the highest numbers of premium recruits. As one can see, winning can have a domino effect on a program and perpetuate a winning tradition for the school.

Franchise Value

Winning appears to have a long-term impact on franchise value (see Table 4–6). In the NFL, after the 1994 season, teams with winning records had franchise values worth $6 million more than teams with losing records. A year later, the franchise value of both winners and losers grew at a pace of 10%, thus widening the gap for winning teams due to the larger base value. Still, the difference between winners and losers is less than 5% of the base franchise.

In the NBA, differences between winners and losers in 1994 averaged $2.4 million in franchise value but the next year the difference was $10.5 million. The growth in franchise value for winners was 14.2% compared to 7.2% for losers. Compared to the 1994 base franchise levels, however, the difference was only 2.1% of the losers' base levels. Similar patterns were shown in the NHL, where the differ-

TABLE 4–6. Impact of winning on franchise value (average per team in $ millions)

	1994	1995	% Change
NFL			
Winners	$162.8	$180.0	10.6
Losers	156.8	172.8	10.2
Difference	$ 6.0	$ 7.2	
NBA			
Winners	$114.4	$130.6	14.2
Losers	112.0	120.1	7.2
Difference	$ 2.4	$ 10.5	
NHL			
Winners	$78.2	$84.0	7.4
Losers	60.6	60.7	0.2
Difference	$17.6	$23.3	

ence between winners and losers was more pronounced the following year. In contrast to the NFL and NBA, the difference between NHL winners and losers in 1994 was substantial—29.2% of the losers' base value.

For franchise value, the differences between winners and losers is not as significant as it was for other outcomes. Why doesn't winning immediately translate to increased value? Certainly winning impacts current revenues and the ability to create new revenue streams. Still, these revenue streams may or may not impact the overall value of the franchise because of other mitigating factors, such as market size, facility lease arrangements or ownership, and the composition of the franchise ownership. Nevertheless, winning matters because it affords the sport entity the opportunity to generate maximum revenue from a variety of sources and does not place the franchise in a situation of being overly dependent upon shared revenue sources. Shared sources, unfortunately, do not necessarily increase substantially from year to year.

As competition for the entertainment dollar increases annually, it is readily apparent that professional and collegiate sport teams that are successful on the field will be the teams most likely to be successful off the field—in the financial ledgers. Teams at both the collegiate and professional levels that have a winning record or qualify for postseason competition are more likely than teams that have not performed successfully to accomplish the following financial objectives:

- have higher gate receipts (both at home and on the road),
- fill a higher percentage of stadium capacities,
- secure revenue increases in local and regional media contracts,
- appear more frequently on television,
- sell more licensed merchandise.

It is important to note that the findings presented are averages across leagues. When one looks deeper, there are discrepancies. For example, the variance between the Dallas Cowboys and Detroit Lions merchandising value is huge, yet both had winning records. In 1994, the Los Angeles Lakers earned $30 million more in total revenue than the Denver Nuggets, although the Lakers had a losing record and the Nuggets had a winning record. These anomalies suggest there is a need for a more complete explanation as to the causes of positive revenue outcomes. Factors such as tradition, head coach, star player, and competitive forces, which contribute to what we call a team's *brand equity*, must all be considered.

Brand Equity in Sport

Over the past decade, evaluating the relative strength of consumer brands, or brand equity, has received significant attention in marketing academic and trade literature. Brand equity has been defined as "a set of assets such as name awareness, loyal customers, perceived quality and associations that are linked to the brand (its name or symbol) and add (or subtract) value to the product or service being offered" (Aaker, 1991). In addition to Aaker's, other definitions of brand equity have been offered. Farquhar (1990) refers to brand equity as the value added to a product by virtue of its name. In the sport industry, teams such as Notre Dame University football and the Boston Red Sox in professional baseball demonstrate significant levels of brand equity. Aside from regular sellouts, Notre Dame is the only university to solely negotiate a network television contract. This would not be possible if Notre Dame did not have brand equity in the marketplace. Similarly, although the Red Sox have not won a championship since 1918, they continue to maintain one of the highest stadium capacity rates in baseball.

Brand equity is created in the minds of consumers in the marketplace. Understanding the marketplace perceptions of a brand is necessary to assessing its equity. *Financial World, Brandweek,* and Landor Associates regularly generate definitions to rank consumer products with respect to brand strength (Stanley, 1995; Ourusoff, 1994; Owen, 1993).

Mainstream marketing studies have focused significant attention on the assessment and measurement of brand equity (Aaker, 1995; Keller, 1993; Aaker, 1991) and the use of brand equity in brand extensions (Dacin and Smith, 1994; Rangaswamy, Burke, and Oliva, 1993; Aaker and Keller, 1993; Herr, Farquhar, and Fazio, 1993; John and Loken, 1992; Bridges, 1992), but little research has been conducted on assessing brand equity in the sport setting. Recently researchers in sport marketing have identified brand equity as an important managerial tool (Gladden, Milne, and Sutton, 1998); still, there have been few empirical studies. One exception is Boone and Kochunny's (1995) study of Major League Baseball teams, but this study used a narrow measurement approach that relied upon financial indicators previously used to establish "franchise values" for professional sports teams (Ozanian, 1994). The only published indicators of brand popularity are the national merchandise sales figures for collegiate licensed merchandise (*Team Licensing Business,* 1995). Although both franchise value and merchandise sales figures may constitute a portion of overall brand equity, they do not reflect the value of the more intangible components of sport. Intangible components are fundamental to the assessment of brand equity since the sport consumer takes nothing away from attending or watching a sporting event other than perceptions and memories (Mullin, Hardy, and Sutton, 1993). Accordingly, a comprehensive measure of brand equity in the sport setting should include a wide range of tangible and intangible factors.

The remainder of this chapter presents a conceptual framework for assessing brand equity in the sport industry based on the previous research of Gladden, Milne, and Sutton (1998). The framework systematically delineates the components of brand equity along with the antecedents and consequences of brand equity in an effort to aid other researchers and sport managers in applying these concepts. Such research efforts should ultimately provide sport managers with models by which to improve the image, awareness, and revenue-generating capabilities of their respective teams and products.

Components of Brand Equity

A brand's equity is comprised of many components. Since these components can provide the basis for enhancing overall brand equity, it is important for sport managers to be aware of them. Such an understanding will allow the sport manager to increase the image and awareness of his/her teams and programs as well as the revenues generated by such programs. Aaker's (1991) model of brand equity suggests there are four main components that contribute to the creation of brand equity: perceived quality, brand awareness, brand associations, and brand loyalty. In creating a theoretical framework for evaluating brand equity in sport, this model provides a useful foundation.

Perceived Quality

The perceived quality of a brand varies with the price and positioning of a product (Aaker, 1991). At the core, perceived quality refers to the importance consumers place on the benefits and attributes associated with the product, or the attribute-based components of brand equity (Park and Srinivasan, 1994). These attributes and benefits allow products to create a position in the consumer's mind. With respect to sport, perceived quality relates to the perception of a team's success, most often defined by wins and losses. Perceived quality is important because it is difficult for products to recover from perceptions of poor quality (Aaker, 1991). Therefore, a sport team experiencing an isolated year of success would likely have a perceived quality in the marketplace lower than that of a team which had experienced long-term, consistent success.

Perceived quality also impacts opportunities to extend a brand name. Research indicates that higher-quality brands have more success with brand extensions. Although an extension can allow a firm to build on its strong name, such a strategy is not without risk. The failure to manage the quality of a brand's family of products will negatively impact the equity accorded the brand name (Dacin and Smith, 1994). Thus, a ski resort conglomerate considering adding another resort to its mix must reflect on how the new resort will impact the perceived quality of its existing resorts.

Brand Awareness

Brand awareness is closely related to the perception of quality. Keller (1993) defined awareness as the likelihood and ease with which a brand name will be recalled. In the sport setting, brand awareness can refer to the familiarity of the sport consumer with a particular team. Aaker (1991) refers to awareness as the starting point in developing equity, providing the anchor to which other associations can be attached. Three reasons that brand awareness is important for measuring brand equity are

1. Awareness increases the likelihood that a brand will be considered by consumers.
2. Awareness can affect decisions about brands in the product category or consideration set.
3. Awareness influences the development and depth of brand associations (Keller, 1993).

Aaker suggests that a pyramid of familiarity with the brand can be created in which "no awareness" is at the bottom of the pyramid and "top-of-mind" awareness is at the top, indicating the small number of products in the position of category dominance (Herr *et al.*, 1993). Such a hierarchy could be created with respect to the sport teams of which consumers are most aware.

Brand Associations

In addition to attribute-based components of brand equity, there are also intangible, nonattribute related components of brand equity (Park and Srinivasan, 1994; Shocker *et al.*, 1994; Bridges, 1992). Intangible associations have received the most attention in marketing literature (Keller, 1993; Bridges, 1992). Such associations have been categorized into experiential (what it feels like to use a product) and symbolic (those benefits which satisfy underlying needs for social approval and personal expression). These intangible qualities have also been distinguished on the basis of three dimensions: favorability (favorable or unfavorable), strength (quantity and quality of processing the brand image), and uniqueness (sustainable competitive advantage) (Keller, 1993).

In the sport context, brand association would represent the experiential and symbolic attributes offered by a particular athletic team. As such, both the emotional identification with a particular team and the exhilaration derived from attending a sporting event would be considered brand associations. Ultimately, some combination of tangible and intangible attributes creates a brand identity, "a unique set of brand associations that the brand strategist aspires to create or maintain," which drives brand associations (Aaker, 1995). It is therefore imperative that sport managers begin to understand the attributes associated with their teams.

Brand Loyalty

Aaker (1991) defines brand loyalty as the ability to attract and retain customers. The inconsistent nature of the sport product accentuates the difficulty of customer retention. In establishing brand loyalty, the emphasis is on customer satisfaction as the main reinforcement tool for repeat purchasing. Because the sport product largely provides only intangible benefits, determining the requirements for generating customer satisfaction is more difficult than in mainstream marketing. However, customer loyalty is critical to maintaining brand equity because it provides (1) protection against aggressive competitors who could undermine brand equity, and (2) the assurance of a predictable level of sales (Grossman, 1994; Shocker *et al.*, 1994). Boone and Kochunny (1995) furthered this notion, suggesting loyalty is critical to maintaining profitability because a loyal customer base provides a steady profit stream.

A Model for Assessing Brand Equity in Sport

Like a traditional product, sport satisfies some basic wants or needs for its consumer, the spectator (either in person or through the media). However, the needs that sport satisfies are the less tangible needs of health, entertainment, and sociability. A major allure for the spectator of sport is its unpredictable outcomes. Unfortunately for sport managers, unpredictable outcomes are born of inconsistent product performance (Mullin, Hardy, and Sutton, 1993). Lack of control over the core product (team performance) is further accentuated by the perishable nature of sport (Mullin, Hardy, and Sutton, 1993). Because the sport product is elusive by nature, measuring its value rests on consumers' perceptions of the product.

Antecedents of Brand Equity

The conceptual framework for assessing brand equity is shown in Figure 4–1. The purpose of this framework is to identify the antecedent conditions that managers can leverage to improve brand equity and to demonstrate how brand equity results in marketplace consequences. Understanding antecedent conditions is important because each has a particular influence on the four components of brand equity. Likewise, the consequences of equity also directly impact the four components of brand equity. Previous research by Cobb-Walgren *et al.* (1995) also utilizes antecedents and consequences to assess brand equity, but their model is narrow and not applicable to sport. Our framework offers a comprehensive basis for understanding the development of brand equity in the sport marketplace.

The linkage between the consequences of brand equity and building brand equity is relevant because the conceptual framework specifies a system whereby the consequences of brand equity form a perception that the sport product holds in the minds of consumers in the marketplace. This perception is the product of antecedents, established equity, and consequences of established equity. *Perception* is a word commonly used when brand equity is discussed in the marketing trade and academic literature, and it is particularly applicable to sport. Due to its intangible and inconsistent nature, the sport consumption experience is nothing but a perception of the association with a particular sport entity. Although seemingly intangible, the conceptual framework for establishing brand equity leads to a greater under-

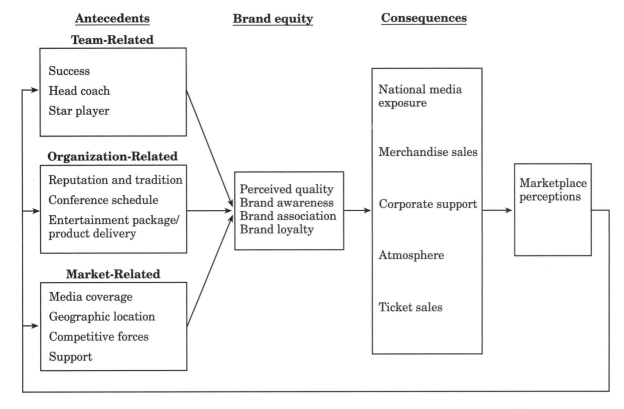

FIGURE 4–1. Conceptual Model for Assessing Brand Equity (Gladden, Milne, and, Sutton 1998)

standing of this perception and so is a means by which to enhance brand equity.

Through continual feedback loops consumer perception impacts both the antecedents and the overall brand equity. Therefore, although the antecedents create the initial levels of equity, the consequences derived from such equity also increase (or decrease) the brand equity of a sport team. This is relevant because sport managers may also be able to maximize the realized effect of each consequence. In an effort to provide the best possible understanding of the model, we will first describe the components of brand equity.

Team-Related Antecedents:

Success Team-related antecedents of equity encompass all attributes of the sport product directly related to performance. As shown earlier in this chapter, there is no substitute for winning athletic contests and receiving postseason invitations. Winning contributes to brand equity by increasing ticket sales, merchandise sales, and donations, and by enhancing the atmosphere at games and attracting national television exposure, thus making the team more attractive to corporate advertisers.

One would expect success to be strictly defined by the ratio of wins to losses and the level of postseason success. Success, however, may also be defined based on expectations. Supporters of a perennially underperforming team would be thrilled by a season of more wins than losses, thus raising the level of brand equity for that team. Success may also be defined by history. Teams with a history of success develop expectations of success to the extent that moderately successful seasons do not generally decrease brand equity because of the high levels previously established and maintained.

Head coach A coach with a proven track record can instantly enhance the brand equity of a team through publicity and expectations of success. Upon hiring Bill Parcels, the New England Patriots saw a jump in season ticket sales. Recently, top college coaches have been visibly decorated by both the media and corporations (Katz, 1994). Television shows, radio shows, and endorsement contracts often increase a head coach's salary by hundreds of thousands of dollars. Such arrangements increase the visibility of the team, and as a result the image of a coach often personifies the image of the team. Similarly, programs that have coaches with established records of success may realize more constant levels of brand equity.

Star player A team that is successful in recruiting or drafting a star player garners immediate national media exposure. Similarly, the race for the Heisman trophy in college football is a practice in publicity generation for both the players and the schools involved. Likewise, the presence of a superstar like Michael Jordan immediately shines the national spotlight on a team and a city. The feats of a star player can also enhance the atmosphere at games, increase merchandise sales, and increase ticket sales (Farrell, 1984).

Organization-Related Antecedents:
Reputation and tradition In addition to success on the field, a continuous commitment from top administrators is essential to the development of brand equity. An emphasis on acquiring the necessary talent, players and coaches, to remain competitive translates into long-term brand equity. The 49ers, for example, have displayed a commitment to their athletes, to their fans, and to the city of San Francisco. Even though winning in sport is cyclical, the key stakeholders can be confident that the 49ers will always remain competitive. This trust helps the organization withstand any off years on the field.

In college athletics, win or lose, a school with a strong academic tradition may generate a faithful following, particularly among alumni and area residents. Even though Northwestern only recently experienced its first successful season on the football field, it has been able to attract average crowds in excess of 30,000 throughout the 1990s (NCAA, 1994, 1996). Such loyalty is visible not only in ticket sales but also in merchandise sales, through which supporters exhibit their desire for association.

Conference and schedule Conference affiliation and schedule considerations are crucial to both college and professional teams. Most universities do not possess enough brand equity to establish national television contracts and create competitive schedules on their own. University athletic programs may have regional appeal but generally lack overall national appeal. Therefore, sport managers often work within the conference framework to gain national television exposure (e.g., "Big Monday" on ESPN, which televises a Big Eight Conference game and a Big East Conference game every Monday night during the college basketball season).

In professional sport, teams playing in strong conferences with well-developed traditional rivalries reap the benefits in terms of attendance and broadcast revenues. In baseball, for example, the American League East has tremendous brand equity because of such teams as the Boston Red Sox, New York Yankees, and Baltimore Orioles. These teams individually have great traditions and followings but also benefit from established rivalries and large markets.

Entertainment package/product delivery Attraction to sport is at least partially attributable to an entertainment value (Sloan, 1979). While performance is difficult to control, the overall environmental experience of spectators can be impacted (Brooks, 1994). Marching bands, mascots, stadium music, tailgate parties (i.e., informal socializing outside of the stadium before the game), and traditional activities such as the entrance of the football team into the stadium may all serve to enhance the overall experience of attending.

Market-Related Antecedents:
Media coverage Agreements with the media, other than those established at the national level, may generate brand equity by increasing affiliation and

interest in sport teams. Tape-delay television coverage and radio broadcasts throughout states and regions build awareness and loyalty for a team. Fans can experience pleasure from sport by following the action after the fact (Smith, 1995). In addition, coaches' shows provide local followings with an opportunity to relive past experiences. Independent media arrangements also allow sport managers and marketers to reach those potential consumers who do not attend or are unable to attend the events.

Geographic location Kapferer (1992) suggests that brand identities are often formed based on geographic location. Despite having an undefeated football team, Appalachian State University does not receive much attention or acclaim (Brewington, 1995). Preferences for a particular sport vary depending on the region. Certain areas of the country are renowned (or not renowned) for specific sports. Men's college basketball is stronger in Illinois, Indiana, North Carolina, and Kentucky (Rooney and Pillsbury, 1992). At the nonprofessional sport level, college baseball is more popular in the Southeast, Southwest, and West, and college wrestling is more popular in the Midwest. As a result, it may be easier to establish brand equity for a Division I men's basketball team in Indiana than it would be in Idaho.

Competitive forces Competition is most influential in the creation of brand equity. The New Jersey Devils versus the New York Rangers is a good example of how rivalry can enhance the value of both teams. At the collegiate level, most universities that compete in Division I athletics are in smaller cities and towns (Rooney and Pillsbury, 1992). If a school is forced to compete with professional sport endeavors or collegiate athletic teams with more brand equity, the availability of corporate support and the ability to sell tickets could be greatly reduced. This disadvantage may be compounded when the university shares its game facility with a professional franchise. For a college team playing its games in a professional arena or sharing its field with another high-profile college team, it is difficult for the athletic department to create a unique and special atmosphere necessary to enhance the attending experience. Competitive forces may also pervade at the state and regional

levels. A school may exist in a mid-sized, noncompetitive market but still be perceived as the second- or third-best offering in the region. If this is the case, then less brand equity will be realized.

Support Central to any team's brand equity is the established group of supporters that attends and helps finance sport. Support is defined by the size and loyalty of a particular team's following. Such support includes, but is not limited to, ticket holders, luxury seat purchasers, and people watching or listening to games.

Consequences of Brand Equity

The benefits of brand equity gained through perceived team quality, awareness, associations, and loyalty can result in increased media exposure, team merchandise sales, corporate support, ticket sales, and heightened atmosphere.

National Media Exposure

National exposure can be defined as live television coverage, televised news stories during live broadcasts and pregame/postgame programs, and national coverage in newspapers, magazines, and on sports talk radio. Notre Dame football, through its independent contract with NBC, illustrates the potential negotiating strength provided by high brand equity. Additionally, the presence and attention of national exposure may also impact the antecedents and, in turn, brand equity. For example, the Dallas Cowboys receive unprecedented media coverage of their on- and off-field exploits. Since television only presents games between the most competitive teams who play in front of full stadiums (Gorman and Calhoun, 1994), national media attention legitimates a particular athletic team and usually results in increased support. In addition, the spectator's overall entertainment package is enhanced when the media is present, particularly in the case of television.

Merchandise Sales

Merchandise sales are defined as the sales of apparel and other items that display the university or athletic name or logo. People purchase school or team logo merchandise because it represents an image that is important to its purchaser (Brooks, 1994). Wearing caps, buttons, T-shirts, and sweatshirts of their favorite teams gives people an identity (Tutko, 1979). Spurred by an appearance of its football team in the 1994 Rose Bowl, the University of Wisconsin's annual royalties from merchandise sales increased from $320,000 to $1.4 million (Bickley, 1995). In professional sport, the Dallas Cowboy's brand equity has resulted in their merchandise sales equaling 25% of total NFL sales. People who wear logo merchandise enhance equity by serving as walking advertisements for their favorite teams. The University of Michigan, Georgetown University, and Florida State University, for example, receive added exposure and enhanced brand equity as the leaders in licensed merchandise sales (*Team Licensing Business,* 1995).

Corporate Support
Corporate sponsorship has become more and more important to sport teams during the past decade. Corporations form alliances with teams with high brand equity in order to transfer the pride in the team to their own product (Stotlar, 1993). The Nike *swoosh* symbol is visible on players' uniforms at Penn State, Michigan, North Carolina, Georgetown, Virginia, and the Dallas Cowboys. Corporate sponsorship dollars can enhance equity through corporate promotions that enhance the entertainment package by building an association with consumer product leaders.

Atmosphere
Brooks (1994) defined atmosphere as the excitement and level of entertainment provided by attending an event. Since the sport consumer takes nothing away from an athletic event other than memories of his or her experience, atmosphere is an important consideration. Brand equity can improve the atmosphere at games. If a team wins more than it loses under the leadership of a charismatic coach while playing before a throng of frenzied fans, the atmosphere surrounding the game is likely to benefit from this energy. Improved atmosphere can lead to increased support and demand for corporate associations with the college and professional athletic product.

Ticket Sales
In line with the basking-in-reflected-glory theory (Cialdini *et al.*, 1976), winning records should correlate with increased spectator attendance. When equity drives ticket sales to the extent that arenas and stadiums are at capacity, colleges are able to require booster club donations as a means of obtaining priority seat locations, and professional sport franchises can limit packages to season ticket holders. Increased ticket sales may also enhance the entertainment package. More attendees generally result in more activity and enthusiasm associated with the attending experience, thus improving product delivery.

Summary

The framework for brand equity provides a starting point for research by describing the elements that contribute to the creation of brand equity in a sport setting. Understanding brand equity should help the sport manager realize a multitude of positive benefits, including enhanced image, increased loyalty, and increased revenues. We suggest that the creation of brand equity is a cyclical process that includes both antecedents and consequences. The antecedents, grouped into three major families, provide a sound understanding of the origins of brand equity. This foundation provides the sport manager with a starting point for manipulating and enhancing brand equity. Although national television exposure, ticket sales, merchandise sales, atmosphere, and corporate support are considered consequences, or outcomes, of brand equity, they can also be managed. Understanding which antecedents produce the desired consequences will allow enhancements to be made that will augment brand equity through feedback loops.

References

1995 Annual Report (1995). *Team licensing business*, June 22–39.

Aaker, D. A. (1991). *Managing brand equity*. New York: The Free Press.

Aaker, D. A. (1995). *Building strong brands*. New York: The Free Press.

Aaker, D. A., and K. L. Keller (1993). Interpreting cross-cultural replications of brand extension research. *International Journal of Research in Marketing*, 10: 53–58.

Antonelli, D. (1994). Marketing intercollegiate women's basketball. *Sport Marketing Quarterly*, 3 (2): 29–33.

Atkin, R. (1995). UConn women rule in high court of fan appeal. *Christian Science Monitor*, March 31, 10.

Barsky, J. (1995). *World-class customer satisfaction*. Burr Ridge, IL: Irwin Professional Publishing.

Basralian, J. (1995). Amateurs at best. *Financial World*, May 10, 117–122.

Berkow, I. (1995). UConn can count on Lobo. *New York Times*, April 3, C1.

Bickley, D. (1995). Cats are cashing in. *Chicago Sun-Times*, November 28, 86.

Blackston, M. (1992). Observations: Building brand equity by managing the brand's relationships. *Journal of Advertising Research*, 32 (3): 79–83.

Boone, L. E., and C. M. Kochunny (1995). Applying the brand equity concept to Major League Baseball. *Sport Marketing Quarterly*, 4 (3): 33–42.

Brewington, P. (1995). Appalachian State earns recognition and shot at title. *USA Today*, October 26, 2C.

Bridges, S. (1992). A schema unification model of brand extensions. *Working Paper, Marketing Science Institute*, August, 1–35.

Brooks, C. M. (1994). *Sports marketing: Competitive business strategies for sports*. Englewood Cliffs, NJ: Prentice-Hall.

Cialdini, R. B., R. J. Borden, R. J. Thorne, M. R. Walker, S. Freeman, and L. R. Sloan (1976). Basking in reflected glory: Three football field studies. *Journal of Personality and Social Psychology*, 34: 366–375.

Cobb-Walgren, C. J., C. A. Ruble, and N. Donthu (1995). Brand equity, brand preference, and purchase intent. *Journal of Advertising Research*, 24 (3): 25–40.

Cohen, W. (1995). Courting big-time commercial success. *U.S. News and World Report*, December 11, 81–82.

Crosset, T. (1995). Toward an understanding of on-site fan–athlete relations: A case study of the LPGA. *Sport Marketing Quarterly*, 4 (2): 31–38.

Dacin, P. A., and D. C. Smith (1994). The effect of brand portfolio characteristics on consumer evaluations of brand extensions. *Journal of Marketing Research*, 31 (May): 229–242.

Dealy, F. X. (1990). *Win at any cost: The sell out of college athletics*. New York: Carol Publishing Group.

Farquhar, P. H. (1990). Managing brand equity. *Journal of Advertising Research*, 30 (4): RC-7–RC-11.

Farrell, C. S. (1984). The Heisman hype: Colleges try to help star players win football's top award. *The Chronicle of Higher Education*, October 3, 25.

Gaskin, J. F., and M. J. Etzel (1985). Collegiate athletic success and alumni generosity: dispelling the myth. In

A. Yiannikis, T. D. McIntyre, M. J. Melnick, and D. P. Hart (eds.), *Sport sociology*, 3d ed. Dubuque, IA: Kendall/Hunt, 166–171.

Gladden, J., G. R. Milne, and W. Sutton (1998). A conceptual framework for assessing brand equity in Division I college athletics. *Journal of Sports Management*, 12 (1): 1–19.

Glenn, P., and P. Cobb (1994). Possible effects of corporate sponsors on intercollegiate athletics. In P. J. Graham (ed.), *Sport business: Operational and theoretical aspects*. Dubuque, IA: William C. Brown Communications, Inc., 93–110

Gorman, J., and K. Calhoun (1994). *The name of the game: The business of sports*. New York: John Wiley and Sons, Inc.

Grossman, G. (1994). Carefully crafted identity can build brand equity. *Public Relations Journal*, 50 (October/November): 18–21.

Herr, P. M., P. H. Farquhar, and R. H. Fazio (1993). Using dominance measures to evaluate brand extensions. *Working Paper, Marketing Science Institute*, November, 1–29.

Hiestand, M. (1995). Northwestern certain to cash in on success. *USA Today*, November 14, 3C.

Howard, D. R., and J. L. Crompton (1995). *Financing sport*. Morgantown, WV: Fitness Information Technology, Inc.

John, D. R., and B. Loken (1992). Diluting beliefs about family brands: when brand extensions have a negative impact. *Working Paper, Marketing Science Institute*, August, 1–27.

Kapferer, J. (1992). *Strategic brand management: New approaches to creating and evaluating brand equity*. New York: The Free Press.

Katz, D. (1994). *Just do it: The Nike spirit in the corporate world*. Holbrook, MA: Adams Publishing.

Katz, D., and R. L. Kahn (1966). *The social psychology of organizations*. New York: John Wiley and Sons, Inc.

Keller, K. L. (1993). Conceptualizing, measuring, and managing customer-based brand equity. *Journal of Marketing*, 57 (January): 1–22.

McDonald, M. A., W. A. Sutton, and G. R. Milne (1995). Measuring service quality in professional team sports. *Sport Marketing Quarterly*, 4 (2): 9–16.

Mullin, B. J., S. Hardy, and W. A. Sutton (1993). *Sport marketing*. Champaign, IL: Human Kinetics.

National Collegiate Athletic Association (1994). *1993 Division IA football attendance*. Mission Park, KS.

National Collegiate Athletic Association (1996). *1995 Division IA football attendance*. Mission Park, KS.

O. C. Hamilton, Jr. (1996). Two leagues of their own? *Business Week*, May 13, 52.

Ourusoff, A. (1994). Brands. What's hot. What's not. *Financial World*, August 2, 40–56.

Owen, S. (1993). The Landor image power survey: A global assessment of brand strength. In D. A. Aaker and A. L. Biel (eds.), *Brand equity and advertising's role in building strong brands*. Hillsdale, NJ: Lawrence Erlbaum Associates, Publishers, pp. 11–30.

Ozanian, M. K. (1994). The $11 billion pastime. *Financial World*, May 10, 50–64.

Park, C. S., and V. Srinivasan (1994). A survey-based method for measuring and understanding brand equity and its extendability. *Journal of Marketing Research*, 31 (May): 271–288.

Rangaswamy, A., R. R. Burke, and T. A. Oliva (1993). Brand equity and the extendability of brand names. *International Journal of Research in Marketing*, 10: 61–75.

Reicheld, F. F. (1993). Loyalty-based management. *Harvard Business Review*, March/April, 64–73.

Rhoden, W. C. (1995). Can women avoid the agents of change? *New York Times,* October 17, B11.

Rooney, J. F., and R. Pillsbury (1992). *Atlas of American sport*. New York: MacMillan Publishing.

Sagarin, J. (1995). Sagarin football ratings. *USA Today*, January 4, 11C.

Sagarin, J. (1996). Sagarin college basketball ratings. *USA Today*, April 3, 11C.

Scully, G. N. (1989). *The business of major league baseball*. Chicago: The University of Chicago Press.

Shocker, A. D., R. K. Srivastava, and R. W. Ruekert (1994). Challenges and opportunities facing brand management: An introduction to the special issue. *Journal of Marketing Research*, 31 (May): 149–157.

Sigelman, L., and S. Bookheimer (1984). Is it whether you win or lose? Monetary contributions to big-time college athletic programs. *Social Science Quarterly*, 347–358.

Sloan, L. R. (1979). The function and impact of sports and fans: A review of contemporary research. In J. H. Goldstein (ed.), *Sports, games and play*. Hillsdale, NJ: Lawrence Erlbaum Associates, 219–262.

Smith, S. M. (1995). Meltdown in marketing professional ice hockey: A survey exploring geographical differences in strategy. *Sport Marketing Quarterly*, 4 (3): 17–23.

Stanley, T. L. (1995). How they rate. *Brandweek*, April 2, 45–48.

Stotlar, D. K. (1993). *Successful sport marketing*. Dubuque, IA: Brown and Benchmark.

Tjafel, H., and J. C. Turner (1985). The social identity theory of group behavior. In H. Tjafel (ed.) *Psychology of intergroup relations*. Cambridge, MA: Cambridge University Press, 15–40.

Tutko, T. A. (1979). Personality change in the American sport scene. In J. H. Goldstein (ed.), *Sports, games and play*. Hillsdale, NJ: Lawrence Erlbaum Associates, 101–114.

Whitney, J. D. (1988). Winning games versus winning championships: The economics of fan interest and team performance. *Economic Inquiry*, 26 (10): 703–724.

CHAPTER 5

Utilizing the Customer Database

Introduction

With the number of competing sport and entertainment options and the subsequent shift of emphasis from acquiring customers to retaining customers, sport marketers are beginning to embrace relationship and database marketing (Milne and McDonald, 1997). Our purpose in this chapter is to review some of the fundamental relationship and database marketing issues that sport marketers need to consider. We will also discuss an empirical study that demonstrates how databases can be used effectively to strengthen customer relationships.

This chapter is divided into two parts. In the first part, we discuss the fundamentals of relationship marketing and database marketing and illustrate how both are being used by sport organizations. We include the following issues:

1. What is database marketing?
2. What is a database?
3. What type of data goes into a database?
4. What are the strategic uses of databases?

In the second part, we use database marketing principles to show how one can calculate the worth of an individual customer to an organization. In par-

ticular, we present a study of a professional basketball team's season ticket base and demonstrate how to measure each customer's relative relationship strength and lifetime value.

Fundamental Concepts

Relationship Marketing

Relationship marketing has been defined as "an integrated effort to identify, maintain, and build a network with individual consumers and to continuously strengthen the network for the mutual benefit of both parties, through interactive, individualized and value added contracts over a long period of time" (Shani and Chalasani, 1992, p. 44). The purpose of relationship marketing is "to establish, maintain, and enhance and commercialize customer relationships (often but not necessarily long term relationships) so that the objectives of the parties are met. This is done by a mutual exchange and fulfillment of promises" (Gronroos, 1990, p. 5).

These definitions stress that relationship marketing is the individual customer–seller interaction that takes place over time, with an emphasis on the expectations and benefits of the relationship. The definitions also imply that customer retention is a valuable goal for marketers. Outside of sport, service marketers have been quick to embrace relationship marketing since it directly affects brand loyalty and long-term profitability. The term *relationship marketing* was introduced into the service marketing literature by Berry (1983, p. 25), who defined relationship marketing as "attracting, maintaining and—in multi-service industries—enhancing customer relationships."

Database Marketing

Database marketing has been called the biggest idea in marketing since "new and improved" (*Business Week*, 1994). Once used primarily by catalog and direct marketing companies, it is now pervasive across many types of organizations using direct marketing. Authors Don Peppers and Martha Rogers (1993) go so far as to call database marketing a paradigm shift. Kotler (1997) defines database marketing as "the process of building, maintaining, and using customer databases and other databases (products, suppliers, resellers) for the purpose of contracting and transacting." As the definition suggests, database marketing is a one-to-one approach to marketing that is information intensive and takes a long-term perspective.

Sport organizations are realizing that the fan or customer base has numerous alternatives for spending its entertainment dollars. Thus, instead of treating the customer base as a faceless mass market, successful firms are getting to know customers on a one-to-one basis in an effort to strengthen individual relationships and keep valuable customers for a lifetime. One strategy to assist sport firms in fostering these relationships is to store marketing information in a database in order to make data-driven decisions (McDonald and Milne, 1997; Milne and McDonald, 1997).

Database marketing is about collecting and storing relevant data about current customers, past customers, and prospective customers. Easy access to this stored data puts the organization in a position to provide better service and keep customers satisfied over the long run simply by recalling

or studying their buying behaviors. Database marketing is about making data-driven decisions to keep customer loyalty high and attrition low. A main advantage of database marketing is that it allows precise targeting of multiple consumer segments. There are many examples of sport organizations using databases and individualized data, some of which include

- ski centers capturing individual data on runs,
- professional sports teams generating and recording season ticket holder databases,
- college athletic fundraising departments implementing priority point systems,
- health and fitness clubs tracking club and equipment usage rates,
- sporting goods stores keeping purchase records.

The adoption of relationship marketing is being fueled by the availability of information technology. Databases allow marketers to store information on consumers, assess their value to the organization, and tailor individualized marketing strategies. Clearly, the use of a marketing database affects how organizations communicate with their constituencies. Consultants Stan Rapp and Tom Collins (1987) highlight this point in their book *Maxi-Marketing*:

> Every established norm in advertising and promotion is being transformed. We are living through the shift from selling virtually everyone the same thing a generation ago to fulfilling the individual needs and tastes of better-educated consumers by supplying them with customized products and services. The shift [is] from 'get a sale now at any cost' to building and managing customer databases that track the lifetime value of your relationship with each customer. As the cost of accumulating and accessing data drops, the ability to talk directly to your prospects and customers—and to build one-to-one relationships with them—will continue to grow.

Establishing a marketing database is crucial for a sports organization to support its attempts to build fan identification, segment its fan base and markets into actionable niches, and control and monitor customer service quality. Further, the database serves as the starting point for managing external stakeholders, such as corporate sponsors and the media, by storing and analyzing key information.

Interestingly, what distinguishes database marketing from a marketing information system (for discussion on MIS, see Mullin, Hardy, and Sutton, 1993) is that the data on customers are at the individual level and therefore can be used for *individualized communication*. This personalized level of understanding helps the organization serve the customer better and ensure retention. With databases, managers can fully engage in one-to-one marketing and deal with customers one at a time. Once the organization identifies an individual's needs, it can then communicate at a more personalized level (such as by making a sales offer) and then record the result of the communication. Thus, the database serves as the organization's memory by which it can refine its future communications.

By using individualized communication, database marketing is concerned with expanding the scope of the relationship with each customer. While traditional marketing focuses on trying to get more people to buy something, database marketing is concerned with getting existing customers to buy more things. As discussed later in this chapter, retaining satisfied customers for their lifetimes can be a valuable and profitable strategic move.

Databases Defined

In its simplest form, a database is a set of organized facts. For example, a Christmas card list or a set of codified receipts could be defined as a database. The data in the database should be interrelated so that the user can sort the data and access subsets of the data. For a database to be effective, the data should serve multiple applications and allow for timely and accurate retrieval of information. Although a database could be stored as a set of index cards, most databases these days are on microcomputers or larger computers. For marketing organizations, the most prevalent database is the customer database. A customer database has been defined by Philip Kotler (1997) as "an organized collection of comprehensive data about individual customers or prospects that is current, accessible, and actionable for such marketing purposes as lead generation, lead qualification, sale of a product or service, or maintenance of customer relationships."

Types of Information in a Database

The data stored in a database are particular to the applications of the marketer. Some general guidelines follow; of course, different data can be added or substituted:

Personal information
- mailing address (including zipcode) and phone number,
- demographics,
- psychographic profile.

Purchase history (transaction data)
- date of purchase,
- dollar amount of purchase,
- services or products consumed,
- method of payment.

Communications history
- pattern of response to past communications,
- media watched, read, or listened to.

Strategic Utilization of Databases

Hughes (1994) notes that "building a database is not difficult. Making money with a database is the real challenge. Keeping it going, building relationships with customers, reducing attrition, increasing sales over a multi-year period have proven to be very difficult for some, while others have mastered the art." In other words, having data is just a start to successful database marketing. To realize the full value from database marketing, it is important for the sport organization to also use it in a strategic manner. To effectively implement strategic database marketing, the following steps are required:

1. **Design a customer database:** All personnel who can benefit from relationship marketing efforts should be involved in designing the database, determining the types of reports to be produced, and scheduling communication programs. This includes

the marketing director, ticket manager, community relations director, sponsorship sales, and licensing/merchandising personnel.

The customer database should include basic information such as names, addresses, telephone numbers, number and type of tickets, and seat locations. Additionally, specific personal data such as birth dates for all household members, alma maters, referred radio station, purchase history, response to previous mailings, preferred activities, preferred opponents, and prior communications should be part of the database. In essence, the more you know about your consumers, the more powerful the database and its applications.

2. **Collect customer-level data:** There are a variety of methods for collecting the information comprising the database. One method is to include a survey in scheduled mailings to existing customers (e.g., ticket renewals). A second method is to distribute surveys at events and provide space for respondents to provide names and addresses to be added to the mailing list. A third way to collect the relevant data is through I.D. cards. Ticket holders can be admitted to games by swiping their bar-coded I.D. cards through a machine. Similar machines can record merchandise and concession purchases to track consumer purchasing habits. In order to ensure involvement from customers, it is important to continually convey the benefits of participation (e.g., improved service, targeted programs). This technique is very similar to the one used by supermarkets that track purchases via store club cards.

3. **Differentiate your customers:** Segment customers based on variables of interest. We focus on measurements of lifetime value and relationship strength. A firm may also segment customers by how they have responded to past communication efforts.

4. **Develop customer incentive programs:** The applications of the database to enhance and measure relationships with customers are nearly unlimited. The most valuable customers could be granted complimentary membership in a preferred membership club. These customers might qualify for opportunities to travel with the team, participate in special events, or gain access to specialty merchandise. Customers could also be provided with coupons for their favorite restaurant on their special days (birthday, anniversary).

An Empirical Study
Measuring Relative Relationship Strength and Lifetime Value

In sport publications as well as in marketing literature efforts toward measuring customer relationship values receive little mention. One measure of the value of a customer to a marketing organization is lifetime value. A customer's lifetime value (LTV) is "the present value of expected benefits (e.g., gross margin) less the burdens (e.g., direct costs of servicing and communicating) from customers" (Dwyer, 1989). Formally, lifetime value is defined as:

$$\Sigma \frac{\text{Revenues} - \text{costs}}{(1 + r)^n}$$

where r is the discount rate (interest rate) and n is number of purchase years in a customer's life. This formula indicates that customers have different value levels to an organization depending on the amount of revenue they may contribute, the costs to serve them, and the estimated length of time a customer is projected to be with an organization. Efficient marketing requires an organization to put more of its marketing budget toward satisfying its most valuable customers.

Despite its appealing conceptual promise, LTV has been utilized primarily by direct marketing companies. The model focuses on identifying differences in current and projected customer financial values, but it does not offer managerial insights for improving retention levels or strengthening relationships with customers. There are other factors that can moderate the strength of a customer's position within an organization. More personal relationship measures—such as loyalty and affiliation—also affect a customer's likelihood of remaining with an organization over the long term. As relationship marketing moves forward, there is a need to develop better measures of customer relationships and to utilize this information to improve individual customer–seller relationships.

In this study, we conceptualized a measure of the intangible bonds between customers and professional sport franchises. We called this relationship measure Relative Relationship Strength (RRS). Additionally, we showed how RRS in conjunction with LTV can be used as a segmentation tool to provide managers with a new approach to understand and improve relationships with current customers. The remainder of the study was divided into four sections. The first section reviews the methodology of the study. The second section details the development of the RRS measure. The third section depicts the results of empirically testing the RRS and LTV measures. Finally, the fourth section describes the managerial implications of using RRS and LTV as segmentation tools.

Study Methodology

Data for this study were collected during the summers of 1994 and 1995. Both the pretest and final data collection phases involved mail surveys of season ticket holders of the Orlando Magic team of the National Basketball Association (NBA). The Magic offered no partial plans, only season ticket packages. Thus, all respondents had significant experiences with the Magic. This sample was selected because of the dual advantages of accessibility and its appropriateness as a service organization. Respondents participating in this research were knowledgeable regarding the Orlando Magic franchise and had attended multiple games at the Orlando Arena during the six months prior to the start of this research.

The pretest phase took place during June and July of 1994. To ensure that the pretest instrument was appropriately tailored to the characteristics of the professional sport context, an initial evaluation was undertaken prior to data collection. Input was provided by both academicians (marketing and sport marketing faculty) and the Orlando Magic management team (marketing research director and managers). Modifications were based on the relevancy of the survey questions to professional sport and grammatical clarity. A cover letter explaining the purpose of the study as well as the survey itself were mailed from the Orlando Magic offices to all 5000 season ticket holders. Mailing addresses were taken directly from the Orlando Magic mailing list. A self-

addressed stamped envelope was included for the respondent to mail the questionnaire back to the Orlando Magic offices. The results were 1611 complete and valid surveys returned, for a response rate of 32.2%.[1] Surveys for the final phase of the research were mailed out in August 1995, with returns accepted through September. As in the pretest phase, 5000 surveys were mailed to season ticket holders. This time, 1380 complete and valid surveys were returned, for a response rate of 27.6%.

Developing an RRS Measure

In the professional sport context, measuring a customer's RRS is complex and requires special consideration beyond the standard financial information. This section conceptualizes an RRS measure applicable to professional sport franchises that incorporates the behavioral and psychological commitment of sport consumers.

Figure 5–1 depicts factors that impact the relationship between customers and a professional sport franchise. These moderators are separated into core and expanded relationship factors. Core relationship moderators relate to the relationship between the customer and the core product. The core relationship is comprised of both the usage index and fan identification index.

Usage refers to the length and intensity of the relationship as well as the frequency and nature of the contact between customers and a franchise. Frequency of utilization is not limited to attendance, but is inclusive of television viewership. If a season ticket holder chooses not to attend a home or away game, but instead views the game on television, this type of utilization still has value to the franchise. Television viewership leads to improved ratings, which translate to increased advertising rates and ultimately result in higher broadcast rights fees for the franchise.

In addition to the usage index, the core relationship is also comprised of the fan identification index. *Fan identification* refers to the level of personal

---

[1]Coincidentally, this is the same sample size and response rate as the sport marketing consumer survey reported in Chapters 2 and 3.

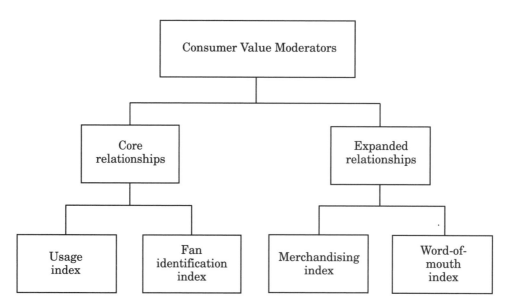

FIGURE 5–1. Factors Impacting the Relationship Between Professional Sport Franchises and Their Customers

commitment and emotional involvement customers have with a franchise (see Chapter 2). Sport differs from other sources of entertainment in that it evokes higher levels of emotional attachment and identification than other forms of entertainment. When a customer identifies closely with an organization, a sense of connectedness ensues and he or she begins to define him- or herself in terms of the organization (Mael and Ashforth, 1992). This identification leads to increased member loyalty to the organization (Adler and Adler, 1987), decreased turnover (O'Reilly and Chatman, 1986), and high brand loyalty and positive word of mouth (Peter and Olson, 1993; Aaker, 1994). It also results in improved retention rates. Given that it can cost an organization six times more to attract new consumers than it does to retain current customers (Rosenberg and Czepiel, 1984), improved retention rates can have a marked impact on the bottom line. Research indicates that identification is equally important for sport organizations as it relates to fan behavior. The degree to which fans identify with a sports team has significant consequences to that team's fiscal success. For example, Wann and Branscombe (1992) found that higher levels of fan

involvement and investment in a team translated into greater attendance and price insensitivity. Additionally, highly identified fans were less likely to disassociate themselves from a team during unsuccessful periods (Wann and Branscombe, 1990).

As presented in Figure 5–1, the second factor comprising RRS is the strength of the expanded relationships. The expanded relationship relates to aspects that transcend usage and identification with the core product. Specifically, it refers to the additional revenue generated from licensing and merchandising as well as the financial impact of developing future customers. As such, the expanded relationship index is comprised of the merchandising index and the word-of-mouth index.

The merchandising index consists of the general proclivity to purchase merchandise through the mail and the specific desire to purchase franchise merchandise through catalogs. In addition to the direct impact merchandise sales have on the revenue of a franchise, individuals wearing logo merchandise further advertise the team. This type of exposure enhances interest in the franchise and indirectly increases the level of support.

The word-of-mouth index refers to the propensity of current customers to encourage others to become franchise customers. Positive word-of-mouth results in the cost-efficient development of a future customer base. Given the high cost associated with attracting new customers, positive word-of-mouth is an extremely cost-efficient way to ensure the continual development of a future customer base.

Conceptually, as the strength of the core and expanded relationships between the customer and franchise increases, so does the overall relationship with the customer. Thus, both core relationship measures (the average of usage factors and fan identification) and expanded relationship measures (the average of merchandising index and word-of-mouth) should have a positive impact on RRS. Both the core and expanded relationship measures are normed by the sample average, with the center at 1.0.

In addition to the core and expanded relationship indices, measuring the strength of the relationship should account for an opportunity cost implicit in choosing to invest time and money in this relationship. This factor is represented in RRS as the *opportunity cost adjustment index*. The opportunity cost adjustment index reflects the implicit opportunity cost of being a season account holder of a professional sport franchise. These customers have chosen to invest their time and money in this relationship. Implicitly, they have chosen this option over other alternative uses of these resources. The opportunity cost index impacts the RRS of customers based on their level of satisfaction with the perceived value of the choice they made. When customers are satisfied (have less opportunity costs), the RRS is positively influenced. In contrast, RRS declines when customers are dissatisfied (have higher opportunity costs). The opportunity cost adjustment index can increase or decrease the RRS. As with the core and expanded relationship indices, this index should be normed by the sample average and centered at 1.0.

The calculation of RRS reflects the impact of all of the preceding factors. Specifically, the strength of the customer relationship is the number of years a person has been with an organization, the core relationship index, the expanded relationship index, and the opportunity cost adjustment index. Formally,

1. Core relationship = $(\text{usage}/\text{usage}_{\text{avg}} + \text{fan}/\text{fan}_{\text{avg}})/2$
2. Expanded relationship = $(\text{merch}/\text{merch}_{\text{avg}} + \text{WOM}/\text{WOM}_{\text{avg}})/2$ (where WOM = word-of-mouth)
3. Opportunity cost adjustment = $(\text{value}/\text{value}_{\text{avg}} + \text{satisfaction}/\text{satisfaction}_{\text{avg}})/2$
4. Relative relationship strength (RRS) = number of years $\times$ [core relationship + expanded relationship] $\times$ (opportunity cost adjustment)

In no. 4 above, "number of years" refers to the anticipated number of years remaining in the relationship. This is calculated by subtracting the current age of the season ticket holder from an upper bound constrained by the age of the oldest season ticket holder in the database.

RRS, in combination with LTV, can be utilized to segment professional sport customers. Many a successful franchise, like the Boston Celtics, has had valuable long-term fans leave when their winning days were over. The franchise is thus left not really understanding which customers to retain through its marketing efforts in order to rebuild the fan base.

Financial Measures

In order to evaluate a customer's worth to an organization, it is necessary to measure both lifetime value and relative relationship strength. Arraying customers on these two principal dimensions should provide an organization with ample information with which to effectively manage its fan base. Table 5–1 presents a framework for segmenting customers based on their LTV and RRS. Customers in a database can be classified according to these variables and arrayed on a two-dimensional space. Customers, based on their LTV and RRS scores, are placed in one of four cells (cell 1: high RRS/high LTV; cell 2: low RRS/high LTV; cell 3: high RRS/low LTV; cell 4: low RRS/low LTV). Sport consumers in cell 1 are referred to as "Core," cell 2 consumers are called "Corporate," cell 3 are known as "Crazed," and cell 4 are classified as "Casual."

Testing the RRS and LTV Measures

Table 5–2 depicts the LTV distribution, divided into deciles, and the corresponding values for mean LTV and mean RRS. The mean LTV for the sample was

$31,492. Decile 1, comprised of customers with the highest lifetime values, has a lower bound of $59,007. Decile 10, containing customers with the lowest lifetime values, has an upper bound of $9,282. The eight deciles between decile 1 and decile 10 range from LTVs of $9,283 to $59,006. For the entire sample, the range of values from low to high was $189,009, indicating the measure has sufficient variance for segmentation purposes.

The RRS shown in the Table 5–2 range from a low of 3.07 to a high of 153.95 ($\mu = 38.9$). The table also shows the mean RRS for each LTV decile. For LTV decile 10, the mean RRS is 19.2. For respondents with the highest lifetime value (decile 1), the mean RRS is 49.3. To better understand the relationship between these two variables, we converted RRS and LTV to a 0–100 scale and graphed the two variables by LTV decile. Figure 5–2 shows the results of this analysis. Generally speaking, as LTV increases, RRS also rises. However, as LTV reaches its highest levels (deciles 1–4), RRS begins to level off. RRS peaks in LTV decile 5. So, while these variables are correlated ($r = .293, p = .001$), increased financial involvement

with a franchise is not always matched by escalating emotional bonds. It appears that RRS provides us with additional insight into the professional sport consumer.

To find how this sample was distributed on the conceptual framework (see Table 5–1), respondents were divided into low and high based on their RRS and LTV scores. The cutoff point for LTV was $35,000, and respondents on RRS were divided at 37.25. Table 5–3 shows the distribution of the sample across the four segments. One-third, or 32.5% of the sample, were classified as cell 1 (Core); 18.2% were in cell 2 (Corporate); cell 3 (Crazed) was comprised of 18.0% of respondents; and 31.3% of the sample were in cell 4 (Casual). Given that these variables are correlated, it is to be expected that the largest groupings are in the high/high and low/low segments. Of greater conceptual interest are the values in each of the high/low cells over 18%. These individuals are either high in financial involvement and low in emotional attachment, or vice versa. The managerial implications of this distribution will be explored later in this chapter.

To profile these segments, we performed a chi-square analysis using the following variables: gender, household income, purpose for game attendance, and location/price preference. The variable location/price preference measured the relative importance of seat price and seat location to survey respondents. The purpose for game attendance indicated the primary motivation for attending games. Although six response options were provided for this item, the vast

TABLE 5–1. Conceptual framework

Relative relationship strength (RRS)	Lifetime value (LTV)	
	High	Low
High	1. Core	3. Crazed
Low	2. Corporate	4. Casual

TABLE 5–2. Comparison of RRS to LTV by decile

Decile number	Low LTV	High LTV	Average LTV	Average RRS
10	$ 2,211	$ 9,282	$ 6,103	19.2
9	9,283	12,110	11,117	16.4
8	12,111	16,724	14,519	34.0
7	16,725	21,013	18,910	35.4
6	21,014	24,220	22,938	49.3
5	24,221	30,019	26,648	38.2
4	30,020	36,330	32,859	47.7
3	36,331	42,683	39,384	49.8
2	42,684	59,006	49,954	48.5
1	59,007	191,220	95,186	49.3
Total Sample	$ 2,211	$191,220	$31,492	38.9

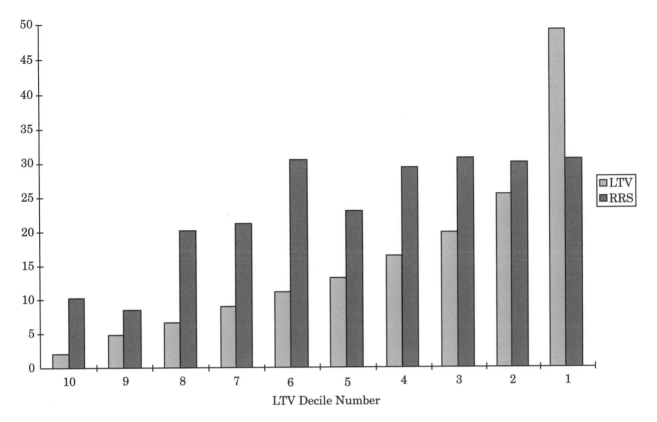

FIGURE 5–2. Relationship Between Lifetime Value (LTV) and Relative Relationship Strength (RRS) by Decile

TABLE 5–3. Relative relationship strength by lifetime value (LTV)

Relative relationship strength (RRS)	Lifetime value (LTV)	
	High	Low
High	32.5%	18.0%
Low	18.2%	31.3%

majority of respondents indicated either business reasons or family entertainment as their purpose for attending.

Table 5–4 displays the results of the chi-square analysis by segment. As shown, 82.1% of "Core" consumers were male. The differences between males and females across segments were not statistically significant ($\chi^2 = 7.02, p = 0.32$). Female basketball fans, often classified as being casual fans, were just as likely to fall into the other three segments. The segments did, however, differ on income ($\chi^2 = 93.09, p = 0.00$) and location/price preference ($\chi^2 = 36.88, p = 0.00$). Not surprisingly, the "Corporate" segment reported the highest business motivation (32.1%), highest percentage of respondents with incomes above \$75,000 (78.7%), and greatest preference for seat location over price considerations (70.9%). In contrast, the "Crazed" segment was price conscious (59.9%), with the majority (60%) having incomes less than \$75,000. This segment, in addition, was overwhelmingly attending for family entertainment purposes (89.9%). The "Core" consumers had profiles remarkably similar to the "Corporate" users. This segment placed a premium on seat location (68.5%)

TABLE 5–4. Profiling RRS/LTV segments by demographics

	RRS/LTV segments*				Chi-square	*p*-value
	Core	Crazed	Corporate	Casual		
Gender						
N	298	287	95	429		
Male	82.1%	75.9%	84.5%	79.2%	7.02	0.32
Female	17.9%	24.1%	15.5%	20.8%		
Income						
N	238	276	91	403		
< $75,000	34.3%	60.0%	21.3%	44.4%	93.09	0.00
> $75,000	65.7%	40.0%	78.7%	55.6%		
Purpose						
N	204	216	84	362		
Business	23.4%	10.1%	32.1%	10.4%	59.81	0.00
Family	76.6%	89.9%	67.9%	89.6%		
Preference						
N	238	282	93	418		
Location	68.5%	40.1%	70.9%	58.7%	36.88	0.00
Price	31.5%	59.9%	29.1%	41.3%		

*Table reports the column percentages.

and was twice as likely to attend for business reasons (23.4%) than the "Crazed" or "Casual" segments.

Since this segmentation depended on both RRS and LTV classification, it is unclear which of these variables was driving the statistically significant differences. Tables 5–5 and 5–6 present the results of additional analysis to clarify this issue. In these tables respondents were classified into high/low categories on RRS and LTV. Chi-square analyses were performed to check for statistical differences between these high/low groups on the same variables as in the previous analysis (see Table 5–4). The only statistically significant difference based on the RRS variable was household income ($\chi^2 = 30.77$, $p = 0.00$). The low RRS group was more likely to have incomes greater than $75,000 (65.1%) than the high RRS group (57.9%). In contrast, three of the four variables had significant differences for the high/low LTV groups. As Table 5–6 shows, respondents classified as high LTV had higher incomes, greater preference for location over price, and were more likely to attend games for business purposes than the low LTV group. In combination, the results in Tables 5–5 and 5–6 support the conclusion that the segment differences reported in Table 5–4 were driven by the LTV variable and not RRS.

Managerial Implications

The conceptual framework we have outlined, segmenting customers based on RRS and LTV, provides sport marketers with new information with which to develop and implement strategies to effectively manage their fan base. A franchise's most valuable customers are its *Core consumers*. These consumers have a high financial and emotional investment in the team. An effective and easily implemented strategy is to recognize and reward these customers for their continued loyalty. Special events in their honor and increased opportunities for contact with players and coaches should be sufficient to continue the quality of these relationships. Recognizing loyalty serves the additional purpose of providing an incentive for other customers to improve their relationships with the franchise to reap similar rewards.

In contrast to Core consumers, *Casual consumers* are not vested emotionally or financially in the team. As such, their relationships with the sport

TABLE 5-5. Profiling RRS segments by demographics*

	RRS		Chi-square	p-value
	Low	High		
Gender				
N				
Male	81.8%	79.7%	1.77	0.41
Female	18.2%	20.3%		
Income				
N				
< $75,000	34.9%	42.1%	30.77	0.00
> $75,000	65.1%	57.9%		
Purpose				
N				
Business	19.0%	19.0%	2.58	0.46
Family	81.0%	81.0%		
Preference				
N				
Location	64.4%	58.7%	5.67	0.13
Price	35.6%	41.3%		

*Table reports the column percentages.

TABLE 5-6. Profiling LTV segments by demographics*

	LTV		Chi-square	p-value
	Low	High		
Gender				
N				
Male	79.0%	83.4%	3.28	0.19
Female	21.0%	16.6%		
Income				
N				
< $75,000	46.6%	26.6%	44.43	0.00
> $75,000	53.4%	73.4%		
Purpose				
N				
Business	12.0%	31.0%	52.16	0.00
Family	88.0%	69.0%		
Preference				
N				
Location	55.3%	71.1%	25.89	0.00
Price	44.7%	28.9%		

*Table reports the column percentages.

organization are likely to fluctuate with team performance. These fans hop on the bandwagon when times are good and will jump ship when team fortunes decline. Since team performance is largely out of the control of sport marketers, few financial resources should be expended on customers in this segment. *Corporate consumers* have high financial investment coupled with low relationship strength. For most franchises, this segment will be comprised of the following two distinct customer groups:

Corporate users: High financial investment could reflect the purchase of a large number of and/or high-priced (e.g., luxury seating) season tickets. A percentage of corporate customers are corporate clients. This accounts for the low level of emotional investment. It is unlikely that these customers will be successfully converted to Core consumers. Fortunately, it doesn't matter—since these customers are purchasing tickets for corporate reasons, including client hospitality, their demand for tickets is inelastic. As a result, these customers will be relatively insensitive to changes in ticket prices and team performance.

These customers, however, will be very sensitive to changing levels of service quality. Corporate users are utilizing the sport product to better serve the needs of their current and future customers. As such, the level of service provided to them and their clients is crucial to continuing the exchange relationship. Marketing dollars expended on Corporate consumers should be allocated to the area of enhanced service quality, which should be delivered in terms of improved business communications and individualized attention during games.

Dissatisfied users: Low relationship strength could reflect high opportunity costs. Customers in this cell might be dissatisfied with the value they are receiving given the time and financial resources they have expended to continue the relationship. This might be a substantial segment, especially for franchises at maximum seating capacity and a correspondingly long waiting list for season ticket holders. Annual price increases and lack of individualized attention might also increase customer opportunity costs. On the other hand, these fans might be continuing the relationship because of superior seat location or team performance.

Customers in this segment offer a prime opportunity for sport marketers to apply the techniques of relationship marketing. These customers need to be rewarded for their continued patronage. Individualized marketing efforts and value-added programs are perfectly suited to this segment.

Customers classified as Crazed fans have high emotional but low financial ties with the team. As such, strategic marketing initiatives have the potential to change these customers to Core fans. Managers must ensure that proper mechanisms are in place for these customers to move up the escalator to higher levels of financial and emotional commitment. For example, a variety of ticket plans must be available to move single-game attendees to more frequent usage. Additionally, all efforts must be made to ensure that these marginal fans have the opportunity to follow the team in the media (television, radio, newspaper, and the Internet) and purchase merchandise and memorabilia at the playing facility as well as off site at easily accessible locations.

A bonus system can also be established to provide additional emotional rewards based on increased financial investment. One such example, a traditional point system, is based on the number of games attended, number of tickets purchased, and concession and merchandise purchasing habits. Rewards should serve to further enhance emotional ties with the team. Especially effective rewards might include the opportunity to travel with the team, the opportunity to sit in the owner's luxury box for a game, or annual access to players and/or coaches prior to a game.

Summary

As competition for consumers' entertainment dollars intensifies and organizations of all types begin to shift emphasis from attracting customers to retaining them, relationship marketing is becoming more important. Crucial to the adoption of relationship marketing is the accessibility to information technology. Databases provide marketers with the opportunity to store information on consumers, assess their current and future values to the organization, and develop individualized marketing efforts.

One measure used to assess customer relationship value is lifetime value (LTV). This measure, however, fails to account for the added benefits derived from customer relationships above and beyond estimated revenue. This chapter, in order to provide a more comprehensive framework for sport marketing, has introduced the concept of relative relationship strength (RRS) to measure the emotional attachment sport consumers have with sport franchises.

The importance of extending the relationship between customers and franchises has resulted in the need to accurately measure the long-term value of these expanded relationships. Limited resources force organizations to choose how best to allocate marketing dollars to optimize customer retention. Franchises should invest more resources (time, energy, and finances) in satisfying those customers who have the greatest long-term impact on the organization's profitability. As marketing evolves from being transaction-based to relationship-based, sport organizations that take the proper steps to develop and manage supplier and customer relationships will have a distinct advantage over the competition.

Limitations of the Study

Although the research just described has made contributions to the understanding of customer LTV and RRS in the professional sport context, it is not without limitations. First, the Orlando Magic is not a typical professional sport franchise. It has been so well managed that it is considered among industry insiders to be one of the premiere franchises in all of sport. This status is reflected in ticket renewal rates approaching 100%, with a long waiting list for season tickets. Furthermore, the Magic experienced tremendous success during the two years this research was conducted. Thus, the results from this study do not necessarily generalize directly to other sport franchises.

Much of the import of calculating LTV is the provision of differential service based on customer profitability levels. Marketers want to identify their best customers and treat them well since higher levels of service will lead to higher retention rates. Alter-

natively, if marketers do not treat customers well, they will become dissatisfied and their probability of leaving will increase, which is of no value to the organization. In the LTV formula, customer dissatisfaction was modeled as part of the opportunity cost index. Although less-satisfied customers have a higher opportunity cost (and are more likely not to renew tickets), this measure is not an exact predictor for retention. A more appropriate measure of retention would be a direct question ascertaining intent to renew tickets the following season and for future seasons.

Another limitation of this study is the estimation of marketing costs. Ideally, this number should vary at an individual or segment level. However, because of lack of available data, customer costs were treated as a constant percentage of revenue in the calculation of LTV and were assumed to be the same percentage for all individuals. Clearly, even in the professional sport context, different customers have different costs associated with maintaining the relationship. Making this number a constant across customers reduced the potential variance in the LTV calculation.

For the purposes of this study, the merchandise purchasing component in the expanded relationship was measured as the propensity to buy merchandise through direct mail opportunities. Valuable customers who preferred to purchase Magic merchandise in person might have received a low merchandise index in spite of frequent purchases. Therefore, data on annual Magic merchandise purchases per customer would have provided a more accurate measure of the value of the expanded relationship.

Future Research

While this research has potentially made contributions to the understanding of lifetime value and relative relationship strength within the professional sport context, several windows of opportunity remain open for future research. Specifically, these research topics could include examining the databases of other professional sport organizations, capturing comprehensive information regarding merchandise purchasing, studying other segments of the sport enterprise, and utilizing LTV and RRS to profile other aspects of the customer/sport organization relationship (e.g., service quality).

Further LTV research could explore expanding the LTV formula by adding a variable to the numerator representing intent to renew tickets. This information could be obtained by adding a question like the following to the survey instrument: "Please rate on a scale from 0 (absolutely not going to renew) to 100 (absolutely sure of renewing), your current intentions regarding season ticket renewal for next season." Intention to renew could then be added into the computation of LTV.

Future research might also focus on the manner of collecting information regarding merchandising. In our study, the two items used to assess propensity to purchase merchandise were focused on responsiveness to direct mail opportunities. While use of these questions reflects future directions for merchandising in professional sport, additional variables need to be added that measure annual merchandise purchases per customer. Combined with the existing direct mail questions, a more complete measure of the value of this expanded relationship should emerge.

The professional sport context was utilized to develop this conceptual framework, but future research could also focus on applying this model to other segments of the sport enterprise. The obvious targets for this extension would be other spectator sport segments, including, but not be limited to, collegiate athletics, the Olympics, and individual sports such as tennis, golf, and skiing. All of these areas charge admission, promote and benefit from fan identification, and provide opportunities to purchase event or team merchandise. It would be interesting and worthwhile to explore the similarities and differences in the four customer segments among these sport areas.

This study profiled RRS and LTV based primarily on demographics. Future research could profile the four segments based on other aspects of the customer/sport organization relationship. Other aspects that could be studied in relation to RRS and LTV are organizational commitment, appropriate advertising vehicles, relative importance of winning, and reasons

for purchasing season tickets. We hope a more complete understanding of RRS and LTV will be derived from exploring the relationship to these other marketing variables.

References

Aaker, D. (1994). Building a brand: The Saturn story. *California Management Review*, 36 (2): 114.

Adler, P., and P. A. Adler (1987). Role conflict and identity salience: College athletics and the academic role. *Social Science Journal*, 24: 443–455.

Berry, Leonard L. (1983). Relationship marketing. In *Emerging perspectives on services marketing*. Leonard L. Berry, G. Lynn Shostack, and Gregory Upah, (eds.). Chicago, IL: American Marketing Association, 25–28.

Business Week (1994). Database marketing: A potent new tool for selling. September 5, 56–62.

Dwyer, F. Robert (1989). Customer lifetime valuation to support marketing decision making. *Journal of Direct Marketing*, 3 (Autumn): 8–15.

Gronroos, C. (1990). *Service management and marketing: Managing the moments of truth in service competition.* New York: Lexington Books.

Hughes, Arthur M. (1994). *Strategic database marketing.* Chicago, IL: Probus Publishing Company.

Kotler, Philip (1997). *Marketing management,* 9th ed. Englewood Cliffs, NJ: Prentice-Hall.

Mael, F. and B. E. Ashforth (1992). Alumni and their alma mater: A partial test of the reformulated model of organizational identification. *Journal of Organizational Behavior*, 13: 103–123.

Milne, George R., and Mark A. McDonald (1997). Introduction to the special issue on relationship marketing in sport. *Sport Marketing Quarterly*, 5 (2): 4.

McDonald, Mark A., and George R. Milne (1997). A conceptual framework for evaluating marketing relationships in professional sport franchises. *Sport Marketing Quarterly*, 5 (2): 27–32.

Mullin, B. J., S. Hardy, and W. A. Sutton (1993). *Sport marketing*. Champaign, IL: Human Kinetics Publishers.

O'Reilly, C., III, and J. Chatman (1986). Organizational commitment and psychological attachment: The effects of compliance, identification, and internalization of prosocial behavior. *Journal of Applied Psychology*, 71 (3): 492–499.

Peppers, D., and M. Rogers (1993). *The one to one future: Building relationships one customer at a time.* New York: Doubleday/Currency.

Peter, J. P., and J. C. Olson (1993). *Consumer behavior and marketing strategy.* Homewood, IL: Richard D. Irwin, Inc.

Rapp, Stan, and Tom Collins (1987). *Maxi-marketing.* New York: McGraw-Hill Inc.

Rosenberg, L. J., and J. A. Czepiel (1984). A marketing approach to customer retention. *Journal of Consumer Marketing*, 1 (Spring): 45–51.

Shani, D., and Suzana Chalasani (1992). Exploiting niches using relationship marketing. *The Journal of Consumer Marketing*, 9 (3): 33–43.

Sutton, W. A., M. A. McDonald, G. R. Milne, and J. Cimperman (1997). Creating and fostering fan identification in professional sports. *Sport Marketing Quarterly* (forthcoming).

Wann, D. L., and N. R. Branscombe (1990). Diehard fans and fair weather fans: Effects of identification on BIRGing and CORFing tendencies. *Journal of Sport and Social Issues*, 14: 103–117.

—— (1992). Role of identification with a group, arousal, categorization processes, and self-esteem in sports spectator aggression. *Human Relations*, 45: 1013–1034.

Managing Niche Markets

Introduction

The marketplace is exploding with new sport options for both participants and spectators. Rollerblading, indoor wall climbing, and bungee jumping have all developed into viable sport participation alternatives. The growth of rollerblading has also impacted the sports of hockey and skiing. Blading has increased access to the sport of hockey by bringing roller hockey to the streets. In skiing, rollerblading has afforded participants an ideal off-season training option. For spectators, the number of viewing options across all sports continues to increase. New sport networks are constantly emerging, including ESPN2, ESPN3, CNNSI, the Golf Channel, and so forth.

Given the competitive nature of today's sport environment, many sport managers are practicing niche strategies and tailoring their sport and fitness services directly to the needs of the target customer markets (Mullin, Hardy, and Sutton, 1993). A niche strategy is the focusing of marketing efforts by managers at a group of customers who are core to the success of the business. A niche is commonly referred to as a habit necessary for a species to exist (Milne *et al.*, 1996). In the sport context, we conceptualize a niche as a habitat, represented by a sport product's core customers (who often have the same demographic and psychographic backgrounds). Niches differ from market segments in that niches reflect only the core customer profile of a single sport, whereas segments are derived independently of specific sports (Milne, McDonald, Sutton, and Kashyap, 1996). Thus, in a market there may be a couple of market segments, but each competitor in a market has a specific niche, which may or may not overlap with those of its competitors.

For managers, serving niches is an attractive means of focusing on the most receptive audiences for the product or message. Evidence of niche strategies can be seen in terms of the proliferation of specialist magazines (e.g., *Triathlete, Cross Country Skier, Skydiving Magazine*); the strong following of special sporting events for new sports like roller hockey and beach volleyball; the TV coverage of new sports on channels like ESPN2 and cable niche channels, such as the Golf Channel; and the interest of sponsors, such as Jose Cuervo and Seagrams, in niche sports.

The attention given to niche strategies may or may not be exclusive to new sports. The existing sport industry is highly fragmented, with numerous options for consumers to participate and spectate. Recent empirical research has shown that for established sport and fitness activities, the consumer market is quite narrow (Howard, 1992). Researchers Rod Warnick and Dennis Howard report that golf and tennis, which are considered mass market sports, are played by less than 5% of the adult population (Warnick and Howard, 1985).

The challenge of pursuing a niche strategy is to constantly monitor competitors within the niche and in the broader product market. This task becomes complicated as the marketplace continues to fragment into numerous options available to the sport consumer. Brooks (1994) has suggested that new golfers, for example, also want to sail, white-water raft, and scuba dive. For managers, it is important to have information about secondary participation sports as well as spectating interests. For leagues with growing sport markets, knowledge about the relationship between participation and spectatorship is critical. By understanding this relationship, managers can better target their communications to increase their overall customer base.

Although the benefits of niche strategies are well known by managers, less is known about how to evaluate the competitive position of a product's niche. In this chapter, we will show the benefits of niche analysis. Specifically, we will measure niches in the sport and fitness markets and use these measures to examine linkages (competitive patterns) that exist among participant and spectator sports.

The chapter is divided into two parts. Part I will provide a conceptual overview of niche marketing and then present the results of two sport studies. The first study utilizes a national sample of syndicated demographic data collected by American Sports Data, Inc., and reports on the competitive participation linkages among seven sports. The second study will utilize demographic and attitudinal data from a national survey of 1611 respondents and show how niche analysis can help assess the spectating and participation linkages for three sports. Part II of this chapter will provide details of the methodology being utilized in this chapter to measure sport niches.

Part I: Niche Analysis in Sport Marketing

Over the years, business researchers have borrowed the competitive theory of niche analysis from ecology and applied it to marketing (Henderson, 1983). Ecologists came to conceptualize the environment, or set of resources that a species relies upon for survival, as the niche (Hutchinson, 1957). However, in many respects the theoretical background for niche strategy dates back to Darwin's (1859) theory of natural selection, which suggests that species that have the best fit with the environment will survive and outperform rivals. The niche has since become an important concept for describing business competition. The Guase Competitive Exclusion Principle was incorporated into the theory of the niche and has been used to explain that no two species (or brands) can fill the identical niche and survive in the long run (Henderson, 1989).

The metaphor of niche theory can be used in marketing contexts, where products are the species and customers are the food source (Milne, 1994; Milne and Mason, 1990). In a sport marketing application, we define a niche as the profile of a sport product customer's background (e.g., demographic, psychographic, and so forth). Depending upon how a niche is measured, customers can be described along a single dimension (such as age) or any number (n) of dimensions (e.g., age, income, education). Consistent with niche theory, each sport in the market has its own niche (or description of its customers). The breadth of the niche depends on the variance of the customers' backgrounds and thus reflects the heterogeneity of customer backgrounds rather than numbers of customers. Competition in the sport and fitness markets is affected by both niche breadth and niche proximity. When two sport activities attract the same customer profile (when their niches overlap), they are, by definition, potentially competing for the same customers.

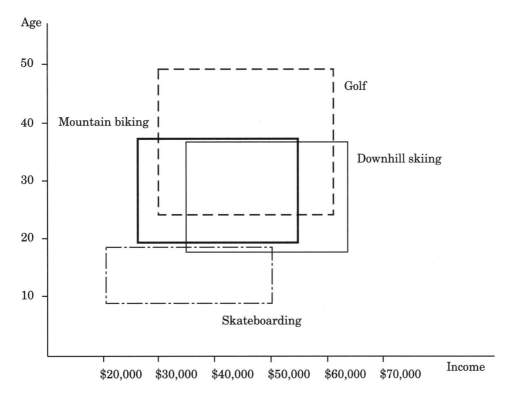

FIGURE 6-1. Niche Overlap Example

In Figure 6–1, we graphically show the niche spaces of golf, downhill skiing, mountain biking, and skateboarding. The niche space in this example is in two dimensions defined by the age and income of each sport's core participants. In this example, the niche breadth of golf (or niche area reflected by that rectangular space) is the broadest, while that of skateboarding is the narrowest. The figure shows different levels of pairwise competition between the sports. For example, golf and skiing compete for participants who have ages between 24 and 37 and income levels between $33,000 and $61,000. On the other hand, golf does not compete with skateboarding, so the two sports' niches do not overlap.

Note that measuring niche overlap is different from measuring the joint occurrence between two activities. For example, managers who wanted to understand the link between media and markets tra-ditionally relied upon joint occurrence information from syndicated data such as Simmons Market Research. Such data might indicate that 40% of readers of *Sport Illustrated* also watch a particular sport on television. Although this information is useful, its application is limited in that it is not tied directly to demographics or motivations of the audience. In niche analysis, we are interested in measuring potential for an individual to engage in similar activities by comparing aggregate profiles of sport consumers. This allows sport marketers to understand the substitute products available to their respective target audience. Sport marketers can use that knowledge to plan joint promotion strategies, define market position, or broaden product-line offerings.

In the following analyses, we will examine the similarities and dissimilarities of customer demographic and/or psychographic backgrounds for

TABLE 6–1. Competitive resource overlap for seven participant sports based on six demographic dimensions[a]

By:	Overlap of these sport categories						
	(1)	**(2)**	**(3)**	**(4)**	**(5)**	**(6)**	**(7)**
(1) Basketball	1.00	0.32[c]	0.45	0.45	0.65	0.28	0.52
(2) Cycling	0.45[b]	1.00	0.75	0.26	0.61	0.71	0.70
(3) Running	0.55	0.66	1.00	0.37	0.69	0.59	0.71
(4) Soccer	0.33	0.13	0.22	1.00	0.29	0.15	0.29
(5) Softball	0.70	0.47	0.60	0.42	1.00	0.43	0.75
(6) Swimming	0.40	0.71	0.67	0.29	0.56	1.00	0.74
(7) Volleyball (sand)	0.56	0.48	0.56	0.38	0.68	0.43	1.00

[a]Niches were defined and based on six demographic variables. These were % male, % white, % living in North Census Region, % living in metropolitan residence, age, and income.

[b]Read this number as 45% of basketball's niche (1) is overlapped by cycling's niche (2).

[c]Read this number as 32% of cycling's niche (2) is overlapped by basketball's niche (1).

several sports. Similarity is based on an index called *competitive resource overlap*, where values range from 0 to 1. A value of 0 indicates 0% overlap between two sports' niches, and an index of 1 suggests 100% overlap (see Part II for details).

Study 1: Evaluating Competitive Links with Syndicated Demographics Data

In Study 1 we used data from the syndicated tracking study *American Sports Analysis* (American Sports Data, 1993). This syndicated data source provided an overview of sports participation in the United States for individuals aged 6 and above. Niche spaces were estimated for basketball, cycling, running, soccer, softball, swimming, and volleyball, and niches were defined based on six demographic variables. Table 6–1 shows the niche structure for these seven participant sports.

The 1.00 values in the table represent a sport's overlap with itself. The competitive overlaps in the table range from a 13% overlap of cycling's niche by soccer to a 75% overlap of volleyball's niche by softball. The data in Table 6–1 show high levels of niche overlaps among groups of sports. For example, 66% and 71% of cycling's niche are overlapped by running and swimming, respectively. Soccer, on the other

hand, appears the least likely of the seven reported sports to overlap or be overlapped by other sports.

In many respects, the results of the niche analysis from Study 1 seem to have a high level of face validity and seem to describe current business practices in the sport and fitness industry. Specifically,

1. Niche overlap has resulted in the creation of new sport events and sport festivals combining one or more activities in a new format. For instance, biathlons and triathlons are direct results of niche overlaps among running, cycling, and swimming.

2. The success of cross training (which has proven extremely lucrative for Nike) is a direct result of the niche overlaps depicted in Table 6–1 between the individual sports of running and cycling, and team sports, such as softball and volleyball. Cross training has also led to new developments in the health club industry in programming, layout and design, and equipment.

3. Astute operators of softball complexes have capitalized on the overlap between volleyball and softball by adding sand volleyball courts to their facilities. Hosting two or more events simultaneously attracts an audience, which also increases concession and merchandise sales.

4. Grass roots sport marketing companies (for example, Triple Crown Sports, Fort Collins, Colorado) have been very successful in the 1990s. These companies originally offered only one sport activity at

a time (e.g., softball). As these businesses have evolved and become more in tune with their consumers' needs, they have started to offer several choices of sports, encouraging teams to compete in multiple activities (softball, basketball, soccer, and so forth).

Study 2: Understanding the Link Between Sport Participants and Spectators

Study 2 utilizes demographic data in a niche analysis to examine links between sport participation and spectatorship. Previous research generally separated these two types of participation. Several researchers have studied socialization and antecedents of leisure sport participation (Sofranko and Nolan, 1972; Sprietzer and Snyder, 1976), whereas other studies have focused on motivations for sport participation (Harris, 1973; Kenyon, 1968). Other studies have focused on spectatorship (Gaskell and Pearton, 1979; Sloan, 1985; Zillman, Bryant, and Sapolsky, 1979). To date, the research is inconclusive regarding the relationship between sport participation and spectatorship. Some researchers, such as Sloan, argue that both types of sport enthusiasts have similar motivations and derive the same benefits. Other researchers, such as Goodhart and Chataway (1968), contend that these activities are contradictory by nature or that socialization into participation is distinctly different from socialization into the secondary sport roles of spectator, viewer, listener, or reader. A recent study by Burnett, Menon, and Smart (1993) concluded that spectators and participants are independent of one another and that sport marketers targeting one of these two groups would fail to reach a large proportion of the other group. It should be noted that the classification of participants and spectators in the Burnett study was based on aggregate sport consumption behavior, with no comparisons made on a sport-by-sport basis. It is likely that the linkage between participation and spectatorship varies by sport based on demographic, motivational, and access variables.

To begin to explore this issue, we used data from a national survey of sport consumers. In conducting the survey, a random sample of 5000 names was drawn from a direct mailing list of individuals who indicated to National Lifestyles, Inc., that they were sport enthusiasts. A prenotification postcard was mailed to each individual asking for cooperation in filling out a subsequent survey. The final survey, which was sent to these individuals a week later, resulted in 1611 responses (32.2% response rate). The theme of the survey was to find out what motivated individuals to play and watch sport in general. As part of the survey respondents indicated which sports were their favorites to watch or play, or both, choosing from a specified list.

As part of the niche analysis we examined the background and attitudes of sport enthusiasts (both participants and spectators) for three sports. We included respondents who said the sport was one of their favorites. Respondents answered in a five-point Likert scale, anchored by "not a favorite" = 1 and "a favorite" = 5). Niche overlaps were calculated between the sports based on five demographic dimensions. The overlaps, shown in Table 6–2, reveal a pattern of strong links between spectator and participant markets. For example, 81% of the basketball participant niche is overlapped by the pro basketball spectator niche. Similarly, 84% of the golf participant niche overlaps the golf spectator niche.

The research study shows subtle differences in audiences for sport. Interestingly, in contrast to pro basketball spectators, the link between basketball participants and college basketball spectators is not relatively strong (43.2%). College basketball spectating is different from pro basketball spectating. This fact is supported by demographics: only 36% of the spectating pro basketball niche is overlapped by the spectating college basketball niche.

In viewing the niche overlaps between spectators and participants, there are many asymmetrical relationships. Not surprisingly, the overlap of the spectator niches by the participant niches is not as strong as the overlap of participant niches by those of spectators. This is because (a) the spectator niches often include individuals who have retired from playing sports, and (b) the audience demographics for spectators is often different and much broader than that for participants. For example, the overlap of golf par-

TABLE 6–2. Competitive resource overlap for sport participant and spectator niches based on five demographic dimensions[a]

| | Overlap of these sport categories | | | | | | |
	(1)	**(2)**	**(3)**	**(4)**	**(5)**	**(6)**	**(7)**
By:							
(1) Basketball (p)	1.00	0.25	0.20	0.42	0.48	0.18	0.16
(2) Golf (p)	0.06	1.00	0.09	0.14	0.05	0.48	0.07
(3) Tennis (p)	0.35	0.62	1.00	0.73	0.32	0.52	0.62
(4) College basketball (s)	0.43	0.57	0.43	1.00	0.36	0.50	0.30
(5) Pro basketball (s)	0.81	0.34	0.31	0.60	1.00	0.32	0.29
(6) Golf (s)	0.08	0.84	0.13	0.22	0.08	1.00	0.11
(7) Tennis (s)	0.32	0.53	0.70	0.59	0.33	0.49	1.00

[a]The five demographic dimensions were age, gender, education, income, and race.

(p) = participant, (s) = spectator.

ticipants by spectators is 84% in contrast to the 48% of spectators by participants.

It should also be noted that the intensity and degree of involvement in spectatorship can affect the linkages. Watching a sport on television may be very different from attending an event. In a 1993 study of 4,079 spectators by Del Wilber and Associates at an LPGA golf event, it was found that 3560, or 87.3%, also played golf (Del Wilber and Associates, 1993).

To further explore the link between participants and spectators, we calculated niche overlap based on individual motivations for spectating and participating in sport using 16 motivational items. In an effort to meet the assumptions of the method, the data were subjected to a principal factor analysis, which revealed the three factors shown in Table 6–3.

The results of the niche analysis conducted on the sports using the three motivation factors are shown in Table 6–4 and indicate that links between spectator and participant niches are not as strong as the links among spectator niches or among participant niches (noted in bold type). The overlaps among the participants range from 63% to 78% and among spectators from 72% to 92%. In contrast, the links between participants and spectators ranged from 18% to 34%. The biggest contributor to the differences between spectators and participants is differences in the personal improvement factor. Compared with sport spectators, sport participants had much

TABLE 6–3. Reasons why people participate in sports

Factor 1: Personal improvement
Release of tension/relaxation, sense of accomplishment, skill mastery, improved health and fitness, other peoples' respect for one's athletic skill, release of aggression, enjoyment of risk taking, personal growth, development of positive values, sense of personal pride
Factor 2: Sport appreciation
Enjoyment of the game, sport competition, enjoyment of beauty of the game, thrill of victory
Factor 3: Social facilitation
Time spent with close friends or family, sense of being member of a group

higher scores for items that constituted the personal improvement factor.

The results of Study 2 suggest that niche analysis can aid in assessing the link between sport audience participants and spectators. In many instances this link remains an elusive, yet important, marketing question. For example, sport researchers in the United States have pondered for years why soccer is popular with players but not with spectators. Clearly, gaining insight into the linkage between the participation and spectator worlds affects a sport's overall competitive position. Anecdotal evidence as well as academic research (Zillman *et al.*, 1979) have shown that for many sports the level of participation increases after a major spectating event. The power of

TABLE 6–4. Competitive resource overlap for sport participant and spectator niches based on three motivation factors

| | Overlap of these sport categories | | | | | | |
	(1)	(2)	(3)	(4)	(5)	(6)	(7)
By:							
(1) Basketball (p)	1.00	**0.70**	**0.77**	0.26	0.28	0.20	0.21
(2) Golf (p)	**0.63**	1.00	**0.78**	0.26	0.28	0.22	0.22
(3) Tennis (p)	**0.64**	**0.74**	1.00	0.23	0.26	0.18	0.19
(4) College basketball (s)	0.28	0.32	0.29	1.00	**0.83**	**0.77**	**0.76**
(5) Pro basketball (s)	0.33	0.37	0.34	**0.88**	1.00	**0.73**	**0.73**
(6) Golf (s)	0.23	0.28	0.24	**0.80**	**0.72**	1.00	**0.84**
(7) Tennis (s)	0.27	0.31	0.28	**0.85**	**0.79**	**0.92**	1.00

(p) = participant, (s) = spectator.

this connection as a marketing tool has not gone unnoticed. *Runner's World*, for example, in an effort to build commitment to the sport, has testimonials from runners saying that reading about running (a related spectating activity) motivates people to actually go out and run. This has been an effective marketing strategy.

The niche analyses presented in this chapter are a new approach for segmenting the industry (Pitts, Fielding, and Miller, 1994). The two studies described illustrate a method of evaluating the link between sporting activities using both syndicated and traditional survey data. Armed with the knowledge gained from niche analysis, managers can plan strategies to

1. *Retain members of the sport.* Membership retention is key to survival in today's markets. Anecdotal evidence suggests that it costs a manager up to 10 times more to attract a customer than it does to keep one. Niche analysis shows the managers what other interests their audience has and on which dimensions (demographic and/or attitudinal) a particular sport may be vulnerable to competitors.

2. *Recruit and motivate new members of the sport.* Niche overlap shows the managers which sports have potential new customers based on similar demographic or attitudinal patterns. New sports, such as boardsailing, for example, can raid established sports of skiing, in-line skating, etc. Niche analysis can also work between spectator and participant markets. Spectator soccer, for example, could benefit from niche analysis of links with participant

soccer and, in turn, motivate participants to watch the sport.

3. *Find opportunities for cross selling.* Niche overlap can highlight opportunities to cross sell and use established facilities. For example, the management team of a ski resort is faced with a facility utilization and marketing dilemma that lasts approximately seven months. Many resorts have added golf courses, mountain bike trails, family fitness complexes, and tennis facilities to attract consumers to the resort in the summer, which increases their revenue bases.

4. *Select proper media vehicles for communications.* Niche demographic profiles can be matched with media vehicle profiles to select effective media. Syndicated data such as *Simmons Market Research* provide data that are well suited for niche analysis. Other sources, such as *The Sponsor Fact Book*, can be utilized in niche analysis to match demographic profiles with promotional activities.

Trends indicate that for sport markets niche strategies will remain an important resource. With the increase of available data, no manager can rely solely on univariate background demographic profiles. Rather, competitive strength will come from combining data in a manner that provides insight and helps guide strategy. Niche analysis is an approach that takes both syndicated and survey data and allows managers to examine sophisticated multivariate connections among sporting activities. Managers who can use these tools should have an upper hand in the competitive sport marketplace.

Part II: Niche Measurement and Validation

The niche-based methodology we use has six steps. To illustrate the methodology, we will show each of these steps for the sports of golf and downhill skiing, using data incorporated in the larger empirical study for validation.

Step 1. Define the Relevant Market

Defining the relevant market entails identifying which collection of sports constitutes a market. The process of market definition is an important marketing management decision. The range of sports included depends upon the purpose of the analysis. For strategic planning, examining a broad spectrum of sports is useful. We used data from the *American Sports Analysis* syndicated tracking study to conduct the research. (The publisher, American Sports Data, is a syndicated data source that provides a comprehensive overview of sports participation in the United States.) The sample for the survey consisted of an NFO research mail panel. The data we used is based on a sample of 14,376 surveys covering the twelve months ended December 1993. Based on data availability, we used 36 sport and fitness activities to define our product market.

Step 2. Define the Relevant Variable of the Resource Space

The variables used to measure the resource space should be selected based on their ability to discriminate among sports; thus, a good variable is one that has substantial variance across the set of sports examined. In selecting variables, the analyst wants to cover the domain of possible discriminating variables without adding redundant dimensions. If syndicated data are used, the available variables include demographics and psychographics. However, it is also possible to include other types of dimensions, such as motivations for participating or benefits sought.

Measures can be used that are based on single variables, such as age, or on multiple-item constructs such as "need for aggression." When using aggre-gated syndicated data (e.g., Simmon's Market Research; American Sports Data) proportions can be used (e.g., % males that participate in sport) or metric means with a standard deviation. If individual-level data from a survey are available, the data can be aggregated.

For this study, we defined niches in six dimensions (e.g., % male, % white, % living in North Census Region, % living in metropolitan residence, age, and income). For clarity, the raw data from American Sports Data for golf and skiing are shown in Table 6–5. Because the data in most syndicated research show percentages, the analyst must calculate the standard deviations. For variables that are represented as proportions (p) (for example, % male), the mean is p and the standard deviation is:

$$\sigma = \sqrt{p(1 - p)}$$

For variables that are categorical (having a distribution of proportions (p) over multiple categories, for example, age), the mean is a weighted average of the category midpoints (m):

$$\mu = \frac{\Sigma mp}{\Sigma p}$$

and the standard deviation is

$$\sigma = \frac{\Sigma \sqrt{(m - \mu)p}}{\Sigma p}$$

The example in Table 6–5 shows the percentages, category midpoints, and resultant means and standard deviations for all variables for the sports golf and skiing. In addition, relevant calculations are provided in full.

Step 3. Compute the Niche Boundaries

The next step is to compute the niche boundaries for each variable and for each sport. This is done using the mean and standard deviation for each variable on each sport. With these two figures, we can calculate the niche boundaries for each variable and sport.

TABLE 6-5. Examples of converting syndicated data percentages into means and standard deviations

Variable	Category midpoint (*m*)	% Golf (*p*)	% Skiers (*p*)	Estimated means Golf (μ)	Estimated means Skiing (μ)	Estimated std. dev. Golf (σ)	Estimated std. dev. Skiing (σ)
Age							
6–11	8.5	4.6	8.7				
12–17	14.5	8.8	16.7				
18–24	21.0	11.9	19.0				
25–34	29.5	26.2	27.9				
35–44	39.5	20.9	18.6				
45–54	49.5	12.5	6.3				
55–64	59.5	7.6	2.9				
65+	65.0	7.4	0.0				
				35.7	27.5	15.6	12.5
Income ($1000s)							
<15	15.0	12.6	5.2				
15–24	19.5	10.2	10.6				
25–34	29.5	13.0	15.4				
35–49	39.5	19.4	20.5				
50–74	62.0	29.2	27.8				
75+	75.0	15.7	20.5				
				45.2[a]	48.1	21.0[b]	20.4
Male		0.756	0.613	.756[c]	.613	.429[d]	.487
White		0.879	0.872	.879	.872	.326	.334
Northern		0.295	0.218	.295	.218	.456	.413
Metro		0.427	0.433	.427	.433	.495	.495

[a]45.2 = [(15 × 12.6) + (19.5 × 10.2) + (29.5 × 13) + (39.5 × 19.4) + (62 × 29.2) + (75 × 15.7)]/(12.6 + 10.2 + 13.0 + 19.4 + 29.2 + 15.7)

[b]21.0 = [((15 − 45.2)$^{.5}$ × 12.6) + ((19.5 − 45.2)$^{.5}$ × 10.2) + ((29.5 − 45.2)$^{.5}$ × 13) + ((39.5 − 45.2)$^{.5}$ × 19.4) + ((62 − 45.2)$^{.5}$ × 29.5) + ((75 − 45.2)$^{.5}$ × 15.7)]/(12.6 + 10.2 + 13.0 + 19.4 + 29.2 + 15.7).

[c]0.756 is the reported percentage in syndicated data source.

[d]0.429 = [.756 × (1 − .756)]$^{.5}$

The boundaries are the mean plus the standard deviation multiplied by a scaling factor. A scaling factor of 0.75 is able to discriminate among competitors while providing substantial levels of overlap.

$$\text{Lower bound} = \mu - 0.75(\sigma)$$
$$\text{Upper bound} = \mu + 0.75(\sigma)$$

Table 6–6 shows the upper and lower bounds for golf and skiing for each of the six dimensions. As shown in Table 6–6, the upper bound for golf on the age dimension is 47.4. This was found by using the esti-mated mean age (35.7) and subtracting the standard deviation (15.6) times 0.75 from Table 6–5.

Step 4. Compute the Niche Breadth for Each Sport

Niche breadth is the volume of the niche and is calculated by multiplying the ranges together; thus, we are calculating an *n*-dimensional volume. We assume a uniform distribution of participants across each variable and across the entire niche volume. While

TABLE 6–6. Examples of calculating niche statistics across six dimensions

Statistic bounds	Age Low	Age Up	Income Low	Income Up	Male Low	Male Up	White Low	White Up	North Low	North Up	Metro Low	Metro Up	Total
Golf	24.0[a]	47.4[b]	29.5	61.0	.433	1.07[c]	.634	1.124	−.047	.637	.056	.759	
Skiing	18.1	36.9	32.8	63.4	.247	.978	.621	1.222	−.092	.527	.061	.805	
Breadth													
Golf	23.4[d]		31.5		.645		.490		.684		.742		118.2[e]
Skiing	18.8		30.6		.731		.501		.619		.744		97.0
Overlap													
Golf–Skiing	12.9[f]		28.2		.545		.488		.574		.737		40.929[g]
Index													
CRO$_{SG}$	.551[h]		.895		.845		.980		.841		.993		.34[i]
CRO$_{GS}$	.686[j]		.922		.746		.974		.927		.991		.42[k]

[a] $24.0 = 35.7 − (.75 \times 15.6)$, mean and standard deviation shown in Table 6–5.
[b] $47.4 = 35.7 + (.75 \times 15.6)$, mean and standard deviation shown in Table 6–5.
[c] Bounds allowed to be less than 0 or greater than 1 in this analysis to capture maximum variance.
[d] $23.4 = 47.4 − 24.0$.
[e] $118.2 = 23.4 \times 31.5 \times .645 \times .490 \times .684 \times .742$.
[f] $12.9 = 36.9 − 24.0$. Note 36.9 is the minimum upper bound, 24.0 is maximum lower bound.
[g] $40.929 = 12.9 \times 28.2 \times .545 \times .488 \times .574 \times .737$.
[h] $.551 = 12.9/23.4$.
[i] $.34 = .551 \times .895 \times .845 \times .980 \times .841 \times .993$.
[j] $.686 = 12.9/18.8$.
[k] $.42 = .686 \times .922 \times .746 \times .974 \times .927 \times .991$.

it is possible to relax this assumption, it does not change the general approach.

In this example we used six dimensions. As shown in Table 6–6 for golf, the difference between the age variable upper bound (47.4) and lower bound (24.0) is 23.4. This niche breadth for age was then multiplied by the other five niche breadths from the other variables for a total niche breadth of 118.2. Niche breadth is a relative measure and can be used to compare the breadth across a set of sports in a market. For reporting purposes, niche breadths are often normalized so that the highest niche breadth among competitors is based on a maximum of 100. In Table 6–6, skiing's normalized niche breadth is 82% the size of golf's niche breadth (97 divided by 118.2); thus, skiing is a relatively more specialized sport.

Step 5. Compute Niche Overlap

To compute niche overlap, we calculated the volume of the intersection of two sports' niches in n-dimensional space. This was done by finding the overlap between any two sports (x, y) on each variable (j). The total pairwise niche overlap is the product of the overlaps across the variables. This is done for each pair of sports in the defined market.

In Table 6–6, the overlap between golf and skiing by age of respondents was found by taking the minimum upper bound between the two sports (36.9) and subtracting the maximum lower bound between the two sports (24.0). The overlap of 12.9 was multiplied by the overlaps of the other five variables for a total overlap of 40.9. This represents the n-dimensional volume that is shared between golf and skiing in six dimensions.

Step 6. Compute the Index of Competitive Resource Overlap

The Competitive Resource Overlap (CRO$_{XY}$) is the niche overlap of sport X and Y divided by the niche breadth of Y. It can be calculated for each dimension, j, as well as overall across all n dimensions. The index can be interpreted as the participant overlap that sport Y faces from sport X. In contrast, CRO$_{YX}$

is the participant overlap that sport X faces from Y. (CRO_{YX} is the niche overlap divided by the niche breadth of X.) Therefore, CRO_{XY} will only equal CRO_{YX} when the niche breadth of X and Y are equal.

Table 6–6 shows the calculations of the CRO between golf and skiing overall and for each of the six variables. For age, CRO_{GS} is .686, which is found by taking the golf–skiing overlap for age from Table 6–6 (12.9) and dividing by skiing's niche breadth from Table 6–6 (18.8). In contrast, for age, CRO_{SG} is .551, which is similarly found by taking the golf–skiing overlap for age (12.9) and dividing by golf's niche breadth (23.4). Total CROs are found by multiplying all the variable CROs together or by dividing total overlap by the respective total niche breadth of the sports. Thus, the total CRO_{GS} is .42 (40.9/97.0) and CRO_{SG} is .34 (40.9/118.2).

Values for CRO_{XY} are from 0 to 1. A value of 1 is obtained when two sports are exact competitors and target the same participants. The index is 0 if two sports do not compete for the same participants (as in the case of golf and skateboarding). CRO_{XY} will be 0 if the two sports do not overlap on at least one dimension. For instance, in the two-dimensional example of Figure 6–1, the index is 0 because golf and skateboarding do not overlap on the age dimension (even though there is some overlap on the income dimension).

It is therefore important not to omit important variables because the resulting index might over-state "true" competition. In contrast, redundant variables (multiple measures of the same dimension) can understate competition. However, these limitations can be mitigated by relying on previous research and/or using syndicated sport research to select variables.

Assessing Method Validity

In order to check the validity and show the usefulness of this approach, we computed niche overlaps among 36 sports and fitness activities reported by American Sports Data. Our approach for calculating all the pairwise overlaps was identical to the six steps we went through in the previous section and which are outlined in detail for golf and skiing in Tables 6–5 and 6–6. To facilitate computation of the 1296 pairwise overlaps across the six dimensions, we wrote a com-

puter program in SAS's Interactive Matrix Language to calculate the competitive resources overlap indices for the 36 sports. The result is the 36 × 36 matrix of CRO indices reported in Table 6–7.

Table 6–7 lists the 36 sports on the left-hand side of the data matrix. Column A is American Sports Data's estimates for the percentage of the U.S. population (> 6 years of age) that plays each sport. Column B shows the niche breadth of each sport. Niche breadth has been rescaled (normalized) to be bounded between 0 and 100 by making the largest niche breadth equal to 100. The following columns are the CROs. The column numbers correspond to sport names to the left having the same numbers. The matrix of CROs has 1.00s down the diagonal, reflecting a sport's overlap with itself. In addition, while the matrix is square, it is also asymmetrical. For example, the number in row 16 (golf), column 27 (skiing) is .42. This is interpreted as 42% of skiing's niche is overlapped by golf. In contrast, the number in row 27 (skiing), row 16 (golf) is .34. Thus, 34% of golf's niche is overlapped by skiing. As shown previously, skiing has a narrower niche breadth than golf.

Table 6–7 reports the percentage of the U.S. population (>6 years of age) that participates in each sport and niche breadth. The niche breadths range from 20.5 to 100. Tackle football and ice hockey (specialist sports) have participant niches that are approximately ¼ the width of bicycle riding and bowling (generalist sports). As shown in the table, niche breadth provides different information from percentage of participants (the correlation between the two measures is .54).

To summarize the 1296 pairwise CRO indices reported in Table 6–7, we mapped the data using a multidimensional scaling program. This procedure is very similar to the ALSCAL mapping procedure and allowed us to handle the asymmetrical matrix. In essence, multidimensional scaling creates maps from distance measures. Multidimensional scaling (MDS) is a standard used in market research for positioning studies and has been used in sport research. For this analysis, the measure of CRO served as the metric distance measure. Sports with high levels of overlap should be closer to each other than sports with small levels of overlap. Figure 6–2 shows

TABLE 6-7. Niche statistics for 36 sports and fitness activities

Sport/Fitness activity	% Pop. A	Breadth B	Competitive Resource Overlap (CRO) Indices															
			1	2	3	4	5	6	7	8	9	10	11	12	13	14	15	16
1 Aerobics	4.43	46.2	1.00	0.00	0.13	0.00	0.00	0.15	0.05	0.04	0.02	0.09	0.00	0.00	0.00	0.00	0.00	0.00
2 Archery	3.78	37.6	0.00	1.00	0.27	0.42	0.35	0.14	0.26	0.29	0.10	0.11	0.36	0.28	0.10	0.34	0.36	0.20
3 Badminton	5.20	57.8	0.17	0.42	1.00	0.21	0.37	0.28	0.31	0.36	0.13	0.21	0.22	0.35	0.09	0.27	0.13	0.12
4 Baseball	6.81	40.5	0.00	0.46	0.15	1.00	0.41	0.11	0.17	0.19	0.06	0.06	0.50	0.13	0.06	0.66	0.79	0.05
5 Basketball	18.42	61.6	0.00	0.58	0.40	0.62	1.00	0.32	0.46	0.47	0.19	0.21	0.55	0.30	0.19	0.72	0.57	0.16
6 Bicycle riding	11.54	86.8	0.28	0.34	0.42	0.25	0.45	1.00	0.71	0.72	0.41	0.61	0.29	0.40	0.42	0.30	0.11	0.39
7 Mountain biking	3.24	49.3	0.06	0.34	0.27	0.21	0.37	0.40	1.00	0.56	0.24	0.28	0.21	0.40	0.34	0.22	0.10	0.28
8 Billiards/Pool	17.60	65.9	0.06	0.51	0.41	0.32	0.50	0.55	0.75	1.00	0.35	0.46	0.32	0.54	0.34	0.34	0.15	0.40
9 Boardsailing	0.36	100.0	0.05	0.26	0.22	0.15	0.31	0.47	0.49	0.53	1.00	0.49	0.22	0.45	0.36	0.18	0.01	0.53
10 Bowling	21.42	93.2	0.18	0.28	0.35	0.14	0.32	0.66	0.53	0.65	0.45	1.00	0.19	0.49	0.51	0.15	0.00	0.53
11 Boxing	0.55	46.1	0.00	0.44	0.18	0.57	0.41	0.15	0.19	0.22	0.10	0.09	1.00	0.16	0.11	0.53	0.62	0.09
12 Fishing (freshwater)	20.89	74.5	0.00	0.55	0.45	0.24	0.36	0.34	0.48	0.61	0.34	0.39	0.26	1.00	0.29	0.25	0.13	0.45
13 Fishing (saltwater)	6.22	55.1	0.00	0.16	0.09	0.08	0.17	0.27	0.38	0.28	0.20	0.30	0.13	0.22	1.00	0.09	0.00	0.33
14 Football (touch)	9.28	48.2	0.00	0.43	0.23	0.79	0.56	0.16	0.22	0.24	0.08	0.08	0.55	0.16	0.08	1.00	0.79	0.06
15 Football (tackle)	5.72	20.5	0.00	0.20	0.04	0.40	0.19	0.02	0.04	0.04	0.00	0.00	0.28	0.03	0.00	0.33	1.00	0.00
16 Golf	10.60	60.2	0.00	0.32	0.13	0.08	0.16	0.27	0.34	0.37	0.32	0.34	0.12	0.36	0.37	0.07	0.00	1.00
17 Hunting	8.89	33.5	0.00	0.28	0.07	0.08	0.08	0.08	0.12	0.16	0.09	0.12	0.12	0.27	0.12	0.05	0.00	0.24
18 Ice hockey	1.11	24.4	0.00	0.36	0.07	0.30	0.18	0.05	0.09	0.10	0.05	0.03	0.19	0.09	0.02	0.20	0.29	0.06
19 Weights (free weights)	13.57	67.6	0.11	0.38	0.33	0.29	0.51	0.63	0.83	0.72	0.37	0.42	0.33	0.38	0.42	0.34	0.14	0.34
20 Racquetball	3.24	63.5	0.00	0.42	0.28	0.32	0.52	0.54	0.81	0.64	0.35	0.34	0.33	0.37	0.39	0.35	0.16	0.38
21 Roller skating (in-line)	5.49	59.0	0.10	0.19	0.30	0.28	0.30	0.21	0.18	0.17	0.06	0.07	0.18	0.09	0.03	0.32	0.17	0.02
22 Running/Jogging	13.17	76.1	0.27	0.37	0.43	0.31	0.55	0.66	0.69	0.56	0.31	0.39	0.37	0.29	0.33	0.41	0.20	0.25
23 Sailing	1.71	50.2	0.08	0.17	0.14	0.06	0.12	0.31	0.36	0.29	0.20	0.27	0.07	0.21	0.25	0.06	0.00	0.40
24 Scuba diving	1.01	36.6	0.00	0.17	0.07	0.05	0.10	0.19	0.28	0.22	0.14	0.15	0.07	0.15	0.28	0.05	0.00	0.40
25 Skateboarding	2.35	31.0	0.00	0.21	0.10	0.44	0.20	0.01	0.01	0.01	0.00	0.00	0.22	0.00	0.00	0.36	0.53	0.00
26 Skiing (cross country)	2.40	48.9	0.09	0.19	0.24	0.05	0.12	0.25	0.26	0.25	0.19	0.26	0.05	0.28	0.13	0.05	0.00	0.34
27 Skiing (downhill)	6.00	49.4	0.09	0.29	0.22	0.14	0.24	0.35	0.54	0.40	0.20	0.22	0.13	0.23	0.20	0.15	0.06	0.34
28 Snowboarding	0.95	24.4	0.00	0.44	0.14	0.32	0.21	0.06	0.09	0.11	0.03	0.02	0.18	0.11	0.01	0.26	0.31	0.03
29 Soccer	7.15	45.3	0.04	0.26	0.27	0.36	0.33	0.13	0.15	0.16	0.01	0.00	0.18	0.09	0.00	0.37	0.33	0.00
30 Softball	13.17	66.2	0.14	0.55	0.60	0.42	0.70	0.47	0.54	0.57	0.22	0.33	0.41	0.35	0.21	0.49	0.32	0.19
31 Swimming	10.33	86.6	0.47	0.25	0.51	0.17	0.40	0.71	0.56	0.57	0.28	0.50	0.20	0.31	0.30	0.26	0.05	0.25
32 Table tennis	7.73	66.9	0.12	0.54	0.52	0.33	0.51	0.50	0.70	0.65	0.30	0.35	0.31	0.41	0.23	0.35	0.21	0.35
33 Tennis	8.46	70.9	0.25	0.32	0.39	0.23	0.40	0.63	0.68	0.52	0.27	0.37	0.25	0.26	0.28	0.27	0.12	0.30
34 Volleyball (hard surface)	3.86	60.8	0.20	0.46	0.77	0.27	0.49	0.38	0.43	0.46	0.17	0.29	0.26	0.32	0.13	0.33	0.16	0.16
35 Volleyball (sand/beach)	5.90	60.4	0.16	0.48	0.58	0.29	0.51	0.48	0.58	0.54	0.24	0.34	0.28	0.35	0.18	0.32	0.17	0.23
36 Water-skiing	5.19	43.1	0.06	0.41	0.30	0.16	0.28	0.32	0.49	0.43	0.21	0.22	0.15	0.30	0.15	0.16	0.08	0.34

TABLE 6-7. (continued)

Competitive Resource Overlap (CRO) Indices

Sport/Fitness activity	17	18	19	20	21	22	23	24	25	26	27	28	29	30	31	32	33	34	35	36
1 Aerobics	0.00	0.00	0.08	0.00	0.08	0.16	0.07	0.00	0.00	0.08	0.09	0.00	0.04	0.10	0.25	0.08	0.16	0.15	0.12	0.07
2 Archery	0.31	0.56	0.21	0.25	0.12	0.18	0.12	0.18	0.25	0.15	0.22	0.68	0.22	0.31	0.10	0.30	0.17	0.28	0.29	0.36
3 Badminton	0.13	0.17	0.28	0.26	0.30	0.32	0.16	0.11	0.19	0.29	0.26	0.34	0.35	0.52	0.34	0.45	0.31	0.73	0.55	0.40
4 Baseball	0.09	0.50	0.17	0.21	0.19	0.16	0.04	0.05	0.58	0.04	0.12	0.53	0.32	0.26	0.08	0.20	0.13	0.18	0.19	0.15
5 Basketball	0.15	0.45	0.46	0.50	0.32	0.45	0.15	0.17	0.41	0.15	0.30	0.54	0.45	0.65	0.28	0.47	0.35	0.50	0.52	0.40
6 Bicycle riding	0.20	0.18	0.81	0.74	0.32	0.75	0.54	0.45	0.04	0.44	0.62	0.21	0.26	0.61	0.71	0.65	0.77	0.55	0.70	0.65
7 Mountain biking	0.18	0.19	0.60	0.63	0.15	0.44	0.35	0.39	0.01	0.26	0.54	0.19	0.16	0.40	0.31	0.52	0.47	0.35	0.48	0.56
8 Billiards/Pool	0.32	0.28	0.70	0.67	0.19	0.48	0.38	0.40	0.04	0.34	0.54	0.29	0.23	0.56	0.43	0.64	0.48	0.50	0.59	0.66
9 Boardsailing	0.28	0.21	0.55	0.56	0.10	0.40	0.41	0.40	0.00	0.40	0.40	0.14	0.04	0.34	0.32	0.45	0.39	0.28	0.40	0.48
10 Bowling	0.33	0.12	0.58	0.51	0.11	0.48	0.51	0.38	0.00	0.49	0.42	0.10	0.02	0.47	0.53	0.50	0.49	0.45	0.53	0.49
11 Boxing	0.16	0.36	0.22	0.24	0.14	0.22	0.06	0.09	0.33	0.05	0.13	0.34	0.19	0.28	0.10	0.21	0.16	0.20	0.21	0.16
12 Fishing (freshwater)	0.61	0.28	0.42	0.44	0.12	0.28	0.31	0.32	0.01	0.43	0.34	0.34	0.15	0.40	0.26	0.46	0.28	0.40	0.44	0.53
13 Fishing (saltwater)	0.21	0.05	0.34	0.34	0.03	0.24	0.28	0.42	0.00	0.15	0.22	0.04	0.00	0.17	0.19	0.19	0.22	0.12	0.17	0.19
14 Football (touch)	0.07	0.40	0.24	0.26	0.26	0.25	0.06	0.06	0.57	0.05	0.15	0.52	0.39	0.36	0.14	0.25	0.19	0.26	0.26	0.18
15 Football (tackle)	0.00	0.25	0.04	0.05	0.06	0.05	0.00	0.00	0.35	0.00	0.02	0.26	0.15	0.10	0.01	0.06	0.03	0.05	0.06	0.03
16 Golf	0.43	0.14	0.30	0.36	0.02	0.20	0.48	0.67	0.00	0.42	0.42	0.07	0.00	0.17	0.17	0.31	0.26	0.15	0.23	0.47
17 Hunting	1.00	0.12	0.10	0.12	0.00	0.06	0.09	0.14	0.00	0.13	0.09	0.07	0.00	0.09	0.04	0.10	0.06	0.07	0.09	0.14
18 Ice hockey	0.09	1.00	0.08	0.10	0.07	0.07	0.04	0.05	0.17	0.04	0.08	0.56	0.14	0.10	0.02	0.13	0.06	0.08	0.12	0.14
19 Weights (free)	0.21	0.22	1.00	0.84	0.22	0.69	0.39	0.40	0.03	0.29	0.62	0.22	0.22	0.57	0.50	0.62	0.61	0.43	0.58	0.62
20 Racquetball	0.23	0.26	0.79	1.00	0.20	0.58	0.36	0.45	0.04	0.28	0.62	0.25	0.21	0.49	0.40	0.58	0.58	0.38	0.52	0.63
21 Roller skating(in-line)	0.01	0.17	0.19	0.19	1.00	0.28	0.07	0.04	0.33	0.09	0.18	0.30	0.59	0.29	0.23	0.30	0.29	0.36	0.34	0.20
22 Running/Jogging	0.14	0.22	0.77	0.69	0.37	1.00	0.39	0.31	0.15	0.28	0.59	0.26	0.37	0.69	0.59	0.69	0.78	0.56	0.71	0.58
23 Sailing	0.14	0.08	0.29	0.29	0.06	0.25	1.00	0.64	0.00	0.49	0.57	0.08	0.03	0.18	0.23	0.27	0.35	0.17	0.23	0.45
24 Scuba diving	0.15	0.08	0.21	0.26	0.02	0.15	0.47	1.00	0.00	0.22	0.39	0.05	0.00	0.10	0.12	0.18	0.21	0.08	0.13	0.30
25 Skateboarding	0.00	0.22	0.01	0.02	0.17	0.06	0.00	0.00	1.00	0.00	0.01	0.33	0.34	0.11	0.03	0.08	0.04	0.09	0.07	0.01
26 Skiing (cross country)	0.19	0.08	0.21	0.21	0.07	0.18	0.48	0.29	0.00	1.00	0.34	0.11	0.04	0.18	0.21	0.28	0.25	0.25	0.27	0.49
27 Skiing (downhill)	0.13	0.18	0.46	0.48	0.15	0.38	0.56	0.53	0.03	0.34	1.00	0.18	0.18	0.30	0.27	0.47	0.50	0.27	0.37	0.67
28 Snowboarding	0.05	0.56	0.08	0.09	0.12	0.08	0.04	0.03	0.26	0.05	0.09	1.00	0.22	0.14	0.05	0.14	0.07	0.14	0.14	0.15
29 Soccer	0.00	0.26	0.14	0.14	0.45	0.22	0.03	0.00	0.50	0.04	0.16	0.41	1.00	0.29	0.15	0.31	0.20	0.28	0.29	0.19
30 Softball	0.17	0.29	0.56	0.51	0.32	0.60	0.24	0.19	0.24	0.25	0.40	0.39	0.42	1.00	0.43	0.61	0.49	0.76	0.75	0.55
31 Swimming	0.10	0.09	0.64	0.54	0.34	0.67	0.41	0.30	0.09	0.37	0.48	0.17	0.29	0.56	1.00	0.54	0.66	0.61	0.62	0.47
32 Table tennis	0.21	0.36	0.61	0.61	0.34	0.60	0.37	0.33	0.18	0.38	0.64	0.40	0.47	0.62	0.42	1.00	0.60	0.61	0.78	0.83
33 Tennis	0.12	0.18	0.64	0.65	0.35	0.72	0.50	0.41	0.10	0.37	0.72	0.22	0.31	0.53	0.54	0.63	1.00	0.51	0.66	0.65
34 Volleyball(hard surface)	0.13	0.21	0.39	0.36	0.37	0.45	0.20	0.14	0.19	0.31	0.33	0.35	0.37	0.70	0.43	0.56	0.44	1.00	0.74	0.49
35 Volleyball (sand)	0.16	0.29	0.52	0.49	0.34	0.56	0.28	0.22	0.14	0.33	0.46	0.35	0.38	0.68	0.43	0.71	0.56	0.73	1.00	0.64
36 Water-skiing	0.19	0.26	0.40	0.42	0.15	0.32	0.39	0.35	0.02	0.43	0.59	0.28	0.18	0.36	0.23	0.53	0.39	0.35	0.46	1.00

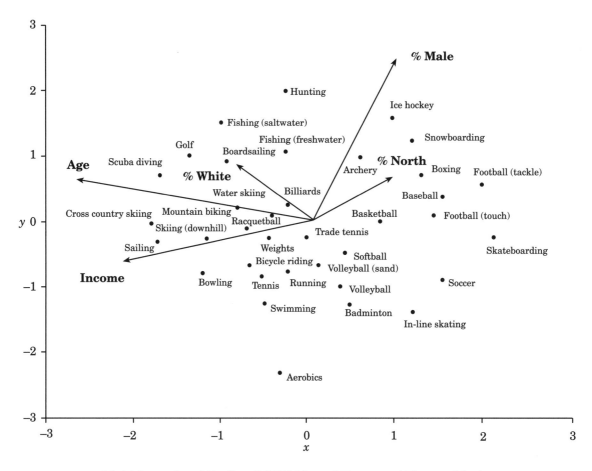

FIGURE 6–2. Multidimensional Scaling (MDS) Map of Sport and Fitness Market

the two-dimensional map based on the 36-sport example.

Although the MDS map shows the relative competitive position of the sports, the map's two dimensional *x-y* space is not directly interpretable. To evaluate the market structure shown on the map, we regressed the coordinates of the MDS space on each of the six variables used to calculate niche overlap. All regressions, except for the equation predicting percent metropolitan residence, were statistically significant. The standardized betas are graphically shown as vectors in the MDS space. The vectors begin from the origin and the endpoint is the coordinate formed from the beta weights. We stretched the vectors from the significant regressions

by a factor of 3 so that they are more visible in the figure. The vectors indicate the direction and magnitude of correlation with the variable and the two-dimensional MDS space.

The table of CRO indices and resulting MDS map (Table 6–7 and Figure 6–2, respectively) seem to reflect the relative competitive position of the sporting activities in terms of the targeted participants. The vectors and the placement of the sports in Figure 6–2 are intuitive because they point to sports that have the same attributes as the vectors. For example, the sports in the top and upper-right-hand corner of Figure 6–2 (hunting and ice hockey) are predominantly played by males. The sports on the right-hand side of the map (snowboarding and boxing) are played proportionally more in the North Census Region. The sports on the extreme left-hand side of the map (golf, cross country skiing, sailing, and scuba diving) are sports played by older, more affluent participants, who are largely white. Finally, sports on the bottom of the map (most notably aerobics) are played by a larger percentage of females than are other sports on the map.

Summary

This chapter outlined and demonstrated a methodology for assessing competitive patterns among sport alternatives. As the sport marketplace continues to fragment, the use of these approaches should provide assistance to managers who want to gain competitive advantage.

References

American Sports Data, Inc. (1993). *American sports analysis report: 1993.*

Brooks, C. (1994). *Sports marketing: Competitive strategies for sports.* Englewood Cliffs, NJ: Prentice-Hall.

Burnett, J., A. Menon, and D. T. Smart (1993). Sport marketing: A new ball game with new rules. *Journal of Advertising Research*, 33 (October): 21–35.

Darwin, C. (1859). *On the origin of species* (reprint). Cambridge, MA.: Harvard University Press (1964).

Del Wilber & Associates (1993). *The Mazda LPGA fan profile study.* St. Louis, MO.

Gaskell, G., and R. Pearton (1979). Aggression and sport. In J. Goldstein (ed.). *Sport, games and play.* Hillsdale, NJ: Lawrence Erlbaum Associates, 263–295.

Goodhart, P., and F. Chataway (1968). *War without weapons.* London: W. H. Allen.

Harris, D. V. (1973). *Involvement in sport: A somatopsychic rationale.* Philadelphia, PA: Lea-Febiger.

Henderson, B. (1983). The autonomy of competition. *Journal of Marketing*, 47 (Spring): 7–11.

Henderson, B. (1989). The origin of strategy. *Harvard Business Review* (November–December): 139–143.

Howard, D. R. (1992). Participation rates in selected sport and fitness activities. *Journal of Sport Management*, 6: 191–205.

Hutchinson, G. E. (1957). Concluding remarks. *Cold Spring Harbor Symposium of Quantitative Ecology*, 22: 415–427.

Kenyon, G. S. (1968). Six scales for assessing attitude toward physical activity. *Research Quarterly*, 39: 566–574.

Milne, G. R. (1994). A magazine taxonomy based on customer overlap. *Journal of Academy of Marketing Science*, 22 (Spring): 170–179.

Milne, G. R., and C. H. Mason (1990). An ecological niche theory approach to the measurement of brand competition. *Marketing Letters*, 1(3): 267–281.

Milne, G. R., M. A. McDonald, W. A. Sutton, and R. Kashyap (1996). A niche-based evaluation of sport participation patterns. *Journal of Sport Management*, 10: 417–434.

Mullin, B. J., S. Hardy, and W. A. Sutton (1993). *Sport Marketing.* Champaign, IL: Human Kinetics Publishers.

Pitts, B. G., F. W. Fielding, and L. K. Miller (1994). Industry segmentation theory and the sport industry: Developing a sport industry segment model. *Sport Market Quarterly*, 3(1): 15–24.

Sloan, L. R. (1985). The motives of sport fans. In J. H. Goldstein. *Sports, games, and play: social and psychological viewpoints*, 2d ed. Hillsdale, NJ: Lawrence Erlbaum Associates, 175–240.

Sofranko, A. T., and M. F. Nolan (1972). Early life experiences and adult sport participation. *Journal of Leisure Research*, 4: 6–18.

Sprietzer, F. A., and E. E. Snyder (1976). Socialization into sport: An exploratory path analysis. *Research Quarterly*, 47: 238–245.

Warnick, R. B. and D. R. Howard (1985). Market share analysis of selected leisure services from 1979–1982. *Journal of Park and Recreation Administration*, 4: 64–76.

Webster's Third New International Dictionary (1976). Springfield, MA: G. & C. Merriam.

Zillman, D., H. Bryant, and B. S. Sapolsky (1979). The enjoyment of watching sport contests. In J. H. Goldstein (ed.), *Sports, games and play.* Hillsdale, NJ: Erlbaum Associates, 298–335.

CHAPTER 7

Sport-Based Segmentation Models

Introduction

The uses of segmentation in sport have generally focused on demographics, with the traditional target market being the 18–49-year-old male. As Hofacre and Burman (1992) point out, however, demographic trends require sport marketers to examine other target groups as well. Specifically, they note trends such as the growing population of older Americans, the increase in Hispanic and Asian populations, the increase of women-headed households, more working women, and generally more leisure time with more competing entertainment options to fill that time.

Sport marketing literature has presented numerous segmentation studies. Fullerton and Dodge (1995) caution sport marketers not to lump all consumers of a single sport into one segment. In their segmentation of the golf market, they found five distinct segments based on demographics, behavior, and attitudes toward golf. Choice-based segmentation was demonstrated by Chang and Johnson (1995) in their conjoint study of the Australian Triathlon Association market. Turco (1996) took a different approach.

Instead of examining a single sport, he examined the generation-X segment to learn more about its attitudes toward sport in general. Other approaches to segmentation have started to move beyond demographics and have segmented markets based on levels of involvement (Lascu *et al.*, 1995) and consumption communities (Shoham and Kahle, 1996). Segmentation has also been done at the industry level (Pitts, Fielding, and Miller, 1994).

Since the world of sport marketing is becoming increasingly competitive, success increasingly depends upon a marketer's ability to further refine approaches for finding target market groups. In previous chapters, we have presented segmentation advances in terms of niche analysis and measuring consumer lifetime value (LTV). In this chapter, we will discuss four additional types of segmentation approaches that can be particularly useful to sport marketers. Specifically, we will introduce the topics of geodemographic segmentation and using motivations to profile spectating and participant sport segments. We will also compare the applications of heavy and light segmentation and the use of activity clusters in grouping similar sporting activities. Following this discussion, we will present four small empirical studies that demonstrate each of these new approaches.

Alternative Segmentation Approaches

Geodemographic Segmentation

Clustering or target marketing to a specified segment within a geographic location has become a widespread practice since the mid-1980s. With the shift toward developing relationships with customers (as opposed to serving larger macromarkets), the availability of demographic, psychographic, and behavioral data for individual zip codes has increased in importance. Geodemographics has become the buzz word for marketing efforts centered on zip code data. Geodemographic segmentation now strives to divide the population into smaller clusters based on similarities in demographics and product preferences (Mitchell, 1995).

Beginning with Joel Garreau's book, *The Nine Nations of North America* (1981), marketers began to see the relevance of segmenting markets based on geographic data. Throughout his travels in North America, Garreau used his qualitative experience to divide the continent into nine distinct areas or nations (Garreau, 1981). Quantitative geodemographic efforts were undertaken in parallel. Even prior to the publication of Garreau's book, Jonathan Robbin was developing a target-marketing system that matched zip code data with lifestyle information generated through census information and other consumer surveys. In attaching both demographic and lifestyle information to each of the 36,000 zip codes nationwide and clustering lifestyles into 40 different categories, Robbin created PRIZM™ (Potential Rating Index for Zip Markets). PRIZM clusters often incorporate more than one adjacent zip code in any given area throughout the United States and is utilized by many different types of businesses, including retail stores, banks, restaurants, and catalog retailers. With this system, Robbin's company, Claritas, generated revenues of $35 million in 1993 (Del Valle, 1994).

In 1988, Michael Weiss combined PRIZM data with qualitative research gathered during his travels throughout the United States in *The Clustering of America*. Weiss employed the PRIZM data to provide an in-depth examination of the 40 clusters delineated by Claritas. Academic research has acknowledged the efforts of Garreau, Claritas, and Weiss. Geographic segmentation was found to be a useful technique for marketers (Kahle, 1986). Practitioners find geographic segmentation to be a productive way of targeting potentially profitable areas. Today, with the rise of database marketing, geographic segmentation is mostly used in conjunction with sophisticated databases.

In the world of sport, geographic segmentation is also very appropriate. Despite the prevalence of national sports fueled by TV exposure, the participation patterns of sport are largely influenced by geographical region. Rooney and Pillsbury (1992) have organized the United States into 11 distinct geographical regions based on sporting behavior. The regions include

1. the Eastern Cradle (New England);
2. Carolinas (North Carolina and South Carolina);
3. Pigskin Cult (Arkansas, Louisiana, Alabama, Georgia, Florida);
4. South Florida;
5. Mills and Mines (Pittsburgh and Buffalo);
6. American Heartland (Michigan, Illinois, Indiana, Ohio, Kentucky);
7. Sport for Sport's Sake (Arkansas, Montana, North Dakota, South Dakota, Minnesota, Nebraska, Missouri, Iowa, Wisconsin);
8. Rocky Mountain High (Idaho, Wyoming, Colorado);
9. Texas Southwest (Texas, Oklahoma);
10. Cowboys and Mormons (Nevada, Utah, Arizona); and,
11. Pacific Cornucopia (Pacific West Coast and Hawaii).

Each region has particular relevance in sport. From the Eastern Cradle comes the birth of most sports, including the trilogy of basketball, baseball, and football. The Carolinas are noted for college basketball and stock car racing. In the Pigskin Cult, as the name suggests, football dominates scholastic sports. South Florida has a strong football tradition, great golf courses, and is a production area for Latin American major league baseball talent. The Mills and Mines region has historically produced NFL football talent—George Blanda, Joe Namath, Dan Marino, Jim Kelly, and Joe Montana. The American Heartland is traditionally a strong basketball region, yet has high participation in all sports. In the Sport for Sport's Sake region, scholastic sport is not the most important part of the community, but is something to be enjoyed. Rocky Mountain High has a large number of world-renowned ski resorts. Texas Southwest is football country, and the Cowboys and Mormons area is noted for rodeo, hunting, and fishing. Finally, the Pacific Cornucopia region is the region most devoted to individual and minor team sports.

Interestingly, although sport has strong geographical roots, sport has generally been examined from a macro, or national, perspective. Given the fluid nature of our society, sport segmentation can benefit by the use of geodemographics to examine sport at the neighborhood level. Next we will describe a study that profiles sport participation and spectating by PRIZM characteristics.

Profiling Sport Segment Membership Using Motivations

Because there are different approaches to segmenting a market, not every segmentation scheme is equally effective. Thus, it is important to evaluate the effectiveness of the segment solution. Kotler (1997) suggests that for market segments to be useful, they must be measurable, substantial, accessible, differentiable, and actionable.

Profiling segments using motivational variables can determine whether segments are differentiable and actionable. By understanding the motivations of members belonging to various sport segments, researchers can check to see if the segments are conceptually distinct. Furthermore, by understanding these motivations it is possible to formulate different marketing mix elements and communication strategies to appeal to member needs. With this knowledge the segmentation approach is actionable, in that effective programs can be implemented to both serve current segment customers and attract new ones.

Simply put, understanding motivations is key to understanding consumer behavior. Marketers would love to understand fully what motivates their customers to buy. Armed with this information, all they would have to do would be to heighten consumers' motivations—similar to what Burger King did a few years back with their ad "Aren't you Hungry?" Sport marketers have tried to tap into motivations by showing why users of sport products keep buying their products. Nike, with its "Just Do It" theme, has tried to tap into sport consumers' "athlete wannabe" and "competitive" motives. "Just Do It" is about fanaticism; it's a call to action, a directive to challenge yourself. However, for most buying situations, measuring consumer motivations is difficult, if not impossible. If a marketer asks a consumer directly for his or her motive for doing something, the consumer will likely provide a socially desirable answer; thus, a more indirect line of questioning is often used (Settle and Alreck, 1989).

In Chapter 3, we formed a typology of sport spectating and participation based on the following thirteen motivational factors: physical fitness, risk-taking, stress reduction, aggression, affiliation, social facilitation, self-esteem, competition, achievement, skill mastery, aesthetics, value development, and self-actualization. In this chapter, we will investigate which of these motivational factors can predict sport segment membership. Specifically, we will use these factors in logit regressions to profile the differences between participants and nonparticipants of 40 sports. In addition, we will profile the differences between spectators and nonspectators in 25 sports.

Heavy/Light Versus Variety Seeking Segmentation

Perhaps one of the oldest forms of segmentation has been identifying heavy users (Twedt, 1964). Early research has shown that heavy users buy more, buy more often, and buy more different brands. This has led marketing to develop the 80/20 rule, which states that 80% of company profits are generated from 20% of the company's customers. The larger implication is that all customers are not equal. In fact, the rule has been extended by William Sherden to the 80/20/ 30 rule. Sherden (1994, p. 77) notes, "The top 20% of customers generate 80% of the company profits, half of which is lost serving the bottom 30% of unprofitable customers."

This old, tried-and-true form of segmentation has been given new life with the advent of the marketing database. Many companies, through examining their records, are discovering that the lion's share of sales is being generated by a small group of loyal consumers. With new customers being harder and more expensive to track, efficient marketing strategy has shifted toward keeping loyal customers happy. As discussed in Chapter 5, lifetime value is an extension of the 80/20 concept. A small portion of the database may account for a large percentage of the lifetime value. Database marketing should focus on groups of individuals who have demonstrated high levels of purchase activity and have the promise of purchasing in the future. While mass marketing focused on increasing market share, database marketing attempts to increase customer share; that is, it attempts to sell more to the heavy user.

Although the 80/20 rule is widely accepted, rarely has it been empirically verified. Anecdotal evidence suggests that for some service industries like airlines, 80% of profits comes from a percentage of the customer base even smaller than 20%. Within sport, it is reasonable to expect that the 80/20 rule might also vary. Such information would be useful for marketers of particular sports, since it would show which customers to target.

Applying the 80/20 rule becomes very interesting when classifying overall sport participation behavior. This is because individuals can engage in multiple sport and fitness activities. Brooks (1994) notes that with the proliferation of sport and the variety-seeking behavior of participants, most pursue multiple activities. For example, unlike traditional golf enthusiasts, new golfers may also want to sail, white-water raft, or scuba dive. For the sport marketer, it would be valuable to segment their customer base not only on the basis of heavy/light usage of their sport but also on heavy/light usage *and* variety-seeking behavior across all sports. In this chapter, we will present such a segmentation approach.

Activity Cluster Segmentation

Although sports are often studied one at a time, they are frequently sold in combination. For instance, retail sporting stores must decide the type of sport product mix they want to offer. The same can be true for catalogs that sell sport merchandise. Camps, resorts, and fitness clubs need to decide the range of the sport products or activities they will offer. When sports are sold in combination, marketers have to be cognizant of how all the sporting options are bundled together. Sport marketers who follow this marketing concept are trying to match their sport product mix to the needs and desires of their target audiences.

Theoretical research suggests that customers gravitate to specific activity clusters. These clusters are often viewed as communities where members have the same set of shared values. Shoham and Kahle (1996, p. 12) define consumption communities based on three types of participant sport activities:

1. the extent to which a consumer engages in competitive sport, such as team sport;

2. the extent to which an individual is active in fitness sport, such as jogging; and,

3. the extent to which an individual participates in nature-related sport, such as backpacking.

One approach to solving this bundling problem is to use empirical methods to group sporting activities into distinct clusters. In this chapter, we will present an empirical study that groups sports into segments based on customer usage patterns.

Study 1—Geodemographic Segmentation

This study used two data sources. Data about sport spectating and participation were collected as part of the national U.S. mail survey of sport enthusiasts mentioned in earlier chapters and described in the appendix of this book. Included as part of this survey was an opportunity for respondents to provide their zip codes, which 87.8% of the 1611 respondents did (28.4% of all respondents included the full zip + 4 information). The 1415 respondents who provided their zip codes were then geocoded using the Claritas PRIZM system.

Claritas' PRIZM Clustering System classifies every neighborhood into 62 distinct lifestyle clusters.

From these 62 clusters, PRIZM also created 15 broader social groups, as shown in Table 7–1. These 15 groups represent a combination of affluence and degree of urbanization. Marketers often use these

TABLE 7–1. PRIZM℠ clustering social groups

1. Elite Suburbs	High levels of education and affluence. Group has high income, education, investment, and spending levels. High index concentrations of wealthy Asian and Arabic immigrants.
2. Urban Uptown	High affluence. High concentrations of executives and professionals in the fields of business, finance, entertainment and education. Recently has absorbed a wave of upscale immigrants from Eastern Europe, Asia, and Middle East.
3. Second City Society	The upper deck in hundreds of America's "second" and "edge" cities. The group has high education and incomes. It also has high home ownership, employment as executives and professionals in essential local industries such as business, finance, health, law, communications, and wholesale. Also conservative.
4. Landed Gentry	A broad geographically based group. The group shows large, multi-income families of school-aged kids, headed by well-educated executives, professionals, and techies. The group likes serenity outside metro beltways.
5. The Affluentials	This group represents the upper-middle income suburbs of major metros. The groups have above average incomes and rentals. There is an eclectic mix of homes, condos, and apartments, a broad spectrum of businesses, technical, and public service jobs, daily commuting, and very little else.
6. Inner Suburbs	This group comprises the middle income suburbs of major metros. Group straddles the average level of affluence for United States. The groups show distinct, variant patterns of employment, lifestyle, and regional concentration.
7. Urban Midscale	The middle-income, urban-fringe neighborhoods of America's major metros. The group exhibits high population densities, ethnic diversity, public transportation, and all the perks and risks of urban life, yet is otherwise unique.
8. Second City Centers	This group represents the midscale, middle-density, "edge" cities surrounding major metros, as well as smaller, second-tier cities, and cover all but 10 minor, agrarian TV markets in the West. The group is better off than peers in the Urban Midscale. The group is predominantly white. There is wide variance in age, marriage, education, occupations, and lifestyle.
9. Exurban Blues	The group consists of midscale, low-density towns lying at the outskirts of all major metros and second cities. High concentration of military group quarters.
10. Country Families	The group represents rural America, consisting of hundreds of small towns and remote exurbs. It is midscale in affluence, has far lower living costs, and suffers low levels of poverty. The group is largely composed of white, married couples, many with children, in industrial and agrarian occupations, living in owned houses and mobile homes.
11. Urban Cores	This group has some of the nation's lowest incomes and highest poverty ratios. This group is multiracial, multilingual communities of dense, rented row and high-rise apartments, shows high indices for singles, solo parents with preschool children, and perennial unemployment.

TABLE 7–1. Continued

12. Second City Blues	The group covers downtown neighborhoods of hundreds of second cities and edges of cities on the fringes of major metros. While lower incomes, there are lower costs of living. Group is better off than big-city cousins in Urban Cores. Coupled with pockets of unemployment, broken homes, and solo parents, there is also a wide range of occupations, including clerical, retail, labor, transportation, agrarian, public and private services.
13. Working Towns	Represents thousands of remote exurbs and satellite towns, lying well outside of major metros and second cities. This group has lower education and income levels, with predominantly blue-collar occupations, and equal mix of owned and rented single-unit houses, religion, home crafts.
14. Heartlanders	The nation's agrarian heartland, broadly geocentered in the Great Plains, South Central, Mountain, and Pacific, with a few pockets East. The group is hardly jet set, but it is comparatively self-sufficient with a low cost of living. They have large multigenerational families, long residential tenure in low-density houses and mobile homes, a mix of Hispanics and Native Americans, and a fierce independence.
15. Rustic Living	This group describes thousands of remote country towns, villages, hamlets, and reservations scattered across the United States. They are neither affluent nor destitute. They are often married, have many elders, mobile homes, kids, carpools, craftsmen, and laborers in agriculture, mining, transport, and construction.

groupings to better understand and target their customers. In our sample of zip codes the 15 groups were represented in the following percentages:

Elite Suburbs (13%)

The Affluentials (12%)

Landed Gentry (10%)

Country Families (10%)

Second City Centers (9%)

Exurban Blues (9%)

Urban Midscale (7%)

Working Towns (7%)

Inner Suburbs (6%)

Second City Society (6%)

Rustic Living (6%)

Urban Uptown (4%)

Second City Blues (3%)

Heartlanders (2%)

Urban Cores (1%)

(totals do not add to 100% due to rounding)

Using only those respondents who provided their zip codes, along with the lifestyle clustering data provided by Claritas, we profiled participation rates for 40 sports and spectating rates for 25 sports by the 15 PRIZM social groups. The summary of this analysis is shown in Tables 7–2a and 7–2b. The tables show the percentage of the sample who participated in or watched a particular sport. For each of the 15 geodemographic segments, we indicate whether the participation or viewing rate was ± 20% of the overall sample. If the rate for a particular geodemographic segment was 20% or higher than average, this is represented by a plus sign. If the rate was less than 20% of the average, this is represented by a zero. For example, in Table 7–2a, tennis participation in the Elite Suburbs and Urban Uptown segments is 20% or higher than the national average rate of 42%. In contrast, it is less than 20% lower than the 42% average participation rate in

TABLE 7–2a. Sport participation rates by PRIZM cluster groups

Participant sport	Rate	Elite Suburbs	Urban Uptown	Second City Society	Landed Gentry	The Affluentials	Inner Suburbs	Urban Midscale	Second City Centers	Exurban Blues	Country Families	Urban Cores	Second City Blues	Working Towns	Heartlanders	Rustic Living
Aerobics	35.64%								+	0			+		+	0
Archery	17.90%		0	0	+		+				+	0	+			
Badminton	38.00%						0	0			+	0	+		0	0
Baseball	43.36%															
Basketball	59.49%															
Bicycle riding	67.54%															
Billiards/Pool	62.84%														0	
Board sailing	4.94%		+	+		0		+		+	0	+	+	+	0	0
Bowling	63.46%												0			
Boxing	6.33%		+		+		0				0	+	0	+	+	0
Bungee jumping	1.74%	0		0	+	0	+			+	0	+	0	+	0	+
Canoeing/Kayaking	25.65%		+				+				+	0	+		0	
Distance running	20.26%		+								+	+	+	0	0	
Freshwater fishing	54.90%		0	0									+	+		+
Saltwater fishing	32.14%		+										+			
Football (tackle)	26.79%		+									0	+			
Football (touch)	37.39%											0	+		0	
Golf	58.43%							0							0	
Hunting	28.33%	0		0		0		0		+	+	0		+		+
Ice hockey	8.55%		+	0			0	+			+	+	0	0	0	0
Ice skating	25.45%	+	+				0				0	+	+	0	0	0
Mountain biking	15.05%		+		+		+	+			0	+	0	0	0	0
Rollerskating (in-line)	14.76%		+	+	+	0			0	0	0	0	+	0		0
Running/Jogging	44.70%		+										+	+	0	
Sailing	16.12%	+	+	+		0				0		0	+		0	0
Scuba diving	8.99%	+	+							0	0	+	+	0	0	0
Skateboarding	6.08%		+		+	0		+	0			0	+		0	0
Skiing (cross-country)	11.76%		+								+	+	+	0		0
Skiing (downhill)	24.42%	+	+	+						0			0	0	0	0
Snowboarding	3.41%	0	+			0	+	+	0	0	+	0	0	0	0	+
Soccer	18.02%		+					+		0	+			0	0	0
Softball	54.51%															
Swimming	76.42%														0	
Table tennis	46.43%												0			
Tennis	42.07%	+	+							0			0			0
Ultimate frisbee	14.00%			0			+			+	0	+	0		+	0
Volleyball (hard surface)	34.77%											+				
Volleyball (beach)	31.51%						+				0	+	0	+	0	0
Water skiing	27.21%						+				0	+	0			
Weightlifting	34.41%		+									+	+			0

Key: + = 20% higher than average participation rate.

0 = 20% lower than average participation rate.

TABLE 7–2b. Sport spectator rates by PRIZM cluster groups

Spectator sport	Rate	PRIZM cluster groups														
		Elite Suburbs	Urban Uptown	Second City Society	Landed Gentry	The Affluentials	Inner Suburbs	Urban Midscale	Second City Centers	Exurban Blues	Country Families	Urban Cores	Second City Blues	Working Towns	Heartlanders	Rustic Living
		1	2	3	4	5	6	7	8	9	10	11	12	13	14	15
Drag racing	36.78%		0	0	+	0					+	0	+	+		+
Sports car racing	50.51%						+				+	0			0	
College baseball	42.38%		0													
Professional baseball	81.25%															
College basketball	73.32%															
Professional basketball	78.71%															
Bowling	45.86%										0	0	+			0
Boxing	48.68%									0		+	+		0	
College football	85.10%															
Professional football	90.69%															
Fishing	41.79%	0	0								+	0	+	+	0	+
Golf	59.94%	+						0								
Horse racing	42.11%												+			0
Ice hockey	51.60%							+							0	0
Ice skating	47.93%			+						0		0			+	0
Rodeo	32.78%					0		0			+	0	+	+	+	+
Skiing	45.32%			+												
Professional soccer	32.73%		+												0	
Tennis	53.06%	+		+				0					+			0
Track and field	44.65%					0							+	+	+	
Truck pulling	21.85%	0		0		0	+	0			+	0	+	+		+
Ultimate frisbee	5.85%		0	0	0	0	+	+		0	+			+		0
Volleyball (hard surface)	32.97%		0										+		+	
Volleyball (beach)	39.47%		+			0	+						+			
Professional wrestling	23.32%		0					+		0			+	+		+

Key: + = 20% higher than average participation rate.

0 = 20% lower than average participation rate.

the Exurban Blues, Urban Cores, and Rustic Living segments.

The pattern of participation rates by geodemographic segments indicates great diversity and variance in participation and viewing rates. The major team sports of baseball, basketball, and football clearly enjoy a national following. For these sports, there are no significant variances by PRIZM social groups. Interestingly, professional soccer, a growing team spectator sport in this country that is benefiting from the introduction of Major League Soccer, also displays nearly universal appeal throughout the clusters analyzed. In contrast, more niche-type sports like auto racing, rodeo, and ultimate frisbee are more confined to certain clusters.

Unlike traditional geographic segmentation that relies upon contiguous groups, the PRIZM system identifies clusters of individuals who are more or less likely to participate or watch a particular sport across the entire country. Segmenting by geodemographics is an important tool for sport marketers to use in conjunction with their database marketing efforts. Geodemographic segmentation can be used to select mailing lists for direct marketing efforts; thus, sport catalogs, sport magazines, and associations can use geodemographic segmentation as a tool for identifying possible new customers. This study has shown that geodemographics is a powerful tool for finding segments of individuals with high or low sport behaviors.

Study 2—Motivation Segmentation

This study examines the effectiveness of motivational factors in profiling the differences among sport segments. The data for this study are from the Sport Consumer Research Project (see the appendix), that has been described in earlier chapters (2 and 3). In brief, this survey was mailed to a random sample of 5000 U.S. sport enthusiasts, of whom 1611 responded. As part of this survey, respondents answered a series of questions that tapped into various motivations they had for participating in their favorite sport. In addition, respondents also indicated their level of in-season participation for 40 sports and their spectating behavior for 25 sports. The response options ranged from every day, to almost every day, to never.

To profile the 40 participation and 25 spectating sports, we used the 13 multi-item participation factors and the 12 multi-item spectating motivation factors that were formulated in Chapter 3. For each of the 40 participant sports, we classified each individual as either a participant or nonparticipant based on their self-reported activity. Similarly, respondents were classified as spectators or nonspectators for each of the 25 spectator sports.

To profile each of the sports, we ran separate stepwise logit regression models, which were then used to examine the relationship between the motivations and the responses (participant or spectating). The dependent variables in the model were binary response measures (participant/nonparticipant)

where participant (spectator) was coded as 1 and nonparticipant (nonspectator) coded as 0. The independent variables were the 12 or 13 motivational factor scores. The general form of the logit models was:

Prob (participating or spectating)

$$= \frac{e^{\Sigma \beta \text{(motivations)}}}{1 + e^{\Sigma \beta \text{(motivations)}}}$$

The package models were estimated using a statistical software package called SAS; specifically, its logistic procedure. The stepwise regression used the forward selection option. Only factors with statistically significant chi-squares ($p < 0.05$) were retained in the final model.

The summary results of 65 logistic regression equations are presented in Tables 7–3 and 7–4, which show the factors that had a statistically significant ($p < 0.05$) positive or negative relationship to the participation/spectating behaviors for each sport. A positive relationship is denoted by a plus sign and a negative relationship is denoted by a zero. For example, in Table 7–3 the motivational profile of someone who participates in aerobics is low competition and skill mastery needs but high physical fitness and self-esteem needs.

The pattern of the tables shows that motivations for people participating in sports vary considerably. As expected, spectator sports in Table 7–4 such as professional basketball and college football, which have been traditionally associated with basking-in-reflected-glow (BIRGing) behavior, are strongly correlated to the motivation of achievement. Physical risk-taking, reflecting an enjoyment of watching athletes place themselves in harm's way, is correlated with the sports of drag racing and sports car racing as well as other dangerous activities like boxing and professional wrestling.

In contrast, competition, which is a very general motivator, is correlated with a number of disparate sports. Sports car racing, boxing, fishing, golf, truck pulling, and ultimate frisbee were all positively related to competition. The thrill of battle, whether against fish or foe, is a powerful motivator of spectator behavior. On the other end of the continuum, only ice hockey was positively related to stress release. If aggression and stress release go hand-in-hand, as

TABLE 7–3. Motivational predictors of sport participation

Participant sport	Achievement	Competition	Social facilitation	Physical fitness	Skill mastery	Physical risk-taking	Affiliation	Aesthetics	Aggression	Value development	Self-esteem	Self-actualization	Stress release
Aerobics		0		+	0						+		
Archery	+					+			+				
Badminton						+							
Baseball	+	+				+							
Basketball		+				+	0	+					
Bicycle riding	+		+			+							
Billiards/Pool	+		+		+	+	0		+				
Board sailing						+							
Bowling		+							+				
Boxing						+		+	+				
Bungee jumping						+							
Canoeing/Kayaking						+							
Distance running	+		0	+		+							
Freshwater fishing						+							
Saltwater fishing									+		+		
Football (tackle)		+				+	0		+				
Football (touch)		+				+	0		+				
Golf	+			+	+						0		
Hunting				0		+			+	+			
Ice hockey						+							
Ice skating		0	+	+		+	0						
Mountain biking				+		+							
Rollerskating (in-line)	+				0				+				
Running/Jogging	+	+		+		+							
Sailing								+					
Scuba diving	+	0				+							+
Skateboarding						+	0		+				
Skiing (cross-country)				+	+								+
Skiing (downhill)	+	0				+			+				+
Snowboarding						+							
Soccer	+					+							
Softball		+			0	+			+				
Swimming				+									+
Table tennis	+				+								
Tennis	+		0	+	+				+	0			
Ultimate frisbee						+							
Volleyball (hard surface)		+				+							
Volleyball (beach)	+					+			+	0			+
Water skiing	+					+			+				
Weightlifting	+					+	0		+				+

Key: + = 20% higher than average participation rate.

0 = 20% lower than average participation rate.

TABLE 7–4. Motivational predictors of sport spectators

Spectator sport	Achievement	Competition	Social facilitation	Skill mastery	Physical risk-taking	Affiliation	Aesthetics	Aggression	Value development	Self-esteem	Self-actualization	Stress release
Drag racing	0	+			+			+				
Sports car racing		+			+							
College baseball										+		
Professional baseball			+									
College basketball			+			+						
Professional basketball	+											
Bowling												
Boxing		+			+			+	+			
College football	+		+					+				
Professional football								+				
Fishing		+			+						+	
Golf		+										
Horse racing						+						
Ice hockey								+				+
Ice skating		0				+	+					
Rodeo	0							+			+	
Skiing								+				
Professional soccer								+			+	
Tennis								+				
Track and field					+			+				
Truck pulling		+			+				+			
Ultimate frisbee		+			+			+		+		
Volleyball (hard surface)					+			+		+		
Volleyball (beach)					+			+	+			
Professional wrestling			+		+							

Key: + = 20% higher than average spectating rate.

    0 = 20% lower than average spectating rate.

some researchers have postulated, one would expect the sports of boxing and both college and professional football to have been related to stress release, yet this was not the case.

While not strongly correlated with sport spectating, achievement was a very powerful motivator for sport participation. Across a vast array of activities, achievement was a prime motivator for participation. Interestingly, achievement as a motivator was most prevalent in activities where athletes have control over their own destinies, as in individual sports. Only one of the team sports listed in Table 7–3, baseball, was associated with achievement. This is to be anticipated because of the emphasis in baseball on the individual skills of throwing, hitting, and catching.

Competition as a motivator was just the opposite of achievement for virtually all team sports. The one motivator that cut across both team and individual sports was physical risk-taking. Pushing oneself to

TABLE 7–5. Sport participant segments

Total number of sports played or participated in last 12 months**	Total number of days played or participated in last 12 months*		
	0 days	1–149 days	150+ days
0 sports	Nonparticipants (43.3%)		
1–2 sports		Minimalists (21.4%)	Specialists (2.8%)
3+ sports		Variety seekers (11.1%)	Enthusiasts (21.4%)

*Number of days can exceed 365 to account for multiple sports played.
**40 sporting activities and 1 "other sport" alternative.

the extreme and even risking injury seem to excite participation in sports and activities.

The results of this study show a variety of motivators influencing participation and spectating in various sports, and this has significant implications for marketers. Marketing plans and advertising campaigns can be targeted to specific motivations to increase either participation in or spectatorship of a specific sport or activity.

Study 3—Heavy/Light Usage Versus Variety Seeking Segmentation

Data for this study are from 19,874 individual respondents to the 1991 Simmons Market Research Study of Media and Markets. Using those study results, we analyzed data on sport participation rates. These data are from a question that asked individuals to mark which of the 41 sports they played or actively participated in during the last 12 months and, for each sport they played or participated in, to mark the duration in total number of days over that 12-month period. The categories for number of days participated were 0, 1–4, 5–9, 10–19, 20–39, 40–59, 60–79, 80–99, 100–149, and 150 or more.

We segmented the 19,874 respondents based on two dimensions: (1) total number of days played or participated (for all sports) in the last 12 months, and (2) total number of sports played or participated in the last 12 months. Based on natural groupings in the data, we formed five market segments (see Table 7–5). The first segment was called "Nonparticipants." This was the large segment of individuals

who did not participate in sport during the past year. Nonparticipants represented 43.3% of the sample. The second segment, called the "Minimalists," represented 21.4% of the sample and was defined as participating in 1–2 sports and playing between 1–149 days. The third segment, which was the smallest (2.8%), was called the "Specialists." Although participating in only 1–2 sports, Specialists played 150 or more days per year. The fourth segment the "Variety Seekers," was made up of 11.1% of the respondents and participated in 3 or more sports and played 1–149 days. The final segment is the "Enthusiast," representing 21.4% of the sample. They played 3 or more sports for a total of 150 or more days.

The usage market segments are profiled by demographics in Table 7–6. The results show there are differences in demographic compositions across the five segments. In particular, Nonparticipants tend to have a higher percentage of females (54.9%), are less likely to have children in the household (27.8%) than Participants, don't work (50.4%), and have lower incomes (30.4% have annual household incomes < $12,500). Based on these demographics, it is possible that a high percentage of this segment are retirees. In contrast, Enthusiasts are 58% male, 42.1% have children in the household, 76.2% are employed, and 91.5% have annual household incomes > $12,500. Overall, sport participation is correlated with economic status. In addition, it appears as though having children in the house increases sport variety-seeking behavior.

We next used the four participation segments (Minimalists, Specialists, Variety Seekers, Enthusiasts) to profile the participants of the 41 sports, as depicted in Table 7–7. The first column of the table

TABLE 7–6. Demographic profile of sport participant segments

	Nonparticipants	Minimalists	Specialists	Variety seekers	Enthusiasts
N	8606	4252	558	2208	4250
% of total	43.30	21.39	2.81	11.11	21.38
Gender					
Male	45.1%	53.2%	50.7%	58.7%	58.0%
Female	54.9%	46.8%	49.3%	41.3%	42.0%
Children					
Children in household	27.8%	33.6%	26.2%	47.8%	42.1%
No children in household	72.2%	66.4%	73.8%	52.2%	57.9%
Marital status					
Married	54.2%	64.1%	65.4%	69.3%	64.5%
Single, not engaged	1.9%	2.5%	1.8%	2.5%	3.3%
Engaged	43.9%	33.5%	32.8%	28.2%	32.2%
Hours worked					
Don't work	50.4%	38.6%	44.4%	22.1%	23.9%
1–39 hours	11.6%	13.4%	9.9%	14.2%	14.5%
40+ hours	38.0%	48.0%	45.7%	63.8%	61.7%
Household income					
<$12,499	30.4%	16.3%	15.6%	10.1%	8.5%
$12,500–$39,999	47.5%	50.9%	52.2%	47.1%	45.9%
$40,000+	22.1%	32.9%	32.3%	42.8%	45.6%
Race					
White	79.9%	87.2%	86.2%	90.0%	91.6%
Black	17.2%	10.4%	10.4%	8.3%	6.5%
Other	3.0%	2.5%	3.4%	1.7%	1.9%

Percentages may not add to 100% due to rounding.

shows the average number of days participants played each sport. Thus, for bowling, the average number of days played was 27. The second column shows the number of days participants of a particular sport spend playing all sports. Looking at bowling again, participants spent an average of 212 days engaged in at least some sporting or fitness activity. The third column is customer share. This is the percentage of all sporting days that are spent on a particular sport (column 1 divided by column 2). Thus, for bowling, customer share is 12.72%, meaning that, on average, bowlers spent 12.72% of their sport participation days bowling. The fourth column is the average number of sports played. Thus bowlers, on average, participated in 5.43 sports. Columns 5–8 show the percentage of participants in a particular sport that fell in the Minimalists, Specialists, Variety Seekers, and Enthusiasts market segments.

In columns 2–8 the top five values are indicated by dark shading. The bottom five values are indicated by borders with no shading. For example, the sports with the highest customer share include

Fitness walking	33.59%
Jogging/Running	20.04%
Stationary bicycling	21.5%
Aerobics	19.79%.

TABLE 7-7. Profile participant sports by heavy/light usage segments

Sport	Avg. days	Avg. days all sports	Customer share	Avg. # sports	Minimalists	Specialists	Variety seekers	Enthusiasts
Bowling	27	212	12.72%	5.43	20.87%	1.79%	25.91%	51.43%
Golf	36	242	15.07%	5.71	18.77%	2.64%	23.07%	55.52%
Tennis	39	319	12.29%	7.13	7.83%	1.49%	18.95%	71.73%
Handball	34	568	6.04%	11.57	5.49%	0.00%	21.98%	72.53%
Racquet ball	38	349	10.98%	8.03	6.43%	2.14%	16.76%	74.66%
Paddle ball	39	486	8.11%	11.13	7.77%	0.00%	23.30%	68.93%
Roller skating	19	271	7.11%	7.23	6.54%	0.82%	29.56%	63.08%
Ice skating	21	343	6.10%	8.73	5.95%	0.38%	23.03%	70.63%
Snowmobiling	31	374	8.41%	8.97	4.62%	0.33%	23.10%	71.95%
Cross-country snow skiing	31	379	8.20%	8.74	3.95%	0.70%	15.12%	80.23%
Downhill snow skiing	26	355	7.35%	8.53	3.49%	0.27%	21.88%	74.36%
Water skiing	25	351	7.09%	8.94	2.90%	0.72%	20.43%	75.94%
Skin diving or snorkeling	31	413	7.45%	9.14	4.66%	0.00%	16.62%	78.72%
Swimming	41	231	17.85%	5.49	15.70%	2.89%	24.42%	56.99%
Power boating	34	293	11.48%	7.01	6.34%	0.79%	25.26%	67.61%
Sailing	33	351	9.32%	8.32	9.31%	1.30%	23.81%	65.58%
Freshwater fishing	36	229	15.57%	5.66	15.35%	2.33%	26.13%	56.19%
Saltwater fishing	29	264	10.99%	6.32	13.91%	0.69%	28.10%	57.30%
Horseback riding	36	332	10.71%	7.74	7.97%	1.00%	21.93%	69.10%
Hunting	38	274	13.83%	6.39	12.29%	1.68%	25.64%	60.39%
Target shooting	33	321	10.26%	7.49	8.95%	0.84%	20.28%	69.93%
Archery	38	396	9.53%	8.49	3.27%	0.00%	16.96%	79.76%
Hiking	37	316	11.63%	7.41	4.70%	0.91%	19.86%	74.53%
Backpacking	33	466	7.01%	10.42	1.98%	0.00%	18.65%	79.37%
Camping trips (overnight)	33	257	12.80%	6.53	10.11%	1.60%	27.73%	60.56%
Fitness walking	73	218	33.59%	4.40	28.39%	6.31%	16.06%	49.24%
Jogging/Running	70	347	20.04%	7.10	8.77%	3.00%	14.47%	73.76%
Distance running	62	400	15.53%	8.06	10.17%	5.08%	11.86%	72.88%
Aerobics	60	305	19.79%	6.38	12.74%	2.44%	16.32%	68.50%
Karate/Martial arts	66	462	14.29%	8.86	7.88%	2.46%	15.76%	73.89%
Free weights	71	387	18.46%	7.60	6.36%	2.36%	13.23%	78.05%
Machine weights	69	418	16.57%	7.90	4.51%	2.11%	11.97%	81.41%
Bicycling (stationary)	62	290	21.50%	5.80	13.65%	5.88%	15.91%	64.56%
Bicycling (outdoor)	47	264	17.90%	6.16	12.02%	2.45%	23.89%	61.64%
Rowing (stationary)	52	406	12.72%	7.93	8.16%	2.37%	14.74%	74.74%
Rowing (outdoor)	32	429	7.47%	9.20	2.75%	0.55%	20.88%	75.82%
Motorcycling (street)	61	330	18.55%	6.93	9.44%	3.99%	16.70%	69.87%
Motorcycling (dirt)	42	390	10.88%	8.86	5.51%	1.27%	21.61%	71.61%
Auto racing	30	324	9.41%	7.00	24.74%	1.55%	28.35%	45.36%
Piloting private planes	50	523	9.65%	9.43	6.42%	1.83%	26.61%	65.14%
Other sports	55	285	19.30%	6.39	14.38%	3.00%	20.30%	62.32%

The sports with the lowest customer share include:

Handball	6.04%
Ice skating	6.10%
Water skiing	7.09%
Roller skating	7.11%

(and so forth).

By looking at the table, we can gain insight into the composition of the four segments. For example, the participants in the Minimalist segment are more likely to participate in fitness walking, auto racing, bowling, golf, or swimming than the other three segments. In contrast, the Enthusiasts branch out into a more diverse set of activities. In addition to traditional activities, they are more likely to use machine weights, cross country ski, and participate in archery, back packing, or skin diving.

In addition to seeing which segments the participants in a particular sport fall into, we also investigated the effectiveness of heavy/light usage patterns within single sports. In Table 7–8, for each of the 41 sports, we show the participation rate and number of participants and how the volume of days played and average number of days played break out across light and heavy usage. For each sport, we formed three segments based on the number of days participated. The first two segments were light and heavy. These were formed by arraying participants of a sport by the number of days played. The light segment was the 50% of participants with the fewest days. The heavy segment was the 50% of participants with the most days. The third segment, which overlapped segment 2, was the top 20% of participants with the most days. For example, in Table 7–8, 15.5% (3072) of the sample participated in bowling. Of the bowlers, the light half accounts for 4.64% of total days bowled (average of 3 days); the heavy half accounts for 95.36% of all days bowled (average of 51 days). Furthermore, the top 20% of bowlers account for 66.76% of all days bowled (average, 90 days).

These results are interesting when compared to the 80/20 rule reviewed in Chapter 5. If these participation numbers were combined with equipment and apparel sales (quantity and quality), many of these sports would approach 80/20, meaning that 20% of the sport's participants buy 80% of the goods. Prior research has indicated that avid golfers, for example, are willing to travel further to play their sport and purchase higher-quality equipment more frequently than do occasional golfers.

This study has demonstrated that participants vary by the number of days they put into sport, the number of sports they participate in, and the customer share of the primary sport. Sport managers of particular sports would be well advised to understand the composition of the customer base for their particular sport. This study has also revealed considerable intersport heterogeneity and that all participants are not equal. Additionally, the study has demonstrated that segmenting customers by combinations of usage levels and the number of competing sporting activities is a useful approach. The next study will address our understanding of related sporting activities.

Study 4—Activity Clusters

This study forms macro-level activity clusters from the data for the 41 sports discussed in Study 3. Again, data for this study are from 19,874 individual respondents to the 1991 Simmons Market Research Study of Media and Markets. In this study, we analyzed cross-classification data—the percentage of participants of one sport who also participated in another sport. The cross-classification data were derived from data from the 19,874 individual survey respondents. The cross-classification matrices are in Table 7–9. The cells of the table show the percentage of participants of the sport number listed in each column who also play the sport listed in each row. For example, 42% of tennis players (column 3) also play golf (column 2). Note that the matrix is asymmetrical; thus, continuing with the previous example, 25% of the golfers (column 2) also play tennis (row 3).

Table 7–9 represents an array of interesting numbers, but it is difficult to see the overall structure of the market. Altogether there are 1640 numbers on the off-diagonals. To cluster the sports into groups, we used the multivariate technique of hierarchical cluster analysis. This analysis groups similar sports together based on their average cross-classification rates. The average cross-classification rates were derived by averaging the two cross-classification rates calculated for each sport-by-sport comparison. Thus, for golf and tennis, the average classification rate was 33.5% [(42% + 25%)/2].

The cluster analyses were done using SPSS for Microsoft Windows (release 6.1), a statistical software package. The average-linkage algorithm was used to form groups. The program started off with 41 groups and kept forming clusters until there was only one final group. The dendrogram in Table 7–10

TABLE 7–8. Profile of consumer participants by segment membership sport type

Sport	Participant rate	# Parts	% Vol. Light $^1/_2$	Heavy $^1/_2$	Heavy 20%	Avg. days Light $^1/_2$	Heavy $^1/_2$	Heavy 20%	Avg. days
1 Bowling	15.5	3072	4.64	95.36	66.76	3	51	90	27
2 Golf	10.9	2163	7.64	92.36	56.15	6	67	102	36
3 Tennis	6.4	1277	8.31	91.69	52.40	7	72	103	39
4 Handball	0.5	91	7.83	92.17	61.38	5	63	105	34
5 Racquet ball	3.8	746	8.43	91.57	53.64	6	70	103	38
6 Paddle ball	0.5	103	9.64	90.36	54.19	8	71	107	39
7 Roller skating	3.7	734	6.48	93.52	86.59	3	36	84	19
8 Ice skating	2.6	521	5.96	94.04	83.83	2	39	88	21
9 Snowmobiling	1.5	303	3.96	96.04	58.88	2	60	93	31
10 Cross-country snow skiing	2.2	430	4.02	95.98	58.47	3	60	91	31
11 Downhill snow skiing	3.7	745	4.78	95.22	70.16	2	50	92	26
12 Water skiing	3.5	690	5.02	94.98	71.46	3	47	89	25
13 Skin diving or snorkeling	1.7	343	4.06	95.94	59.74	2	59	92	31
14 Swimming	22.5	4471	12.05	87.95	47.63	10	73	98	41
15 Power boating	5.7	1136	8.15	91.85	56.98	5	62	96	34
16 Sailing	2.3	462	5.97	94.03	56.82	4	61	93	33
17 Freshwater fishing	11.9	2365	9.06	90.94	53.31	6	65	95	36
18 Saltwater fishing	3.7	726	4.76	95.24	64.62	3	55	94	29
19 Horseback riding	3	602	3.57	96.43	61.60	3	69	110	36
20 Hunting	5.7	1131	9.69	90.31	50.45	7	68	95	38
21 Target shooting	3.6	715	6.19	93.81	58.43	4	62	96	33
22 Archery	1.7	336	10.32	89.68	53.92	8	68	102	38
23 Hiking	6.6	1319	7.03	92.97	52.76	5	68	97	37
24 Backpacking	1.3	252	4.41	95.59	59.81	3	63	98	33
25 Camping trips (overnight)	9.5	1879	6.08	93.92	56.39	4	62	93	33
26 Fitness walking	24.3	4833	19.19	80.81	40.99	28	118	150	73
27 Jogging/Running	6.7	1334	17.34	82.66	42.56	24	115	148	70
28 Distance running	1.8	354	16.01	83.99	45.73	20	104	142	62
29 Aerobics	5.8	1146	17.51	82.49	45.56	21	100	138	60
30 Karate/Martial arts	1	203	11.70	88.30	45.51	15	117	150	66
31 Free weights	4.9	975	19.13	80.87	41.17	27	116	147	71
32 Machine weights	3.6	710	17.80	82.20	42.04	25	114	146	69
33 Bicycling (stationary)	9.3	1854	17.49	82.51	45.46	22	103	142	62
34 Bicycling (outdoor)	10.7	2122	13.97	86.03	47.42	13	81	112	47
35 Rowing (stationary)	1.9	380	15.14	84.86	47.49	16	88	122	52
36 Rowing (outdoor)	0.9	182	4.72	95.28	67.15	3	61	108	32
37 Motorcycling (street)	2.8	551	13.63	86.37	47.94	17	106	147	61
38 Motorcycling (dirt)	1.2	236	9.51	90.49	49.49	8	77	105	42
39 Auto racing	1	194	7.35	92.65	61.68	4	56	94	30
40 Piloting private planes	0.5	109	9.70	90.30	51.17	10	91	129	50
41 Other sports	6.4	1266	15.77	84.23	46.35	17	93	127	55

shows which sports group together. Sports and groups of sport that are most similar group together; eventually, all groups form one group. For example, power boating and water skiing are the first sports grouped together due to their high average cross-classification rate, as are target shooting and hunting, camping and hiking, machine weights and free weights, and so forth. When sports link up, they form

TABLE 7–9. Sport cross-classification percentages

	1	2	3	4	5	6	7	8	9	10	11	12	13	14	15	16	17	18	19	20	21
1 Bowling	1.00	0.39	0.39	0.57	0.45	0.60	0.48	0.51	0.47	0.30	0.39	0.47	0.30	0.34	0.36	0.34	0.31	0.30	0.38	0.29	0.34
2 Golf	0.27	1.00	0.42	0.40	0.43	0.33	0.21	0.36	0.37	0.37	0.36	0.33	0.30	0.22	0.25	0.38	0.23	0.24	0.24	0.26	0.25
3 Tennis	0.16	0.25	1.00	0.43	0.39	0.36	0.19	0.29	0.24	0.28	0.32	0.26	0.32	0.15	0.16	0.34	0.12	0.13	0.23	0.11	0.12
4 Handball	0.02	0.02	0.03	1.00	0.06	0.25	0.03	0.03	0.07	0.04	0.02	0.03	0.03	0.01	0.02	0.04	0.01	0.02	0.02	0.02	0.02
5 Racquet ball	0.11	0.15	0.23	0.47	1.00	0.37	0.14	0.21	0.18	0.24	0.21	0.16	0.25	0.08	0.11	0.18	0.07	0.08	0.13	0.10	0.14
6 Paddle ball	0.02	0.02	0.03	0.29	0.05	1.00	0.04	0.06	0.06	0.04	0.03	0.03	0.06	0.01	0.02	0.05	0.01	0.02	0.03	0.01	0.03
7 Roller skating	0.11	0.07	0.11	0.23	0.14	0.32	1.00	0.26	0.10	0.13	0.12	0.17	0.10	0.11	0.10	0.10	0.08	0.10	0.16	0.07	0.10
8 Ice skating	0.09	0.09	0.12	0.20	0.15	0.31	0.18	1.00	0.18	0.17	0.18	0.17	0.17	0.08	0.10	0.18	0.06	0.08	0.13	0.07	0.09
9 Snowboarding	0.05	0.05	0.06	0.23	0.08	0.17	0.04	0.11	1.00	0.10	0.09	0.13	0.08	0.04	0.08	0.08	0.06	0.06	0.09	0.10	0.06
10 Cross-country snow skiing	0.04	0.07	0.10	0.18	0.14	0.18	0.07	0.14	0.14	1.00	0.17	0.11	0.17	0.07	0.08	0.16	0.05	0.04	0.10	0.06	0.05
11 Downhill snow skiing	0.09	0.12	0.19	0.20	0.21	0.20	0.12	0.26	0.22	0.30	1.00	0.29	0.31	0.11	0.17	0.24	0.09	0.13	0.18	0.09	0.11
12 Water skiing	0.11	0.10	0.14	0.23	0.15	0.21	0.16	0.22	0.31	0.17	0.27	1.00	0.22	0.12	0.31	0.24	0.04	0.12	0.16	0.15	0.15
13 Skin diving or snorkeling	0.03	0.05	0.09	0.13	0.12	0.20	0.05	0.11	0.09	0.14	0.14	0.11	1.00	0.05	0.09	0.19	0.04	0.10	0.10	0.05	0.08
14 Swimming	0.50	0.45	0.54	0.53	0.48	0.53	0.69	0.70	0.62	0.70	0.67	0.51	0.69	1.00	0.65	0.58	0.45	0.44	0.60	0.41	0.50
15 Power boating	0.13	0.13	0.15	0.20	0.16	0.23	0.15	0.22	0.32	0.20	0.26	0.51	0.31	0.16	1.00	0.30	0.18	0.24	0.20	0.19	0.21
16 Sailing	0.05	0.08	0.12	0.21	0.11	0.21	0.06	0.16	0.12	0.17	0.15	0.16	0.26	0.06	0.12	1.00	0.05	0.09	0.11	0.06	0.07
17 Freshwater fishing	0.24	0.25	0.22	0.23	0.23	0.26	0.26	0.25	0.44	0.28	0.29	0.35	0.27	0.24	0.37	0.27	1.00	0.52	0.30	0.59	0.51
18 Saltwater fishing	0.07	0.08	0.07	0.15	0.08	0.17	0.10	0.12	0.13	0.07	0.12	0.12	0.21	0.07	0.15	0.15	0.16	1.00	0.13	0.12	0.14
19 Horseback riding	0.07	0.07	0.11	0.16	0.10	0.17	0.13	0.15	0.18	0.13	0.14	0.14	0.17	0.08	0.11	0.15	0.08	0.11	1.00	0.11	0.11
20 Hunting	0.11	0.13	0.10	0.20	0.15	0.16	0.10	0.16	0.39	0.16	0.13	0.24	0.17	0.10	0.19	0.14	0.28	0.19	0.21	1.00	0.44
21 Target shooting	0.08	0.08	0.07	0.19	0.13	0.20	0.10	0.12	0.14	0.08	0.11	0.15	0.17	0.08	0.13	0.10	0.15	0.14	0.14	0.28	1.00
22 Archery	0.04	0.04	0.05	0.27	0.06	0.17	0.05	0.07	0.12	0.08	0.05	0.09	0.06	0.04	0.06	0.04	0.06	0.05	0.08	0.18	0.20
23 Hiking	0.15	0.12	0.22	0.29	0.19	0.33	0.22	0.27	0.23	0.43	0.30	0.23	0.30	0.18	0.18	0.24	0.17	0.15	0.28	0.17	0.26
24 Backpacking	0.04	0.03	0.05	0.23	0.08	0.21	0.06	0.08	0.11	0.13	0.09	0.09	0.11	0.03	0.04	0.05	0.04	0.05	0.09	0.06	0.07
25 Camping trips (overnight)	0.22	0.16	0.21	0.31	0.26	0.27	0.31	0.32	0.32	0.40	0.35	0.40	0.30	0.23	0.29	0.28	0.31	0.25	0.34	0.33	0.30
26 Fitness walking	0.37	0.40	0.44	0.53	0.41	0.53	0.48	0.45	0.31	0.53	0.42	0.38	0.44	0.44	0.39	0.45	0.37	0.36	0.41	0.27	0.35
27 Jogging/Running	0.14	0.18	0.27	0.42	0.34	0.31	0.21	0.24	0.20	0.22	0.32	0.28	0.29	0.16	0.17	0.28	0.13	0.14	0.23	0.13	0.18
28 Distance running	0.04	0.05	0.08	0.34	0.12	0.25	0.05	0.07	0.09	0.10	0.07	0.08	0.09	0.04	0.04	0.08	0.04	0.05	0.06	0.04	0.06
29 Aerobics	0.13	0.09	0.19	0.24	0.16	0.21	0.22	0.19	0.16	0.20	0.18	0.18	0.17	0.14	0.11	0.16	0.07	0.08	0.21	0.06	0.09
30 Karate/Martial arts	0.03	0.02	0.04	0.24	0.07	0.23	0.04	0.07	0.09	0.04	0.04	0.05	0.09	0.02	0.03	0.06	0.02	0.04	0.07	0.03	0.06
31 Free weights	0.11	0.13	0.18	0.21	0.25	0.22	0.14	0.18	0.21	0.12	0.22	0.23	0.20	0.11	0.14	0.14	0.11	0.13	0.14	0.14	0.22
32 Machine weights	0.08	0.09	0.13	0.27	0.22	0.23	0.10	0.12	0.12	0.14	0.14	0.09	0.17	0.09	0.08	0.13	0.06	0.08	0.13	0.08	0.13
33 Bicycling (stationary)	0.17	0.18	0.21	0.32	0.24	0.30	0.21	0.25	0.22	0.31	0.25	0.20	0.24	0.20	0.19	0.23	0.14	0.13	0.21	0.10	0.16
34 Bicycling (outdoor)	0.22	0.23	0.32	0.27	0.28	0.39	0.35	0.39	0.28	0.44	0.40	0.33	0.37	0.27	0.27	0.39	0.21	0.22	0.31	0.19	0.24
35 Rowing (stationary)	0.04	0.05	0.07	0.13	0.10	0.11	0.06	0.08	0.06	0.10	0.08	0.06	0.11	0.04	0.04	0.09	0.03	0.04	0.07	0.04	0.05
36 Rowing (outdoor)	0.02	0.03	0.05	0.21	0.04	0.17	0.04	0.05	0.07	0.04	0.03	0.04	0.05	0.02	0.04	0.09	0.03	0.05	0.05	0.03	0.05
37 Motorcycling (street)	0.06	0.05	0.08	0.14	0.08	0.09	0.10	0.10	0.18	0.07	0.08	0.13	0.16	0.06	0.10	0.09	0.07	0.08	0.12	0.11	0.16
38 Motorcycling (dirt)	0.04	0.03	0.02	0.13	0.04	0.10	0.04	0.07	0.13	0.04	0.06	0.10	0.07	0.03	0.06	0.07	0.05	0.07	0.06	0.08	0.09
39 Auto racing	0.02	0.01	0.02	0.10	0.03	0.11	0.04	0.03	0.10	0.02	0.04	0.05	0.07	0.02	0.04	0.04	0.02	0.04	0.04	0.04	0.06
40 Piloting private planes	0.01	0.01	0.02	0.10	0.03	0.09	0.02	0.04	0.04	0.03	0.02	0.02	0.07	0.01	0.03	0.05	0.01	0.03	0.04	0.02	0.03
41 Other sports	0.16	0.14	0.20	0.31	0.22	0.35	0.20	0.22	0.16	0.20	0.21	0.18	0.20	0.15	0.13	0.16	0.14	0.12	0.16	0.14	0.20

TABLE 7–9. [continued]

	22	23	24	25	26	27	28	29	30	31	32	33	34	35	36	37	38	39	40	41
1 Bowling	0.38	0.34	0.45	0.35	0.24	0.33	0.36	0.34	0.38	0.35	0.34	0.29	0.32	0.30	0.36	0.33	0.46	0.29	0.26	0.40
2 Golf	0.25	0.20	0.25	0.18	0.18	0.29	0.33	0.17	0.26	0.28	0.27	0.21	0.23	0.28	0.31	0.21	0.26	0.16	0.25	0.24
3 Tennis	0.17	0.21	0.27	0.14	0.12	0.26	0.30	0.21	0.22	0.24	0.23	0.14	0.19	0.24	0.36	0.17	0.13	0.16	0.23	0.20
4 Handball	0.07	0.02	0.08	0.01	0.01	0.03	0.09	0.02	0.11	0.02	0.04	0.02	0.01	0.03	0.10	0.02	0.06	0.06	0.08	0.02
5 Racquet ball	0.13	0.11	0.24	0.10	0.06	0.19	0.25	0.10	0.27	0.19	0.23	0.10	0.10	0.20	0.18	0.11	0.13	0.10	0.18	0.13
6 Paddle ball	0.05	0.03	0.09	0.01	0.01	0.02	0.07	0.02	0.12	0.02	0.03	0.02	0.02	0.03	0.09	0.02	0.04	0.06	0.08	0.03
7 Roller skating	0.11	0.12	0.16	0.12	0.07	0.11	0.10	0.14	0.12	0.11	0.10	0.08	0.12	0.11	0.15	0.13	0.13	0.13	0.15	0.12
8 Ice skating	0.11	0.11	0.16	0.09	0.05	0.09	0.11	0.09	0.14	0.09	0.09	0.07	0.10	0.11	0.15	0.09	0.14	0.09	0.18	0.09
9 Snowboarding	0.11	0.05	0.13	0.05	0.02	0.05	0.08	0.04	0.17	0.07	0.05	0.04	0.10	0.05	0.11	0.10	0.17	0.15	0.11	0.09
10 Cross-country snow skiing	0.10	0.14	0.22	0.09	0.05	0.07	0.12	0.08	0.09	0.05	0.09	0.07	0.09	0.11	0.10	0.05	0.08	0.05	0.13	0.04
11 Downhill snow skiing	0.12	0.17	0.26	0.14	0.06	0.18	0.14	0.12	0.16	0.17	0.15	0.10	0.14	0.15	0.14	0.10	0.19	0.16	0.16	0.07
12 Water skiing	0.19	0.12	0.25	0.15	0.05	0.14	0.15	0.11	0.16	0.17	0.09	0.07	0.11	0.11	0.15	0.16	0.29	0.19	0.14	0.12
13 Skin diving or snorkeling	0.06	0.08	0.15	0.05	0.03	0.07	0.08	0.05	0.15	0.07	0.08	0.04	0.06	0.10	0.09	0.10	0.10	0.12	0.23	0.10
14 Swimming	0.53	0.60	0.56	0.54	0.41	0.53	0.46	0.55	0.49	0.51	0.55	0.47	0.56	0.52	0.59	0.48	0.59	0.46	0.47	0.54
15 Power boating	0.22	0.16	0.19	0.18	0.09	0.14	0.12	0.11	0.19	0.17	0.13	0.12	0.14	0.13	0.23	0.21	0.29	0.22	0.34	0.12
16 Sailing	0.06	0.08	0.09	0.07	0.04	0.10	0.10	0.06	0.13	0.07	0.08	0.06	0.08	0.11	0.22	0.07	0.14	0.10	0.19	0.06
17 Freshwater fishing	0.43	0.31	0.37	0.39	0.18	0.22	0.23	0.15	0.24	0.26	0.19	0.18	0.24	0.20	0.37	0.30	0.48	0.28	0.29	0.26
18 Saltwater fishing	0.11	0.08	0.15	0.10	0.05	0.08	0.10	0.05	0.15	0.09	0.08	0.05	0.08	0.08	0.19	0.11	0.20	0.13	0.17	0.07
19 Horseback riding	0.14	0.13	0.23	0.11	0.05	0.10	0.10	0.11	0.21	0.09	0.11	0.07	0.09	0.11	0.18	0.13	0.16	0.12	0.23	0.08
20 Hunting	0.62	0.15	0.25	0.20	0.06	0.11	0.14	0.05	0.18	0.16	0.13	0.06	0.10	0.12	0.21	0.23	0.16	0.24	0.26	0.12
21 Target shooting	0.42	0.14	0.19	0.11	0.05	0.10	0.12	0.06	0.20	0.16	0.13	0.06	0.08	0.09	0.19	0.21	0.39	0.21	0.22	0.11
22 Archery	1.00	0.08	0.15	0.07	0.02	0.05	0.11	0.03	0.14	0.07	0.06	0.03	0.04	0.07	0.17	0.12	0.19	0.08	0.11	0.06
23 Hiking	0.29	1.00	0.63	0.32	0.15	0.21	0.22	0.22	0.20	0.21	0.20	0.19	0.25	0.22	0.34	0.17	0.22	0.13	0.25	0.22
24 Backpacking	0.11	0.12	1.00	0.10	0.02	0.06	0.10	0.04	0.11	0.06	0.08	0.04	0.05	0.08	0.10	0.06	0.08	0.05	0.18	0.06
25 Camping trips (overnight)	0.37	0.45	0.73	1.00	0.15	0.20	0.24	0.20	0.26	0.22	0.18	0.19	0.26	0.29	0.41	0.28	0.40	0.26	0.38	0.24
26 Fitness walking	0.29	0.54	0.40	0.39	1.00	0.50	0.51	0.64	0.39	0.42	0.51	0.61	0.46	0.59	0.42	0.30	0.28	0.23	0.38	0.38
27 Jogging/Running	0.20	0.21	0.33	0.15	0.14	1.00	0.40	0.24	0.33	0.38	0.35	0.18	0.20	0.26	0.20	0.17	0.21	0.13	0.30	0.22
28 Distance running	0.11	0.06	0.13	0.05	0.04	0.10	1.00	0.06	0.15	0.11	0.10	0.05	0.05	0.08	0.15	0.06	0.06	0.09	0.16	0.06
29 Aerobics	0.11	0.19	0.20	0.12	0.15	0.21	0.20	1.00	0.18	0.20	0.28	0.20	0.14	0.22	0.13	0.12	0.09	0.10	0.17	0.12
30 Karate/Martial arts	0.09	0.03	0.09	0.03	0.02	0.05	0.08	0.03	1.00	0.08	0.07	0.02	0.03	0.07	0.14	0.06	0.07	0.09	0.16	0.03
31 Free weights	0.21	0.15	0.23	0.11	0.08	0.28	0.30	0.17	0.37	1.00	0.48	0.16	0.12	0.24	0.23	0.21	0.21	0.16	0.26	0.19
32 Machine weights	0.13	0.11	0.22	0.07	0.07	0.18	0.20	0.17	0.24	0.35	1.00	0.19	0.09	0.31	0.13	0.11	0.15	0.14	0.23	0.14
33 Bicycling (stationary)	0.18	0.26	0.33	0.19	0.23	0.25	0.27	0.32	0.19	0.30	0.49	1.00	0.21	0.64	0.21	0.14	0.14	0.13	0.24	0.18
34 Bicycling (outdoor)	0.24	0.40	0.42	0.29	0.20	0.31	0.28	0.26	0.28	0.25	0.27	0.25	1.00	0.27	0.32	0.26	0.25	0.19	0.28	0.28
35 Rowing (stationary)	0.08	0.06	0.13	0.06	0.05	0.07	0.09	0.07	0.13	0.09	0.16	0.13	0.05	1.00	0.13	0.04	0.07	0.06	0.18	0.05
36 Rowing (outdoor)	0.09	0.05	0.08	0.04	0.02	0.03	0.08	0.02	0.12	0.04	0.03	0.02	0.03	0.06	1.00	0.05	0.06	0.07	0.09	0.04
37 Motorcycling (street)	0.19	0.07	0.14	0.08	0.03	0.07	0.09	0.06	0.16	0.12	0.08	0.04	0.07	0.06	0.16	1.00	0.29	0.24	0.23	0.08
38 Motorcycling (dirt)	0.13	0.04	0.08	0.05	0.01	0.04	0.04	0.02	0.08	0.05	0.05	0.02	0.03	0.04	0.08	0.12	1.00	0.15	0.11	0.04
39 Auto racing	0.05	0.02	0.04	0.03	0.01	0.02	0.05	0.02	0.09	0.03	0.04	0.01	0.02	0.03	0.07	0.08	0.12	1.00	0.15	0.02
40 Piloting private planes	0.04	0.02	0.08	0.02	0.01	0.02	0.05	0.02	0.08	0.03	0.04	0.01	0.01	0.05	0.05	0.05	0.05	0.08	1.00	0.02
41 Other sports	0.21	0.21	0.28	0.16	0.10	0.21	0.22	0.14	0.19	0.25	0.24	0.12	0.17	0.17	0.29	0.19	0.22	0.14	0.25	1.00

TABLE 7–10. Activity clusters shown in dendrograms

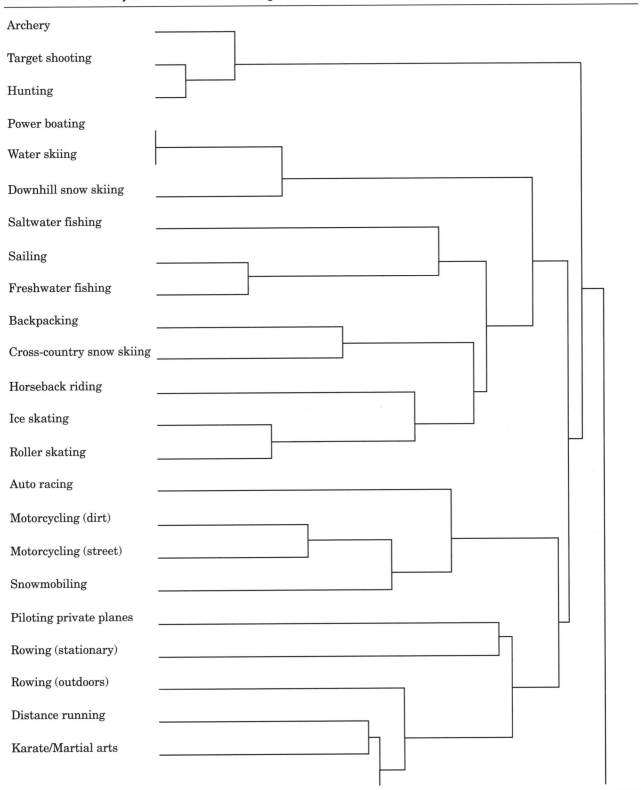

TABLE 7–10.   (continued)

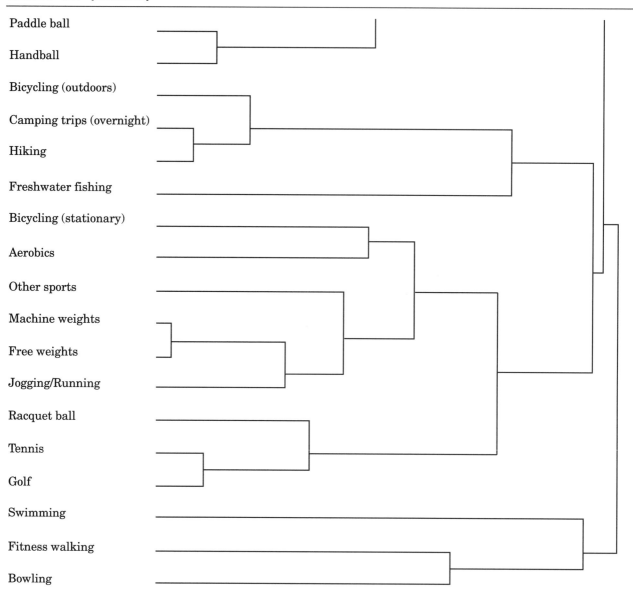

clusters. Thus, the target shooting/hunting segment forms a larger activity segment when it links up with archery. This segment, being different from many of the other sports, does not link up with other sports until the end of the process.

Table 7–10 shows other natural groupings of sports and provides a unique summary of the 41 sports that cannot be readily obtained from raw numbers. Depending on the level of analysis desired, managers can organize groups of sports into activity clusters. For example, there exists a natural grouping of "fitness sports" that includes stationary bicycling, aerobics, machine weights, free weights, and jogging/running. The next most related grouping is "corporate exercise," which includes golf, tennis, and racquet ball. If a retail store was considering how wide its product line should be, examining activity clusters could provide a useful start.

Summary

This chapter presented four new segmentation approaches for managers to consider as they try to better understand the sport marketplace. Given the tremendous number of competing sports, it is imperative for managers to understand where their customers live, what motivates them, what defines their usage and variety-seeking levels, and in what other activities they are likely to participate. Together, the segmentation approaches introduced in this chapter begin to address these issues.

References

Brooks, C. M. (1994). *Sports marketing: Competitive business strategies for sports*. Englewood Cliffs, NJ: Prentice-Hall.

Chang, Martin G. S. J., and Lester W. Johnson (1995). Segmenting the Triathlon Association membership market: An Australian example. *Sport Marketing Quarterly*, 25–28.

Del Valle, C. (1994). They know where you live and how you buy. *Business Week*, Feb. 7, 89.

Fullerton, S., and H. Robert Dodge (1995). An application of market segmentation in a sports marketing arena: We all can't be Greg Norman. *Sport Marketing Quarterly*, 4(3): 43–47.

Garreau, J. (1981). *Nine nations of North America*. Boston: Houghton Mifflin Company.

Hofacre, Susan, and Thomas K. Burman (1992). Demographic changes in the U.S. into the twenty-first century: Their impact on sport marketing. *Sport Marketing Quarterly*, 1(1): 31–36.

Kahle, Lynn R. (1986). The nine nations of North America and the value basis of geographical segmentation. *Journal of Marketing*, 50(2): 37–47.

Kotler, Phillip (1997). *Marketing management: Analysis, planning, implementation, and control*. Upper Saddle River, NJ.: Prentice-Hall.

Lascu, Dana-Nicoleta, Thomas D. Giese, Cathy Toolan, Brian Guehring, and James Mercer (1995). Sport involvement: A relevant individual difference factor in spectator sports. *Sport Marketing Quarterly*, 4(4): 41–46.

Mitchell, S. (1995). Birds of a feather. *American Demographics*, February, 40–48.

Pitts, Brenda G., Lawrence W. Fielding, and Lori Miller (1994). Industrial segmentation theory and the sport industry: Developing a sport industry segmentation model. *Sport Marketing Quarterly*, 3(1): 15–24.

Rooney, John F., and Richard Pillsbury (1992). *Atlas of American sport*. New York: MacMillan Publishing Co.

Settle, Robert B., and Pamela L. Alreck (1989). *Why they buy: American consumers inside and out*. New York: John Wiley & Sons.

Sherden, William A. (1994). *Market ownership: The art & science of becoming #1*. New York: Amacon.

Shoham, Aviv, and Lynn R. Kahle (1996). Spectators, viewers, readers: Communication and consumption communities in sport marketing. *Sport Marketing Quarterly*, 5(1): 11–19.

Turco, Douglas M. (1996). The x factor: Marketing sport to generation x. *Sport Marketing Quarterly*, 5(1): 21–26.

Twedt, Dik Warren (1964). How important to marketing strategy is the 'heavy user'? *Journal of Marketing*, 23 (January): 71–72.

Weiss, M. J. (1988). *The clustering of America*. New York: Harper & Row Publishers.

Measuring Service Quality

Introduction

As competition for customers intensifies, shifting the focus from acquiring customers to retaining them, a firm's ability to provide consistent high-quality service is becoming a prime source of competitive advantage. Service quality has been identified as one of the most important issues facing management across a broad range of industries (Dean and Evans, 1994; Greising, 1994). The inability to control the core product in professional sports serves to further heighten the need to provide high-quality service. Sport managers, therefore, are searching for tools to measure service quality effectively.

In this chapter, we will review a scale developed to measure service quality effectively in professional sport settings. To this end, the chapter is divided into three parts. The first part will review the literature on service quality as it applies to sport. Part II will describe the development of an instrument to measure service quality in a professional sport setting. In the last section, Part III, we will discuss the validation of this instrument through a comparison of expectations and perceptions of service quality by lifetime value deciles (see Chapter 5). This is accomplished by segmenting the respondents according to their lifetime values to the professional sport franchise and comparing scores on service quality dimensions across these segments.

Part I: Service Quality in Sport

A major draw of professional sport is the unpredictable nature of its outcomes (Mullin, Hardy, and Sutton, 1993). A game played today will be different from tomorrow's game, even if the starting lineups do not change. The downside is that unpredictable outcomes result directly from the inability of sport managers to exert control over the composition of the core product. A team's general manager and coaching staff are responsible for recruiting, drafting players, trades, and acquisitions—not actual playing.

Furthermore, schedules are typically developed by the league office, with limited input from individual teams. Thus, two key aspects of the core product, players and scheduling, are not under the control of sport marketers (Mullin, Hardy, and Sutton, 1993). This is in stark contrast to most industries, which expend considerable effort and financial resources on attempting to produce and deliver consistent goods and services.

Professional sport has a large service component. For the most part, consumers take nothing away from attending a sporting event other than the experience. Attending a sporting event, however, often includes tangibles such as food and drinks, a ticket stub, a program, memorabilia, and merchandise of the team and/or the arena or stadium. The service requires a capital-intensive good—an arena/stadium—for its realization, but the primary item is a service—entertainment.

This service component, coupled with an organization's inability to control the core product, provides a great challenge and opportunity to influence customer satisfaction by providing high-quality service. Recent evidence indicates that service quality is highly valued by professional sport consumers. A survey of 1000 sport fans by *Money Magazine* (Kasky, 1995) ranked National Football League (NFL), National Basketball Association (NBA), and Major League Baseball (MLB) teams by the "value" they offered to fans. *Value*, for this study, was defined as a combination of price and quality considerations. The fans surveyed had been to at least one game in the past three years, with the average respondent having attended eight games. The top seven consumer priorities, ranked from a comprehensive list of factors, each involved aspects of customer service. Surprisingly, none of these top priorities related to the team, the sport, or the game itself, but instead reflected concerns ranging from the convenience of public transportation to the comfort of the arena or stadium.

Brown, Sutton, and Duff (1993) note that service is one of the most crucial concerns of consumers attending events. Even the most vested consumer can be discouraged by poor ticket procurement procedures, slow or unfriendly concession service, inefficient entrance and exit traffic patterns, and unclean restroom facilities (Brown, Sutton, and Duff, 1993). Given the importance of service to properly managing events, some sport organizations have invested sizable amounts of time and money to enhance this aspect of their operations. The San Jose Sharks, for example, have recruited a core of community volunteers to serve on their Teal Team. The sole responsibility of this group is to greet customers at home games and be attentive and responsive to ticket holder needs during the staging of the event. For their efforts, people participating in this program receive one free ticket per month to a Shark home game (San Jose Sharks, 1996).

Given that service quality is important to professional sport consumers, how can it be accurately measured? For services, the measurement of quality is more difficult than it is for physical goods, because of the unique characteristics of services (intangible, inseparable, perishable, and variable). As Parasuraman, Zeithaml, and Berry (1991) note:

> The intangibility of services implies that precise manufacturing specifications concerning uniform quality can rarely be set for services as they can for goods. This difficulty is compounded by the fact that services, especially those with a high labor content, are heterogeneous: their performance often varies from producer to producer, from customer to customer, and from day to day. As a result, uniform quality is difficult to ensure . . . . The inseparability of production and consumption of services implies that quality cannot be engineered and evaluated at the manufacturing plant prior to delivery to consumers. Perishability means that goods and services cannot be saved, and this can lead to unsynchronized supply and demand problems. Clearly, goods-quality principles are not directly pertinent to services (p. 253).

With physical products, quality can be measured objectively using indicators such as number of defects or durability (Crosby, 1979; Garvin, 1983). In contrast, with services it is first necessary to identify the relevant dimensions. Lehtinen and Lehtinen (1982) indicate that a consumer could perceive "process quality" (e.g., the customer's qualitative evaluation of his/her participation in the service production process) and "output quality" (the consumer's evaluation of the results of a service production process). Lovelock (1983), however, identified two basic dimensions of service: (1) the nature of the act and (2) the degree of customization in service delivery. Lovelock's work was extended by the development of a service classification scheme that categorized the nature of the act into three groups: (1) services directed toward tangibles, (2) services directed toward intan-

CONSUMER

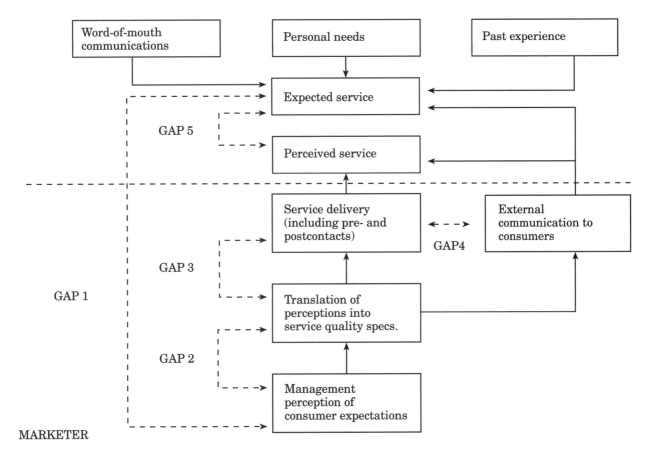

FIGURE 8–1. Gap Model of Service Quality (Zeithaml, Berry, and Parasuraman, 1988)

gibles, and (3) services directed toward people (Kelly, Donnelly, and Skinner, 1990).

The Gap Model of Service Quality

The primary model that has been applied to both academic research and consulting efforts is the Gap Model of Service Quality, which has been adapted in Figure 8–1 (Zeithaml, Berry, and Parasuraman, 1988). This model conceptualizes customer service satisfaction as being a function of the following five perceptual gaps that occur between service design and delivery:

Gap 1: The difference between consumer expectations and management perceptions of consumer expectations.

Gap 2: The difference between management perceptions of consumer expectations and service quality specifications.

Gap 3: The difference between service quality specifications and the service actually delivered.

Gap 4: The difference between service delivery and what is communicated about the service to consumers.

Gap 5: The difference between perceived service and expected service on the part of consumers.

As a result of testing the Gap Model, the original authors (Parasuraman, Berry, and Zeithaml, 1985) have developed the Extended Gap Model (Parasuraman, Berry, and Zeithaml, 1988), which is reviewed in the following section.

The Extended Gap Model

The Extended Gap Model in Figure 8–2 (Parasuraman, Berry, and Zeithaml, 1990) includes a set of antecedents that influence the four gaps that together determine the service performance gap. Two studies, Parasuraman, Berry, and Zeithaml (1991) and Parasuraman, Berry, and Zeithaml (1990), referred to as PBZ91 and PBZ90, respectively, present the results of testing these relationships. The following sections will review the relationships among the antecedents and the four gaps in service quality and the results of empirical tests of these relationships.

Gap 1: Marketing Information Gap.

Three factors influence the effectiveness of the marketing information system: levels of management, marketing research orientation, and upward communication. Levels of management refers to the number of layers between top management and the customer. Since each layer may inhibit communication and lead to distortion of messages, more levels should be associated with a greater marketing information gap.

Marketing research orientation refers to the utilization of market research information. This includes the degree to which marketing information is collected and used, as well as the extent to which such information focuses on service quality issues. Additionally, this variable includes the extent to which managers deal directly with customers. The size of the marketing information gap should be inversely related to the level of market research orientation.

Upward communication refers to the extent and type of communication that flows from contact personnel to top management. Both formal and informal communication are to be considered, as well as the appropriateness of communication channels utilized

to distribute information. The size of the marketing information gap should be inversely related to effective and extensive upward communication. Two studies, PBZ90 and PBZ91, found direct support for these relationships among the variables; however, the effect of the marketing research orientation was not statistically significant in these studies. Additionally, some survey items representing upward communication and levels of management did not yield significant regression coefficients, meaning they were not statistically significant either.

Gap 2: Standards Gap.

Four factors influence the degree to which management delineates service quality specifications in line with their perceptions of what customers expect:

1. goal setting,
2. management commitment to service quality,
3. perception of feasibility, and
4. task standardization.

Goal setting refers to establishing and monitoring performance and formal goals relating to service quality. Service quality goal setting should reduce the size of the standards gap.

Management commitment to service quality refers to the degree to which management emphasizes service quality as a priority in organizational goals. Clearly, firms choose among a variety of strategies, including, but not limited to, short-term profit maximization, cost reductions, or service quality. Commitment to service quality by management should also result in a smaller standards gap.

Perception of feasibility refers to the degree to which managers perceive that they have the ability and resources to meet their customers' expectations. Some services cannot be delivered at the level customers would prefer, and some levels of service delivery are not economically feasible in that the consumers are not willing to pay enough to cover the cost of desired service improvements. Like the first two factors, the perception that customers' service expectations are feasible leads to a smaller standards gap.

Finally, task standardization refers to translating service quality standards into specific tasks that

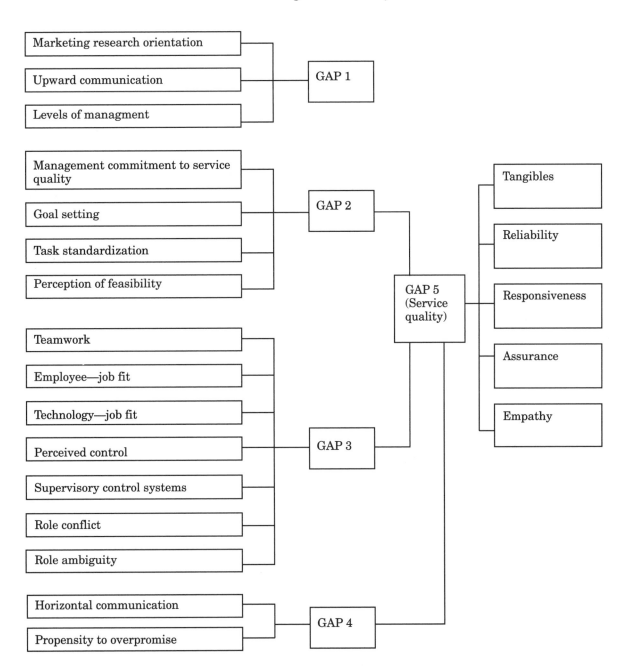

FIGURE 8-2. Extended Gap Model of Service Quality (Zeithaml, Berry, and Parasuraman, 1990)

can be standardized and bench marked. Two options are available for task standardization: substituting hard technology for humans and improving work methods. As with the other factors, task standardization (using one or both options) should lead to a smaller standards gap.

Examination of the two studies, PBZ90 and PBZ91, lends support to the contention that management commitment to service quality, goal setting, and task standardization all tend to decrease the standards gap. The perception of feasibility, however, was not significantly related to the standards gap. In PBZ90, for example, this variable was negatively related to the standards gap in three companies and positively related in two companies.

Gap 3: Service Performance Gap.

Seven factors influence the degree to which customer-contact personnel are able and willing to deliver the level of service quality desired by management:

1. employee-job fit,
2. technology fit,
3. teamwork,
4. perceived control of the employee,
5. supervisory control systems,
6. role conflict, and
7. role ambiguity.

Employee-job fit refers to whether the organization hires employees who are well-suited to their positions. The high turnover experienced in service industries may lead to haphazard hiring and training practices that fail to identify and correct skill deficiencies. Attempts to appropriately match employees to their jobs should result in a smaller service performance gap.

Technology-job fit means the appropriateness of work systems and equipment to the tasks to be performed. Equipment that fails or is too complex for employees will hinder job performance. Likewise, tasks or procedures that interfere with an employee's ability to provide service could be counterproductive. Therefore, appropriate matches between technology and jobs should result in a smaller service performance gap.

Teamwork refers to how much the delivery of service quality depends on employees and managers working together. Critical variables included in this concept are organizational commitment, supportive management style, and the fostering of a cooperative work ethic. Greater levels of teamwork should lead to a smaller service performance gap as well.

Perceived employee control is the degree to which employees feel they have control over their work situations. Employees who perceive that they have flexibility in dealing with problems have greater control and should perform better. Thus, perceived control should result in a smaller service performance gap.

Supervisory control systems can either be behavior based or outcome based. Behavior-based control systems are those where an employee's behavior is scripted, with the goal of the system being to monitor whether the employee performs the specified behavior. Outcome-based control systems monitor and reward results that are positive for the organization and ignore the employee behaviors that produced those results. Zeithaml et al. (1988) contend that the outcome-based approach may ignore critical aspects of service delivery, such as long-term activities that build customer loyalty. Therefore, behavioral control systems, and not outcome-based control systems, will generally result in a smaller service performance gap.

Role conflict refers to the amount of conflict employees experience in satisfying the interests of different constituents. Front-line employees are very susceptible to conflicting demands, as they are positioned directly between management and customers. Role conflict can lead to poor performance and widen the service performance gap.

Finally, role ambiguity measures an employee's uncertainty about management expectations and evaluation methods. Training that emphasizes an organization's expectations through appropriate communication from upper management helps reduce role ambiguity. Additionally, role ambiguity can be lessened through the proper use of a behavioral control system. A system that lessens role ambiguity will also reduce the service performance gap.

These relationships were tested in the PBZ90 and PBZ91 studies, with mixed results. The direction of the effect of behavioral control systems was unclear and weak. The effects of role conflict and role ambiguity were inconsistent across the companies studied. In contrast, teamwork, employee-job fit, technology-job fit, and perceived control were all statistically significant and negatively related to the size of the service performance gap.

Gap 4: Communication Gap.

Two factors impact the difference between the service delivered and what is communicated regarding what constitutes appropriate customer service: (1) horizontal communication and (2) propensity to overpromise.

Horizontal communication refers to the degree to which departments discuss with each other the service to be delivered. Customers will not develop unreasonable expectations of service if there is communication regarding the feasibility of providing the service. Therefore, high levels of communication between service personnel and departments responsible for designing external communications will reduce the communication gap.

Propensity to overpromise refers to the tendency to promise more than can be delivered, either implicitly or explicitly. This behavior is prevalent because many managers feel the need to overpromise in order to remain competitive, both interdepartmentally and industrywide. Overpromising will inflate customer expectations, thus increasing the size of the communication gap.

The relationship between horizontal communication and the propensity to overpromise was tested in the PBZ90 and PBZ91 studies. Horizontal communication was found to reduce the size of the communication gap; however, the propensity to overpromise did not significantly increase the size of the communication gap as theoretically proposed.

Gap 5: Service Quality Gap.

The service quality gap refers to the difference between customers' expectations and their perceptions of service, which is largely a function of the first four gaps. Tests of this gap have not resulted in statistically significant results. The R^2 value for the regression of Gap 5 on the other four Gaps, for example, was only 0.04 (Parasuraman, Berry, and Zeithaml, 1991).

Through extensive research within five consumer service categories—appliance repair and maintenance, retail banking, long-distance telephone, securities brokerage, and credit cards—Parasuraman, Zeithaml, and Berry (1988) identified the following five dimensions of service quality (see Figure 8–2):

- *Tangibles:* physical facilities, equipment, and appearance of personnel,
- *Reliability*: ability to perform the promised service dependably and accurately,
- *Responsiveness:* willingness to help customers and provide prompt service,
- *Assurance:* knowledge and courtesy of employees and their collective ability to inspire trust and confidence,
- *Empathy:* caring, individualized attention the firm provides its customers.

Although each of these dimensions has a positive impact on service quality, it should be noted that respondents rating a variety of service businesses have consistently rated reliability as the most important (Parasuraman, Berry, and Zeithaml, 1990; Zeithaml, Berry, and Parasuraman, 1991).

In order to accurately measure service quality, Parasuraman, Zeithaml, and Berry (1985) developed a 22-item instrument identified as SERVQUAL. SERVQUAL has been widely used in a number of service industries (e.g., Brown and Swartz, 1989; Webster, 1989), but the instrument has since been criticized because (1) some argue that the use of difference scores results in the measurement of satisfaction rather than performance (Bolton and Drew, 1991; Cronin and Taylor, 1992), and (2) some say the dimensionality of the construct varies depending on the service industry being studied (Carmen, 1990).

Cronin and Taylor (1992) have questioned the difference between satisfaction and service quality conceptualized as a comparison of consumers' expectations with their perceptions of an organization's performance. They argued that the literature has viewed these two concepts as being nearly identical. Parasuraman *et al.* (1988) have responded that expectations leading to levels of satisfaction consist of what a customer thinks a service organization has to offer, while expectations leading to perceptions of service quality are what a customer thinks a service firm *ought* to offer.

A study by Cronin and Taylor (1992) found that a performance measure of service quality was superior to a difference score measure. In that study, the authors provided empirical support suggesting that service quality should be measured as an attitude. Cronin and Taylor also developed a SERVPERF scale, changing the 22-item SERVQUAL scale into performance-based items. Confirmatory factor analyses supported their contention that SERVPERF resulted in a superior explanation of service quality.

Carmen (1990) studied four service settings different from those initially tested with SERVQUAL. Evidence of five to nine distinct dimensions was found to exist, depending on the type of service setting. Variances in the number of dimensions resulted partially from modifications in words and phrases to suit the settings under investigation.

Service Quality and Sport

The importance of service quality within the sport context has been recognized by both academicians and practitioners. Bill Veeck, a sports pioneer, was interested in the impact of service quality as it related to repeat attendance. Veeck, while running the St. Louis Browns, made it a practice to wander around the stadium and informally interact with all types of fans (Veeck and Linn, 1962). This "wandering" served as a primitive but effective form of assessing organizational effectiveness in providing service quality as well as assessing customer responsiveness. Veeck also made contributions to hospitality management by emphasizing comfort and cleanliness. In St. Louis, he added a nursery/day care facility, remodeled restrooms, and provided free plastic rain capes to fans (Veeck and Linn, 1962).

Shilbury (1994) noted the importance of, and the obstacles to, achieving service quality when staging professional sport contests. Specifically, the simultaneous production and consumption of the sport experience was considered to lead to tensions between operations and marketing staff. The operations staff was primarily concerned with efficiently moving people in and out of the stadiums, while the marketing staff focused on providing high-quality service during the interactions between staff and spectators (Shilbury, 1994). The convergence of these two functions—marketing and operations—ultimately determined the quality of the consumer's "service experience" (Bateson, 1989; Lovelock, 1988, 1991).

Sport managers and researchers, specifically in the health and fitness industry, have also begun to modify SERVQUAL to meet their objectives. Graff (1994), for example, augmented the original instrument with items specifically related to European sports centers. The added dimensions included, among others, consumer perceptions of the quality of training provided by fitness staff and attention paid by the center to an ill or injured member. Additionally, questions were included to ascertain if club members felt they were receiving value-added benefits by participating in the activities of the sports center and to determine the frequency of their facility/service usage.

Kim and Kim (1995) developed the QUESC (QUality Excellence of Sports Centers) instrument to identify the kinds of services customers wanted, the level of service they desired, and which specific areas required managerial attention. The QUESC instrument is in the form of an attitude model based on customer's importance-weighted evaluations of performance for specific dimensions. QUESC consists of 33 items measuring 11 dimensions of service quality in Korean sports centers. These 11 dimensions are ambiance, employee attitude, employee reliability, information available, programs offered, personal considerations, price, privilege, ease of mind, stimulation, and convenience.

Part II: Measuring Service Quality

Within sport and other industries, measuring service quality has clearly received a great deal of attention. This section of the chapter will describe the development of a scale to measure the quality of service in professional sport settings.

The data for this study were collected in the same research project detailed in Chapter 5, "Utilizing the

Customer Database." In brief, pretest and final data collection involved mail surveys distributed to season account holders of the Orlando Magic team of the National Basketball Association (NBA). The pretest phase occurred during June and July of 1994. A total of 5000 surveys were mailed to account holders and 1611 complete and valid surveys were returned, for a response rate of 32.2%. The final phase of this study took place in August and September 1995. The same number of surveys were mailed and 1380 complete and valid surveys returned, for a response rate of 27.6%. Since no items were dropped based on the analysis of the pretest instrument, this chapter will only report the results of the final phase of the research project.

The survey instrument was an adaptation of the well-established and tested SERVQUAL instrument. Based on their conceptual model, Parasuraman, Zeithaml, and Berry (1988) developed SERVQUAL, a 22-item instrument designed to measure five dimensions of service quality (see the appendix). This instrument was designed to be administered in two parts, with the first half comprising items measuring expectations of service quality and the second half containing the corresponding perceptions items. Each statement was attached to a seven-point Likert scale ranging from (1) strongly disagree to (7) strongly agree.

From a practitioner's perspective, the prime benefit of this instrument is accuracy in the measurement of consumer expectations and perceptions, which in turn helps managers pinpoint areas requiring managerial action to improve service quality. The developers of SERVQUAL envisioned its use across a wide variety of service and retailing organizations. Because this instrument was initially created to be generic and applicable across a broad spectrum of services (Parasuraman, Zeithaml, and Berry, 1988), it required modification and adaptation to make it suitable to a professional sport context.

The survey instrument (see the appendix) closely resembled the original SERVQUAL. The instrument consisted of 80 items, 40 each to measure expectations and perceptions. In addition to the original 22 SERVQUAL questions, items were added to account for the multifaceted nature of service encounters

within professional sports. Specifically, items were included to measure the quality of service provided by ticket ushers, concessionaires, merchandisers, and customer service representatives.

The analysis of the adapted SERVQUAL instrument was multifaceted. First, the factor structure of the instrument was tested. A principal factor analysis was performed, setting commonality to squared multiple correlation and using Varimax rotation. Next, scale and subscale reliabilities were tested on both the original 22 items and the additional professional sport-specific items. The reliability of the service quality dimension subscales was determined by calculating Cronbach alphas for the expectation, perception, and gap score scales.

To assess the validity of SERVQUAL, these measures were profiled to see if they were different across customer segments. Specifically, survey respondents were divided into deciles based on their lifetime values to the franchise. Once the database was segmented into deciles, these segments were compared based on their ratings of overall service quality. Next, comparisons were made based on ratings provided on the five service quality dimensions and the sport-specific service areas. Essentially, the segmented sample was compared using service quality dimension scores to see if customers with greater lifetime values to the franchise were perceiving higher levels of service.

The adequacy of the SERVQUAL scale for assessing season ticket holders' perceptions of service quality was examined in accordance with the recommendations provided in the measurement literature (Churchill, 1979). Thus, the analyses performed related to the scale's reliability and validity. Reliability assessments were based on the internal consistency of the items as measured by the coefficient alpha. Validity assessment was based on correlation and factor analyses.

Items for each subscale (e.g., empathy) were subjected to reliability assessment. Reliabilities were tested for perception scores, expectation scores, and the derived gap scores (expectation minus perception). Using criteria suggested by Peter (1981), scales with reliabilities around 0.8 were deemed acceptable. Corrected item-to-total correlations were also exam-

TABLE 8-1. Adapted SERVQUAL subscale reliability analysis

	Number of items	Coefficient alpha
SERVQUAL expectation subscales		
Tangibles	4	0.897
Reliability	5	0.897
Responsiveness	4	0.906
Assurance	4	0.910
Empathy	5	0.926
SERVQUAL perception subscales		
Tangibles	4	0.873
Reliability	5	0.935
Responsiveness	4	0.923
Assurance	4	0.927
Empathy	5	0.935
SERVQUAL gap score subscales		
Tangibles	4	0.800
Reliability	5	0.864
Responsiveness	4	0.865
Assurance	4	0.855
Empathy	5	0.900

ined; that is, the correlation between scores for an item and the summed scores of the remaining items within a subscale. A cut-off value of 0.35 was utilized for corrected item-to-total correlations, as suggested by Saxe and Weitz (1982).

Reliability for the scales corresponding to each of the service quality dimensions was calculated for expectation, perception, and gap scores. As depicted in Table 8–1, the tangibles, reliability, responsiveness, assurance, and empathy expectation scales all proved to be sufficiently reliable (e.g., alpha coefficients > 0.80). The alphas for the standardized variables, adjusted for rounding, were 0.90, 0.90, 0.91, 0.91, and 0.93, respectively. Additionally, all items had item-to-total correlations over 0.60, well above the suggested cut-off value of 0.35 suggested by Saxe and Weitz (1982).

Table 8–1 also shows perception scores for the reliability, responsiveness, assurance, and empathy scales. Alphas for the standardized variables for these scales were 0.87, 0.94, 0.92, 0.93, and 0.94, respectively. Alphas for the tangibles, reliability, responsiveness, assurance, and empathy gap score

scales were 0.80, 0.86, 0.87, 0.86, and 0.90. All subscales had alphas above 0.8, and were thus deemed acceptable.

In order to examine the dimensionality of the scale, the gap scores were analyzed using common factor analyses with Varimax rotation. The analysis was constrained *a priori* to five factors, based on conceptualization of service quality (consisting of five dimensions) (Parasuraman, Zeithaml, and Berry, 1985, 1988). Items with loadings over 0.4 were considered significant (Hair *et al.*, 1995, p. 385) and are underlined on all factor loading tables.

Factor analysis of the gap scores produced three factors with Eigenvalues greater than 1.0, accounting for 57.5% of the variation in item scores (Table 8–2). The first factor accounted for more than 43% of the variability. All five factors combined accounted for 61.6% of the variation in item scores. The Varimax rotation produced a factor-loading matrix that was relatively easy to interpret. With few exceptions, items assigned to each dimension consistently had high loadings (>0.5) on only one of the five factors. Results showed items loaded according to expec-

TABLE 8-2. Factor analysis[1] of adapted SERVQUAL gap score items

Adapted SERVQUAL gap score items	Factor loadings				
	Factor 1	Factor 2	Factor 3	Factor 4	Factor 5
Orlando Arena . . . modern-looking equipment.	0.02	0.04	−0.05	0.83	−0.10
The Orlando Arena's physical facilities are visually appealing.	0.01	0.04	0.00	0.85	−0.14
The Orlando Magic's employees are neat in appearance.	0.12	0.11	0.19	0.58	0.18
Materials . . . are visually appealing at the Orlando Magic.	0.15	0.09	0.19	0.56	0.10
. . . promise to do something by a certain time they will do it.	0.21	0.65	0.09	0.10	0.26
When you have a problem . . . sincere interest in solving it.	0.35	0.60	0.31	0.03	0.23
The Orlando Magic performs the service right the first time.	0.28	0.70	0.27	0.09	−0.03
. . . provides its services at the time it promises to do so.	0.21	0.77	0.21	0.06	0.02
The Orlando Magic insists on error free records.	0.21	0.61	0.22	0.12	−0.24
Employees . . . tell you exactly when services will be performed.	0.28	0.55	0.40	0.10	−0.14
Employees of the Orlando Magic give you prompt service.	0.33	0.50	0.47	0.08	−0.11
Employees of the Orlando Magic are always willing to help you.	0.40	0.41	0.57	0.08	0.19
Employees . . . are never too busy to respond to your requests.	0.37	0.34	0.62	0.13	0.03
The behavior or employees . . . instills confidence in customers.	0.39	0.26	0.62	0.18	0.00
You feel safe in your transactions with the Orlando Magic.	0.31	0.35	0.51	0.12	−0.08
Employees of the Orlando Magic are consistently courteous with you.	0.44	0.31	0.59	0.08	0.08
Employees . . . have the knowledge to answer your questions.	0.53	0.27	0.38	0.18	0.06
The Orlando Magic gives you individual attention.	0.75	0.25	0.29	0.09	−0.02
The Orlando Magic has operating hours convenient to all customers.	0.68	0.21	0.14	0.11	0.06
The Orlando Magic has employees who give you personal attention.	0.77	0.17	0.33	0.13	−0.11
The Orlando Magic has your best interests at heart.	0.67	0.31	0.27	−0.01	0.05
Employees of the Orlando Magic understand your specific needs.	0.73	0.33	0.22	0.04	0.03
Eigenvalue	9.54	1.97	1.12	0.55	0.34
Percent variance explained	43.4	9.0	5.1	2.5	1.6

[1]Common factor analysis with Varimax rotation: loadings of ≥0.4 are underlined.

tations on the tangibles, reliability, and empathy subscales. However, items contained on the responsiveness subscale loaded across three factors (factors 1, 2, and 3). Furthermore, no items on the scale loaded significantly on factor 5, which accounted for only 1.6% of the variance.

These results are consistent with other research (Carmen, 1990), which found that some SERVQUAL items did not load on the same component when compared across different types of services. Although the conceptualization of the SERVQUAL scale consisting of five distinct components has been

TABLE 8–3. Service quality gaps (expectations less perceptions) by LTV decile

Decile	Tangibles	Reliability	Responsiveness	Assurance	Empathy
1	0.03	0.88	1.12	0.89	1.12
2	0.10	0.60	0.79	0.62	0.95
3	−0.29	0.62	0.71	0.37	0.69
4	−0.22	0.53	0.55	0.38	0.80
5	−0.27	0.29	0.41	0.22	0.62
6	−0.12	0.55	0.64	0.30	0.66
7	−0.06	0.57	0.79	0.57	1.09
8	−0.03	0.55	0.41	0.15	0.69
9	0.09	0.53	0.55	0.34	0.78
10	−0.46	0.07	0.23	0.00	0.40
Total	−0.11	0.54	0.63	0.39	0.78
F-value	2.08	2.14	2.63	3.82	1.53
F. Prob.	0.03	0.03	0.01	0.00	0.14

questioned (Carmen, 1990), the validity of the 22 individual items comprising the scale has been well supported by the literature (cf. Carmen, 1990).

Summary statistics on all variables included in the final version of the survey instrument can be found in the appendix at the back of the book. Data included in these tables are the number of observations, means, and standard deviations by variable. Information is tabled for expectation and perception scores is also included.

Part III: Service Quality and Lifetime Value

Part II of this chapter provided insight into the reliability and validity of the adapted SERVQUAL instrument. This section will explore the relationship between service quality gap scores and customer lifetime value (see Chapter 5). For this analysis, respondents were divided into deciles based on their financial involvement with the franchise. Customers with the greatest financial value to the team were placed into decile 1. Customer lifetime value declines for each decile thereafter, with the least valuable customers (from a financial perspective) being placed in decile 10.

The relationship between lifetime value and service quality was explored by performing an analysis of variance (ANOVA) on service quality gap scores by LTV decile. Results of ANOVAs on gap scores are provided in Table 8–3. ANOVAs were statistically significant at the 0.05 level for each of the dimensions of service quality by LTV decile, with the exception of empathy ($F = 1.53$, $\rho = 0.14$). In general, mean service-quality-dimension gap scores were higher for customers with higher lifetime values and lower for customers with lower lifetime values. Thus, customers with higher financial investments in the franchise perceived that they were not receiving service commensurate with their levels of investment in the franchise. Therefore, it is likely that customers who provided more value and profitability to the firm had higher expectations than clients with less investment.

One of the objectives of this study was to adapt the SERVQUAL survey instrument for the professional sport context. To this end, SERVQUAL items were altered and new items were added to reflect the multifaceted nature of this service experience. Assessments of the reliability of this adapted instrument indicate that items on the subscales were internally consistent. The validity of the instrument was tested utilizing factor analysis with Varimax rotation. Some of the items did not load on the same component when compared with prior studies across different types of services. Additionally, this analysis questions the validity of SERVQUAL's five distinct components, which is consistent with previous research. The results of the reliability analysis in this study were consistent with previous studies. Thus, while the SERVQUAL items appear to hold together well in their pre-established subscales, the dimensionality of these five subscales continues to be suspect.

The last analysis conducted assessed the relationship between the expanded LTV model and service quality. Perceptions and expectations of service quality increased with higher levels of customer investment for both dimensions of service quality and service areas. However, the overall impact of LTV on service quality gap scores (perception minus expectation) was negligible.

Summary

The economics of professional sports in the 1990s, coupled with increased competition for the entertainment dollar, reinforce the need to constantly strive for improvements in service. Inability to control the core product in sport, a severe obstacle not faced by other industries, serves to further heighten the need to provide high-quality service within this context. Since winning in professional sports is cyclical by nature, service quality is one area under a sport marketer's control that can be utilized to gain a competitive advantage.

Quality of service is directly related to renewal— whether it be ticket plans, sponsorship, or licensing agreements. Dissatisfied consumers who feel they are not receiving service commensurate with their investments will not renew their relationships with the sport organization (McDonald, Sutton, and Milne, 1995). Enhanced service, in contrast, helps to retain current customers and encourage expansion of their relationships with the franchise. This expanded relationship can include television viewership, game attendance, participation in profitable seat licensing programs, and the purchase of licensed merchandise.

Expansion of the marketing relationship is heavily dependent on customer satisfaction with the primary contacts with the franchise (McDonald, Sutton, and Milne, 1995). Franchises must establish service quality bench marks, both qualitative and quantitative, through ongoing assessments.

Another contribution of this study is the adaptation of the SERVQUAL instrument to the professional sport context. This adaptation incorporates changes in wording for the five dimensions of service quality as well as adding subscales to measure the various service areas necessary to stage a professional sport contest (e.g., ticket ushers, concessionaires, and so forth). Analysis of the psychometric properties of this adapted instrument support the conclusion that this modified instrument is both highly reliable and valid.

By using the measures from the model to assess service quality, this study provides guidance on how to strengthen marketing relationships through improving service quality. The model stresses the importance of differentially managing the expectations and perceptions of service quality based on customers' lifetime values. Additionally, given the ability of the various subscales to discriminate among the expanded LTV deciles, this adapted instrument provides results that are both relevant and interpretable for sport marketers.

References

Bateson, J. E. G. (1989). *Managing services marketing.* Orlando, FL: Dryden Press.

Bolton, R. N., and J. H. Drew (1991). A longitudinal analysis of the impact of service changes on customer attitudes. *Journal of Marketing,* 55: 1–9.

Brown, S. C., W. A. Sutton, and G. Duff (1993). The event pyramid: An effective management strategy. *Sport Marketing Quarterly,* 2 (4): 29–35.

Brown, S. W., and T. A. Swartz (1989). A gap analysis of professional service quality. *Journal of Marketing,* 53: 92–98.

Carmen, J. M. (1990). Consumer perceptions of service quality: An assessment of the SERVQUAL dimensions. *Journal of Retailing,* 66: 33–55.

Churchill, G. A., Jr. (1979). A paradigm for developing better measures of marketing constructs. *Journal of Marketing Research,* 16: 64–73.

Cronin, J. J., and S. A. Taylor (1992). Measuring service quality: A reexamination and extension. *Journal of Marketing*, 56: 55–68.

Crosby, P. B. (1979). *Quality is free: The art of making quality certain*. New York: New American Library.

Dean, James W., Jr., and J. R. Evans (1994). *Total quality management, organization, and strategy*. Minneapolis, MN: West Publishing Company.

Garvin, D. A. (1983). Quality on the line. *Harvard Business Review*, 61 (Sept.–Oct.): 65–73.

Graff, A. J. van der (1994). Service quality and sport centers. *European Journal for Sport Management*, 1 (1): 42–57.

Greising, David (1994). Quality, how to make it pay. *Business Week*, August 8, 54–59.

Hair, Joseph F., Jr., R. E. Anderson, R. L. Tatham, and William C. Black (1995). *Multivariate data analysis*. Englewood Cliffs, NJ: Prentice-Hall.

Kasky, J. (1995). The best ticket buys for sport fans today. *Money Magazine*, October, 146–155.

Kelly, S. W., J. H. Donnelly, and S. J. Skinner (1990). Customer participation in service production and delivery. *Journal of Retailing*, 66: 315–334.

Kim, D., and S. Y. Kim (1995). QUESC: An instrument for assessing the service quality of sport centers in Korea. *Journal of Sport Management*, 9: 208–220.

Lehtinen, J. R., and U. Lehtinen (1982). Service quality: A study of quality dimensions. *Unpublished working paper*. Helsinki: Service Management Institute.

Lovelock, C. H. (1983). Classifying services to gain strategic marketing insights. *Journal of Marketing*, 47 (Summer): 9–20.

——— (1988). *Managing services marketing, operations, and human resources*. Englewood Cliffs, NJ: Prentice-Hall.

——— (1991). *Services marketing*, 2d ed. Englewood Cliffs, NJ: Prentice-Hall.

McDonald, M. A., W. A. Sutton, and G. R. Milne (1995). TEAMQUAL: Measuring service quality in professional sports. *Sport Marketing Quarterly*, 4 (2): 9–15.

Mullin, B. J., S. Hardy, and W. A. Sutton (1993). *Sport marketing*. Champaign, IL: Human Kinetics Publishers.

Parasuraman, A., V. A. Zeithaml, and L. L. Berry (1985). A conceptual model of service quality and its implications for future research. *Journal of Marketing*, 49: 41–50.

——— (1988). SERVQUAL: A multiple-item scale for measuring consumer perceptions of service quality. *Journal of Retailing*, 64 (Spring): 12–40.

Parasuraman, A., L. L. Berry, and V. A. Zeithaml (1990). An empirical examination of relationships in an extended service quality model. Cambridge, MA: *Marketing Science Institute, Report #90–122*.

——— (1991). Perceived service quality as a customer-based performance measure: An empirical examination of organizational barriers using an extended service quality model. *Human Resource Management*, 30 (Fall): 335–364.

Peter, J. P. (1981). Construct validity: A review of basic issues and marketing practices. *Journal of Marketing Research*, 18 (May): 133–145.

R. Saxe, and B. A. Weitz (1982). The SOCO scale: A measure of the customer orientation of salespeople. *Journal of Marketing*, 19 (August): 343–351.

San Jose Sharks (1996). *San Jose Sharks Web Page*.

Shilbury, D. (1994). Delivering quality service in professional sport. *Sport Marketing Quarterly*, 3 (1): 29–35.

Veeck, B., and E. Linn (1962). *Veeck—As in wreck*. New York: Putnam.

Webster, C. (1989). Can consumers be segmented on the basis of their service quality expectations? *Journal of Services Marketing*, 3: 35–53.

Zeithaml, Valarie A., L. L. Berry, and A. Parasuraman (1988). Communication and control processes in the delivery of service quality. *Journal of Marketing*, 52 (April): 35–48.

Sport Sponsorship Personality Matching[1]

In the U.S., mass-media advertising has long been the cornerstone of most brand-building efforts. But that norm is threatening to become obsolete. Fragmentation and rising costs are already inhibiting marketing through traditional mass media like television. To build strong brands in this uncertain environment, U.S.-based companies would do well to study their counterparts in Europe . . . who have long relied on alternative communication channels to create public awareness, convey brand associations and develop loyal customer bases.

From Joachimstaler, Erick,
and David A. Aaker (1997). Building brands
without mass media, *Harvard Business
Review,* January–February: 39.

Introduction

Proper brand positioning and adequate product exposure to the target market are both vital considerations when developing a marketing plan. However, as markets have become saturated, communicating the features, strengths, and identity of a brand/firm has become increasingly challenging. Amid the growing clutter of traditional media outlets, brand-building pursuits have become more expensive and less efficient. A need exists to supplement traditional communication strategies with more effective, cost-efficient alternatives. In order to convey brand-related information in such a dense competitive marketplace, an organization must be prepared to adopt new strategies. One such alternative is the use of strategic partnering to serve the dual goals of increased product exposure and brand-image enhancement.

The benefits of marketing alliances have been widely documented in marketing literature. Numerous studies have highlighted the efficiencies that arise when firms engage in symbiotic marketing. Just as

[1]This chapter was adapted from a working research paper titled *Evaluating Sponsorship and Co-branding Matches Using Brand Personality Measures* written by Michael Musante, George Milne, and Mark McDonald.

alliances have yielded synergistic, cost-efficient, and effective results in achieving various goals, these formal relationships may also have a place in the pursuit of stronger brand positioning. Organizations can aid positioning efforts by effectively articulating the brand's identity through strategic partnering with entities outside their product categories.

In the sport industry, strategic partnering with outside entities is often in the form of sponsorship. Sponsorship has been defined as a business relationship between a provider of funds, resources, or services and a sports event or organization that offers the sponsor some rights and an association that may be used for commercial advantage (Sleight, 1989). More broadly, sponsorship is defined as investing in causes or events to support overall corporate objectives and/or marketing objectives (Cornwell, 1995). When one considers that corporate sponsorship has grown from $2.3 billion in 1989 to $9.6 billion in 1993 (Cornwell, 1995), it becomes evident that sponsorship is now a legitimate marketing vehicle. The dramatic rise of sponsorship has resulted in part as firms are exploring new, more efficient opportunities to communicate with consumers. Organizations in nearly every product category are now recognizing sponsorship as a viable marketing tool and an effective complement to existing promotional efforts.

Corporate sponsorship of sporting events has fueled much of the growth in total sponsorship expenditures. It is estimated that sport sponsorship accounts for two-thirds of all event sponsorship spending, with corporate sponsorship of sport in the United States expected to exceed $3 billion in 1995 (*IEG Sponsorship Report*, 1994). Even though the number of sport sponsorship opportunities has increased, the demand for marquee sponsorships continues to outstrip supply. The allure of sponsoring a big-time event also contributes to escalating sponsorship fees. For example, the price tag to become a Centennial Olympic Partner for the 1996 games was $40 million. To be affiliated with the 1994 World Cup, individual companies such as MasterCard spent about $30 million in advertising and promotional dollars. In total, the renowned soccer event generated an estimated $300 million in sponsorship fees (Carter, 1996).

Given the expense of sponsorship, a logical question is just what is driving firms to become event

TABLE 9–1. Sponsorship objectives ranked in order of importance (Fortune 1000 firms)

1. Increase company awareness
2. Improve company image
3. Demonstrate community responsibility
4. Increase awareness of specific products
5. Provide a forum for corporate hospitality
6. Improve product image
7. Increase short-term sales revenue
8. Increase long-term sales revenue
9. Foster employee pride and motivation

(Kuzma, Shanklin, and McCally, 1993)

sponsors? Firms cite a number of corporate and product-related objectives for investing in a sport sponsorship (see Table 9–1). While utilizing sponsorship as a vehicle for name exposure is most often acknowledged as the primary goal, image-enhancement is also commonly noted as a sponsorship objective (Gardner and Shuman, 1988; Marshall and Cook, 1992; Irwin and Sutton, 1994; Thwaites, 1995; Copeland, Frisby, and McCarville, 1997; Cornwell, 1995; Lough, 1996). Many firms view sponsorships as an opportunity to foster a favorable image for their brand or firm (Gardner and Shuman, 1987; Meenaghan, 1991; Irwin and Assimakopoulas, 1992; Kuzma, Shanklin, and McCally, 1993; Javalgi *et al.*, 1994; Cornwell, 1995).

The growing popularity of sponsorships, and the corresponding rise in sponsorship fees, increases the pressure on marketing researchers to more closely examine this communication vehicle. To date, a majority of the research in this area has addressed sponsorship's effectiveness in meeting awareness objectives. Although acknowledged as one of the primary reasons for engaging in a sponsorship, considerably less research attention has been paid to the objective of enhancing an image through sponsorships. Although research exploring brand-image enhancement via sponsorship is slowly surfacing, further research in this area is clearly warranted as many questions remain unanswered.

In this chapter, we will review work completed on this topic, utilizing brand equity principles as a foundation, and build upon prior findings. The focus of our analysis will be selecting the proper sponsorship opportunity, which is the key to achieving brand-image goals through such an affiliation. Specifically, we will present a new methodology for linking brands and sponsorship opportunities. Through a series of studies, we will document the development of a personality scale and demonstrate its usefulness in assessing the match between sporting events and sponsors.

The balance of the chapter is organized into five sections. In the first section, we will discuss the role that sponsorship can play in brand management. In particular, we will highlight sponsorship selection and the importance of brand and event/sport perceptual fit. In the second section, we will discuss our objectives and present hypotheses to help us validate the proposed methodology. In the third section, we will test our personality matching methodology and review the context, procedures, and measures used to evaluate sponsorship fit. The results of our analysis will be presented in the fourth section. In the fifth, and last, section, we will discuss implications of the findings and research methodology, outline strengths and weaknesses of the approach, and offer suggestions for future research.

Brand Management and Sponsorship

Managing brands, and in particular brand equity, is an area of growing concern in marketing. At the same time, the importance of brand equity is also beginning to be acknowledged in other areas, such as sport (Gladden, Milne, and Sutton, 1998). Some argue that consumer-based brand equity is the outcome of brand knowledge, which is largely a function of brand awareness and image (Keller, 1993). If this is true, brand-building efforts must begin by creating brand awareness and establishing brand image. Of the two components, brand awareness would appear to be more easily managed, as it can be directly controlled through efforts to increase exposure to the brand name. Managing brand image, on the other hand, appears to be the more challenging and critical task.

Prior research has stressed the importance of a firm taking steps to elaborate and fortify the images of its brands (Park, Jaworski, and MacInnis, 1986).

In creating a clear, rich brand image, firms should seek to build brand associations that share meaning or are congruent (Keller, 1993; Aaker, 1996). Brand associations are the perceived characteristics of the brand or the images with which it is associated. Presenting consistent associations is believed to help define the "personality" of the brand (Aaker 1996). Since the concept of brand personality is one gaining acceptance as a viable measure of image, it will be highlighted in our analysis.

A brand personality is the set of human characteristics associated with given brand (Aaker, 1996). Like a person, a brand can be perceived as being upscale, fun, active, formal, and so forth. Aaker notes that just as one's perceptions of a person are affected by nearly everything associated with that individual—friends, activities, and so forth—so too is a brand's personality. While the drivers of brand personality may be product related (such as its attributes), nonproduct-related characteristics also play a contributing role. Ad style, age, user image, country of origin, company image, symbols, and celebrity endorsers all help to define the personality. In addition, another nonproduct-related association thought to influence brand personality is sponsorships (Aaker, 1996; Brooks, 1994).

Previous research has offered support for the theory that sponsorship can enhance a corporate image and, in particular, impact specific dimensions of the image (Javalgi *et al.*, 1994; Stipp and Schiavone, 1996; Turco, 1994). A sponsorship helps define a brand personality through its inferred association with the sport property. In an unobtrusive fashion, the salient public affiliation between the brand and the sport is thought to alter image perceptions of the brand (Brooks, 1994). Meenaghan (1991) has noted that this "image by association" effect is the result of an image "rub-off." For example, take a case where a firm enters into public affiliation with a sport perceived to be sophisticated or upscale, like golf or tennis. The firm's new association will act as new input to be processed by consumers, a cue that may influence perceptions of the firm. Thus, the result of the affiliation will be that the firm will be more likely to be perceptually positioned closer to the upscale sport. Employing such a strategy, a firm seeking a certain identity would pursue an affiliation with an entity that represents the desired image or personality traits.

Sponsorship Selection

As was noted earlier, many firms utilize sponsorships as a vehicle to increase awareness in a target market. Thus, not unlike other media selection efforts, a common practice for a firm selecting a sponsorship has been to seek opportunities where demographic profiles of the event audience match the demographic profiles of the firm's target audience (Meenaghan, 1983, 1991; Carter, 1996). A better approach is to evaluate a sponsorship opportunity on its ability to achieve several specific objectives (Meenaghan, 1983, 1991; Irwin and Assimakopoulas, 1992; Cornwell, 1995). Thus, while matching demographics may be useful to meet the "awareness" objective, other criteria are necessary for image-enhancing objectives. Unfortunately, it appears that many firms continue to rely on identification of a demographic match even while pursuing image-enhancement or positioning as an objective (Javalgi *et al.*, 1994). We will attempt to show that a good demographic fit between a brand's target market and a sport audience, however, does not always correspond to an appropriate "image" match.

In order to achieve image-enhancement goals via sponsorship, a firm's primary selection criteria when evaluating a potential affiliation should be the image of the event (Meenaghan, 1983, 1991; Irwin and Asimakopoulas, 1992). Meenaghan (1983) notes, "The very fact that a particular sponsorship has its own personality and perception in the public's mind is a key criterion in sponsorship choice. The ability of a particular sponsorship proposal to deliver a required message by association becomes a critically important criterion in the sponsorship selection process" (p. 29). Practitioners appear to agree. Research suggests that firms are concerned with finding the appropriate image match for their firm/brand in order to attain image association benefits (Irwin, Assimakopoulas, and Sutton, 1994; Marshall and Cook, 1992; Copeland, Frisby, and McCarville, 1994).

As noted, there appears to be a consensus among researchers and practitioners that given image-

enhancement goals, finding the right match or image fit is vital to effective sponsorship selection. This relationship only highlights the need to understand more clearly how, and indeed if, the public perceives natural image fits between brands and sports. Thus, we will now turn our attention to determinants of perceived sponsorship fit.

Sponsorship Fit

The concept of perceptual fit is commonly used in marketing. Because we view perceptual fit as the heart of personality matching in sponsorship, we utilize the term *sponsorship fit* to represent an individual's perception of the compatibility between brand and sport. We believe sponsorship fit is grounded in the perceived image congruency between each entity.

Schema congruity theory (Fiske, 1982; Fiske and Taylor, 1991) appears to be a useful lens from which to gauge an individual's assessment of sponsorship fit. A schema is a "cognitive structure that represents knowledge about a concept or type of stimulus, including its attributes and the relations among those attributes" (Fiske and Taylor, 1991, p. 98). In essence, a schema is a preconception that has been developed through experience.

Previous brand research has noted that consumers maintain schemas for individual brand names (Sujan and Bettman, 1989), and the same is thought to hold true for individual sports. Applying congruity theory to sponsorship, we believe when the brand and the sport's association becomes salient, the perceiver will assess the congruency of the schemas between the two. Theory suggests that the perceived congruity between the brand's image and the sport's image largely determines perceived sponsorship fit. Those brands that maintain shared perceptual characteristics are likely to have more congruent schemas and in turn be viewed as better affiliates or partners. This logic implies that assessments of perceived sponsorship fit between a given sport and sponsor would increase as the personalities become more aligned or congruent.

Evaluating the proper fit between a brand and sport based on image congruency is supported by work in the area of matching. In marketing, matching theory has been used extensively in the area of media selection. The process of selecting the most appropriate "match" has been examined by numerous marketing researchers (Sissors, 1971; Winter, 1980; Cannon, 1985). Often, a generalized distance measure is used to evaluate the closeness of fit.

Image-based matching is not a new concept in brand management. Perhaps the most well-known use of image-based matching in brand research has occurred in the area of celebrity endorsers. Here too, findings show that congruency between the celebrity image and the brand image is key to achieving brand image enhancement (McCracken, 1989; Kamins, 1990). It has also been noted that when the celebrity endorser is from the sports world, the image of the sport plays a role in the evaluation. Martin (1996) found the greater the dissimilarity between the product and sport images, the lower the endorsement evaluation.

Given the importance of selecting a sponsorship with a good perceptual fit, researchers have now begun to explore "image-based" matching in sponsorships. In one study, a perceptual map was used to examine how sports are viewed differently by consumers (Martin, 1994). Although useful in capturing the dimensionality of 10 sports, this analysis stopped short of proposing a method to match brands and sports. Ferrand and Paages (1996) proposed a model of image sponsoring based on the concept of social representation. In their study, each event and sponsor pair was analyzed for common characteristics. Their methodology proposes the use of adjective matching and analyzing the data through a factor analysis. While the Ferrand and Paages method is thorough, assessing entities on 300 adjectives, it may be cumbersome and difficult to implement for practitioners. Both studies make some contribution, and we will add to these efforts by presenting an approach that is simultaneously comprehensive and parsimonious. The strength of our method is that it employs an established brand-based scale that adequately captures the identity of both sports and brands. We believe our method offers the potential for universal application across a wide range of product categories and sports. In sum, our matching technique offers firms insight when considering which

sport is most appropriate for their brands, as well as aiding sport properties in the selection of image-enhancing brands.

Hypotheses

The literature reviewed indicates that it is crucial to match a sport's personality with a brand's to achieve image enhancement via sponsorship. Brands having shared perceptual characteristics with a sport are likely to be viewed as a good match for that sport. This would imply that assessments of perceived sponsorship fit between a given sport and sponsor would increase as the personalities became more aligned or congruent.

Based on these implied linkages, a primary objective of our research was to test the concept that individuals perceive natural matches between brands and sports and that perceptions of a good sponsorship fit are based on the congruency of the brand/sport images. Confirmation of these relationships will provide support for personality congruency as a foundation for image enhancement via sponsorship. We also seek to establish that given a sponsorship objective of brand-image enhancement, personality, not demographics, is a superior matching criterion. In the studies that follow, we will test the following two hypotheses.

> **H₁:** Perceived sponsorship fit increases with the personality match between the sport and the brand.

> **H₂:** Perceived sponsorship fit has a stronger positive relationship with brand/sport personality match than with brand/sport demographic match.

Methodology

In our effort to develop and validate the use of our personality-matching methodology, we conducted two independent empirical studies. The first was a student-based study that focused on examining the measurement properties and internal validity of the approach. In the second, we used the personality-matching technique to assess perceptions of sponsorship fit between actual sponsors and a sport at a popular national sporting event.

Study 1

Study 1 employed two subject groups. The first group consisted of 28 graduate students (18 male and 10 female) majoring in sport management at a major northeastern university. The subjects completed a questionnaire for course credit. These subjects were considered appropriate for this study because they were knowledgeable about sport and each possessed some form of playing, coaching, or sport administrative experience. The average age of the group was 24, with an average of six years of work experience in sport. The second group consisted of 45 undergraduate business majors from the same university. The average age of this group was 21. In the following empirical work, data from both groups were combined after it was determined that there were no differences in the pattern of responses.

Each subject completed a questionnaire in which he/she evaluated the personality of five brands and five sports on an identical scale. The sports in the study (tennis, auto racing, baseball, golf, and beach volleyball) were chosen based on their diversity and their documented associations with corporate sponsorship. The brands utilized in the study (Marlboro, Cadillac, Mountain Dew, Jack Daniels, and Bud Light) represented various product categories and were selected based on their perceived unique personalities. In the last section of the questionnaire, each respondent rated the level of fit for the 25 brand/sport combinations in a sponsorship setting.

Questionnaire Format.

The questionnaire consisted of the following format. Subjects rated their overall favorability of five sports on a nine-point scale (anchors: 9 = favorable/1 = not favorable*)*. Subjects rated their likability of five brands on a nine-point scale (anchors: 9 = very likable/1 = not likable). Subjects then evaluated five brands and five sports on the Brand Personality Scale (anchors for BPS: 1 = least represents how I view the sport/brand, and 5 = best represents how

I view the sport/brand). Finally, subjects rated sponsorship fit on a nine-point scale when brands and sports were matched (anchors: 9 = good fit/1 = poor fit).

Development of the Brand–Sport Personality Scale.

To measure brand and sport personality traits, we adopted and modified the Brand Personality Scale (BPS) developed by Aaker (1995). Aaker's original BPS is a compact set of traits designed to both measure and structure brand personality. In her empirical study, Aaker was able to identify five personality factors that explained 93% of the observed differences between brands. These factors were Exciting, Sincere, Rugged, Sophisticated, and Competent. Each of the five factors was comprised of a number of traits or facets that represented a common theme for each factor. We assumed that the personality scales would also maintain meaning for sports even though they were derived as a personality measure for brands. The robustness of using personality scales in new contexts is supported by other research that has found personality measures to be interpretable and consistent across people (Aaker, 1996).

The original number of scale items for each factor varied, ranging from 5 to 20 traits. While maintaining the essential structure and integrity of the Aaker scale, we modified and condensed the scale to make it appropriate for the sports setting. After reviewing the relevant sport literature, and seeking expert advice from other sport researchers, we eliminated the Competent factor, and renamed the Sincerity factor as Wholesome (a major facet of Sincerity in the scale). We selected 5 scale items to represent each of the four factors, bringing our modified BPS to 20 scale items. We were comfortable that the modified BPS employed in the study was an instrument that was applicable to both brands and sports.

A common factor analysis was conducted in order to assess the data structure of the 20 personality items as well as the reliability of the resulting four subscales (see Table 9.1). An examination of the factor loadings yielded anticipated findings, as four distinct factors emerged that explained 68% of the variance. Only one item (blue collar) loaded in an unexpected manner (Rugged instead of Wholesome).

TABLE 9–2. Study 1: Factor analysis results

	Factor 1 Sophisticated	Factor 2 Rugged	Factor 3 Exciting	Factor 4 Wholesome
Upper class	**.91**	−.18	−.09	.17
Sophisticated	**.86**	−.11	−.08	.25
Pretentious	**.77**	−.16	−.06	.12
Refined	**.74**	.03	−.08	.34
Mature	**.69**	.22	−.18	.38
Rugged	−.17	**.88**	.01	−.04
Tough	−.08	**.86**	.17	.04
Strong	.08	**.81**	.08	.23
Masculine	−.08	**.80**	−.06	.14
Bold	.04	**.73**	.22	.07
Lively	−.18	.08	**.90**	−.11
Exciting	−.08	.15	**.88**	.01
Fun	−.04	.01	**.84**	.14
Young	−.24	−.01	**.76**	−.07
Flashy	.12	.15	**.58**	−.11
Classic	.37	.19	−.16	**.72**
Genuine	.16	.26	.02	**.69**
Old-fashioned	.38	.16	−.33	**.60**
Wholesome	.38	−.09	.24	**.55**
Blue collar	−.41	**.45**	.00	.18
Alphas	**.92**	**.91**	**.89**	**.70**
% of variance explained	20%	19%	18%	11%

Factor loading >.45 are indicated in bold type.

The coefficient alphas for each of the four constructs were strong (Exciting, $\alpha = 0.89$; Wholesome, $\alpha = 0.70$; Rugged, $\alpha = 0.91$; Sophisticated, $\alpha = 0.92$). The high level of reliability not only helps provide confidence in the validity of the BPS as a brand measure but also indicates the usefulness of the scale in assessing the personalities of various sports. The alphas were very consistent across both brands and sports (sports: Exciting, $\alpha = 0.88$; Wholesome, $\alpha = 0.80$; Rugged, $\alpha = 0.90$; Sophisticated, $\alpha = 0.92$; brands: Exciting, $\alpha = 0.91$; Wholesome, $\alpha = 0.64$; Rugged, $\alpha = 0.90$; Sophisticated, $\alpha = 0.92$).

Calculating Brand–Sport Personality Fit Indices.

Personality fit indices were calculated for all 25 combinations of brands and sports. These calculations were made at the individual level; thus, for each subject, 25 fit indices were created. The fit indices are the Euclidean distance between the personality measures of a sponsor and that of a particular sport. The Euclidean distance was based on the factor scores of 20 personality measures. The factor scores were formed by averaging the individual items with significant loadings. This method of forming factor scores is often done in applied market research (Hair *et al.*, 1995). Formally,

Brand − Sport personality fit

$$= \sqrt{\sum_{i=1}^{4} (bpf_i - spf_i)^2}$$

where bpf_i is the ith brand personality factor score and spf is the ith sport personality factor score. The indices representing the 25 brand–sport combinations used in subsequent analysis were found by averaging individual level scores.

Calculating Brand–Sport Demographic Fit Indices.

Demographic fit indices were based on aggregate level data for each sport and brand. Specifically, we formed a matching index based on five demographic

TABLE 9–3.   Matching coefficients

	Fit coefficient	Bud Light	Marlboro	Cadillac	Mountain Dew	Jack Daniels
Tennis	Personality[a]	0.51	0.24	0.70	0.38	0.40
	Demographic[b]	0.60	0.37	0.21	0.22	0.58
	Sponsorship[c]	0.13	0.00	0.73	0.68	0.19
Baseball	Personality	0.61	0.57	0.41	0.42	0.60
	Demographic	0.69	0.44	0.27	0.37	0.77
	Sponsorship	0.86	0.47	0.31	0.65	0.45
Golf	Personality	0.22	0.10	0.87	0.00	0.31
	Demographic	0.34	0.16	0.37	0.13	0.51
	Sponsorship	0.31	0.18	1.00	0.35	0.46
Racing	Personality	0.54	0.74	0.23	0.52	0.64
	Demographic	0.79	0.53	0.05	0.61	0.83
	Sponsorship	0.93	0.92	0.24	0.58	0.68
Volleyball	Personality	0.76	0.32	0.09	1.00	0.28
	Demographic	1.00	0.60	0.00	0.58	0.87
	Sponsorship	0.80	0.17	0.18	0.95	0.31

[a]Personality matching coefficient for Study 1 was based on Euclidean distance, where low disance was good fit and high distance was bad fit. For the purposes of this table, the coefficient was transformed to be bounded between 0 and 1, where 0 was worst fit and 1 was best fit.

[b]Demographic fit was originally bounded between 0–1.

[c]Personality fit was measured on a 9-point scale, with 0 a worst fit and 9 a best fit. For purposes of this table, the coefficient was transformed to be bounded between 0 and 1, where 0 was worst fit and 1 was best fit.

variables reported in *Simmons Media and Markets*. Variables utilized in this assessment included average age, average income, race, gender, and region of the country. Brand users were those who had bought the brand in the last 12 months. The sport demographic data was for those who reported watching the sport on television. The matching procedure utilized to derive this brand–sport demographic fit coefficient was identical to the one proposed by Milne (1994). This niche overlap technique highlights the degree of congruency between two variables in the form of a metric coefficient. The higher the coefficient, the greater the demographic profile overlap between the brand and sport.

Perceived Sponsorship Fit (Dependent Variable).

In order to derive a measure for sponsorship fit, subjects were presented with sponsorship scenarios displaying each of the 25 potential brand–sport sponsorship combinations. The respondents were asked to rate the level of perceived sponsorship fit they felt existed for each scenario on a nine-point scale.

Brand and Sport Favorability (Covariates).

Finally, as individuals' perceived functional congruity assessments have been shown to be biased by individuals' preferences or self-congruity (Sirgy *et al.*, 1991), each respondent was also asked to rate his or her overall feeling for each brand and sport. These variables were used as covariates in the study.

Results.

Table 9–3 reports three matching coefficients for each combination among the five sports and the five brands. For each of the 25 cells, the table reports coefficients for personality fit matching, demographic fit, and perceived sponsorship–brand fit. The fit coefficients, for comparison purposes in this table, were transformed so that all were bounded between 0 and 1, where 1 = best fit and 0 = worst fit.

The table shows that the appropriateness of fit depends on whether one looks at personality or demographics. Although the personality fit between Cadillac and golf is quite high, the demographic match is not high. This pattern also is true for Cadillac and

TABLE 9–4. Regression results (DV = sponsorship fit)

	Full model		Personality model		Demographics model	
	Std. beta.	T-value	Std. beta	T-value	Std. beta	T-value
Intercept						
Personality	−0.81	−5.61[a]	−0.76	−6.23[a]		
Demographics	−0.09	−0.66			0.32	1.66
Sport favorability	0.20	1.59	0.20	1.62	0.29	1.50
Brand favorability	−0.22	−1.75	−0.21	−1.75	−0.17	−0.89
Adj. R^2	0.64		0.65		0.12	
F-value	11.67[a]		15.84[a]		2.07	

[a]Significant at the 0.05 level.

tennis. The perceived sponsorship fit for both of these pairs is quite high, suggesting that personality is a driving factor of this perception. The match between Bud Light and racing has a strong perceived sponsorship and demographic fit, yet a moderate personality fit. If Bud Light were attempting to align its personality more closely with another sport, it might consider beach volleyball. Not having the right personality fit could also hurt a sponsor. For example, although the demographic fit between beach volleyball and Jack Daniels is quite high, beach volleyball might not want this sponsorship because the personality fit is so low. Clearly, the data show that demographic fit explains only part of the picture.

In order to further examine the research questions, we conducted regression analysis. The dependent variable (sponsorship fit) was regressed upon the two independent variables (personality fit and demographic fit). The two covariates (brand favorability and sport favorability) were also included in the analysis. Three models were estimated. The first was a full model, but because of the multicollinearity between personality fit and demographic fit (correlation of 0.51), two other models were run that included just one of these variables. The results of this analysis are shown in Table 9–4.

The regression results show that personality match has a statistically significant relationship with perceived sponsorship fit. In the models that contain personality fit, the overall model is statistically significant [full model: adj. $R^2 = 0.64$ ($p < 0.01$); personality only model: $R^2 = 0.65$ ($p < 0.01$)]. In these models, the personality fit parameter is significant at the 0.05 level. In contrast, demographic fit is not statistically significant in either the full model (with personality fit) or in the reduced model. This implies that in terms of an individual's perceptions of sponsorship fit, personality congruency is a better gauge than demographic congruency. This result suggests that for those firms who seek image-enhancement benefits from sponsorship, the sport's image and not demographic fit should be the main sponsorship selection criteria.

In order to assess which of the four personality constructs offered the greatest contribution to overall sponsorship fit, that variable was independently regressed upon each of the constructs. It was found that three of the four factors were independently significant in their contribution to personality fit. While all factors except Wholesome were significant at the 0.05 level, the constructs Sophisticated and Exciting accounted for much of the variance. In total, the four factors accounted for 72% of the variance of sponsorship fit. It is important to note that the results of this particular analysis may be influenced by the particular brands and sports used in the sample. Wholesome may well have been significant had other brands and sports been utilized.

Study 2

To assess further the potential of personality matching between sports and brands, a second study was conducted. Study 1 supported our personality-

TABLE 9–5. Brand personality for NBA sample*

	Sophisticated		Rugged		Exciting		Wholesome	
	Mean	**s.d.**	**Mean**	**s.d.**	**Mean**	**s.d.**	**Mean**	**s.d.**
NBA	3.58	1.17	3.19	1.39	3.97	1.30	3.43	1.37
Amex	3.54	1.20	2.60	1.31	2.64	1.32	3.27	1.20
McDonald's	3.33	1.35	2.59	1.37	3.14	1.35	3.51	1.25
Gatorade	3.35	1.16	2.94	1.37	3.31	1.33	3.44	1.24
Sprint	3.10	1.19	2.54	1.31	2.71	1.34	3.08	1.29
Nike	3.63	1.31	3.23	1.39	3.81	1.24	3.47	1.29
Wendy's	2.85	1.25	2.59	1.34	2.75	1.31	3.27	1.34
Visa	3.49	1.23	2.58	1.36	3.01	1.38	3.21	1.29
All Sport	3.14	1.26	3.02	1.36	3.25	1.30	3.31	1.28
AT&T	3.54	1.23	2.59	1.36	2.85	1.40	3.20	1.31
Reebok	3.47	1.25	3.19	1.33	3.56	1.30	3.38	1.29

*5-point scale where 1 = strongly disagree and 5 = strongly agree.

matching methodology; the purpose of Study 2 was to further validate personality matching with a larger, more diverse sample.

Methodology.

As part of the 1997 National Basketball Association (NBA) All-Star Weekend, the city of Cleveland hosted a fan festival called Jam Session. During the weekend event, 153 individuals completed a survey similar to the one we employed in Study 1. The 153 respondents were demographically diverse: of the survey respondents, 72% were male, 46% had completed a college education, 44% had household incomes of $30,000 to $75,000, and one-third (34%) were African-American.

The questionnaire we utilized in Study 1 asked respondents to evaluate five brands and five sports on personality traits. The instrument used in Study 2 differed slightly, in that subjects were asked to assess one sport (pro basketball) and ten brands on the four personality factors. The brands represented various product categories and included American Express, Visa, McDonald's, Wendy's, Gatorade, All Sport, Nike, Reebok, Sprint, and AT&T. Five of these companies were official sponsors of the 1997 NBA Jam Session (American Express, McDonald's, Gatorade, Reebok, and AT&T). Unlike Study 1, where a complete 20 item BPS was used, in Study 2 the NBA and each brand was directly evaluated on the

four personality factors. This consolidation was done to reduce respondent fatigue. In a pilot test conducted at the 1997 National Hockey League (NHL) All-Star Weekend, we found that respondents did not have the patience to answer all 20 BPS scale questions for each stimuli. Survey length resulted in straight lining and partial completion of survey instruments. We were comfortable with the consolidation given the high degree of internal scale validity demonstrated in the first study. Thus, each respondent was asked to what extent they considered the NBA and each brand to be Wholesome, Rugged, Exciting, and Sophisticated on a five-point scale.

Results.

Just as in Study 1, personality congruency between each brand and the NBA was derived via the personality-fit index formula. Mean scores for the NBA and the ten brands on each of the four factors are highlighted in Table 9–5. Results of this analysis reflect the diversity of personalities among brands. Ratings of sophistication, for example, range from Wendy's ($\mu = 2.85$) to Nike ($\mu = 3.63$). Likewise, mean scores on Exciting range from 2.71 (Sprint) to 3.81 (Nike). Interestingly, the NBA was rated more exciting ($\mu = 3.97$) than all of the brands listed. The only brands approaching the NBA in terms of excitement were in the athletic footwear category (Nike and Reebok). Brands in other product catego-

TABLE 9–6. Sponsorship fit with NBA (1 = best fit, 0 = worst fit)

Sponsor	Personality match
Nike	1.00
Reebok	0.83
Gatorade	0.74
McDonald's	0.64
All Sport	0.57
Amex	0.39
Visa	0.35
AT&T	0.30
Sprint	0.19
Wendy's	0.00

ries such as telecommunications (Sprint, AT&T) could be perceived as more exciting by associating with the NBA. The personality factor displaying the least variance was Wholesome, going from 3.08 (Sprint) to 3.51 (McDonald's).

NBA and sponsor personality congruency (Euclidean distance) results are presented in Table 9–6. Sponsorship fit scores range from 0 (worst fit) to 1 (best fit). The brands displaying the highest personality fit with the NBA, athletic footwear and isotonic beverage, are functionally related to the sport of basketball. For the athletic footwear category, Nike (1.00) and Reebok (0.83) both had extremely high personality fits. Gatorade (0.74), an isotonic beverage, had the third-highest personality fit with the NBA of the brands analyzed. All three of these brands, it should be noted, have had long associations with sports in general and with basketball in particular. The brand with the poorest fit is Wendy's (0.00). The results once again demonstrate that consumers clearly perceive natural image links between certain brands and sport.

In order to test for the presence of differences within the sample in terms of personality ratings of the NBA, the sample was divided into subgroups based on gender, NBA interest, NBA attendance, NBA viewership, and income. For the latter four categories, the sample was split based on the median response. Overall, the results indicated little difference among the subgroups. The only significant difference worth noting was for the NBA interest

category. The results shown in Table 9–7 indicate that those with high NBA interest evaluated the NBA significantly higher on three factors, Sophisticated, Exciting, and Wholesome. In contrast, behaviors directly related to NBA interest (attendance and viewership) had no significant differences between high and low groupings of respondents.

Discussion

The regression analysis findings from Study 1 indicate that the perceptual sponsorship fit between a sport and a brand increases as their personalities become more congruent. This would suggest that in a salient sponsorship setting people consider the images held by the sport and the sponsor to assess the brand–sport affiliation. This conclusion was also reached in Study 2. These results support the first hypothesis (H_1), that perceived sponsorship fit increases with the personality match between the sport and the brand. The Study 1 regression analysis also revealed that while personality fit was found to be a significant predictor of perceived sponsorship fit, demographic fit was not. This result clearly lends support to the second hypothesis (H_2) that perceived sponsorship fit has a stronger positive relationship with brand–sport personality match than with brand–sport demographic match.

The results of these studies are important for firms seeking to use sponsorship for image-enhancing purposes, as they establish that individuals perceive image links between a brand and a sport. This finding supports the contention that sponsorship holds the potential to be an effective image-enhancing promotional vehicle. Our results highlight the impact of personality links, which establishes a basis for (and suggests the plausibility of) an image transfer from sport to brand in a sponsorship relationship.

The ability to help define a brand's image via affiliation with a sport appears to be a strategy that is gaining momentum. Thus, research into the selection of an appropriate sponsorship opportunity to achieve such goals is clearly warranted. At this stage it is important for researchers to explore methods that will assist firms in finding the best match for the desired image they wish to project. We feel our

TABLE 9-7. Personality scale ratings of the NBA by selected subgroups*

Subgroup	N	Sophisticated Mean	s.d.	Rugged Mean	s.d.	Exciting Mean	s.d.	Wholesome Mean	s.d.
Gender									
Males	110	3.50	1.21	3.22	1.34	4.05	1.20	3.41	1.28
Females	43	3.76	1.15	3.17	1.52	3.77	1.54	3.49	1.58
*Interest**									
High	71	**3.79**	1.13	3.28	1.45	**4.33**	1.05	**3.92**	1.12
Low	82	**3.39**	1.18	3.10	1.33	**3.66**	1.41	**3.00**	1.42
*Attendance***									
High	71	3.77	1.07	3.35	1.32	4.07	1.23	3.46	1.28
Low	82	3.40	1.23	3.05	1.43	3.89	1.36	3.40	1.44
*Viewership***									
High	75	3.64	1.11	3.36	1.39	4.17	1.19	3.57	1.35
Low	68	3.53	1.21	2.98	1.36	3.83	1.32	3.26	1.44
*Income***									
High	70	3.38	1.22	3.22	1.42	3.94	1.31	**3.16**	1.39
Low	83	3.73	1.11	3.15	1.36	4.00	1.29	**3.66**	1.32
Race									
Black	34	3.70	1.16	3.35	1.51	4.18	1.31	**3.82**	1.26
White	79	3.43	1.10	3.13	1.24	4.07	1.10	**3.12**	1.36

*5-point scale where 1 = strongly disagree and 5 = strongly agree. Statistically significant differences between groups are in bold.

**For the groupings interest, attendance, viewership, and income, an attempt was made to split the sample based on the median for the category. Category explanations are as follows:

Interest: References the survey question: "Please rate your level of interest in the NBA using a scale from 1 (no interest) to 7 (extremely interested)." Low = Responses 1–5 (n = 82), High = Responses 6 and 7 (n = 71).

Attendance: References the survey question: "How many NBA games do you attend each season?" Low = One or fewer games each season (n = 82), High = Two or more games each season (n = 71).

Viewership: References the survey question: "In an average month, approximately how many NBA games do you watch on television?" Low = 1–6 games (n = 68), High = 7+ games (n = 75).

Income: Annual household income. Low = Less than $50,000 ($n$-83), High = Over $50,000 ($n$-70).

studies present a viable methodology that allows firms to best select a sponsorship that meets image-enhancement goals. Furthermore, we feel the personality-matching technique advances current practices for sponsorship selection. In particular, our method is unique in that it takes a brand perspective and evaluates sport on dimensions shown to have high relevance for brands.

Consider a firm pursuing a sponsorship with an image-enhancement goal—it must first be able to examine the sport in terms of traits that will offer

meaning to the brand. It may be difficult for managers to assess the appropriateness of a sponsorship by examining the sport on a multitude of characteristics. Thus, we condone the use of the established Brand Personality Scale (BPS) as a basis of evaluation. Utilizing that scale offers firms operating in a wide variety of product categories the opportunity to assess how various sports or events fit with their brands on factors that impact brand image. By employing the BPS to match compatible brands and sports on dimensions shown to maintain high relevance to brands, we believe our studies present a methodology that advances previous research and that offers proven relevance in a condensed format.

Summary

As noted earlier, in order clearly to establish and fortify the image of a brand, brand managers must ensure that brand associations are consistent. A sponsorship is a brand association. This would suggest that in a circumstance where a firm is considering a sponsorship, it should also be acutely aware of the perceived image of the sport or event. Based on the image-by-association hypothesis, while a good personality match might enhance the image of a brand, so a poor match may actually dilute a brand's image by confusing what the brand stands for. Schema theory would also support this possibility and suggests that while a sponsorship that appears image consistent would strengthen the brand's image schema, a sponsorship association that lacks image fit may disrupt the existing schema.

This result would also have implications for firms entering into a sponsorship for reasons other than image enhancement. There are numerous objectives for engaging in a sponsorship role, but it is important for managers to recognize that there are benefits and risks of sponsorship on a number of fronts. A good personality match may serve both awareness and image functions as a contribution to brand equity. In this case, a sponsorship that maintains a good personality match as well as a good demographic match literally stands to achieve two benefits for the price of one. The value for the sponsorship dollar is increased as the sponsorship is used as an identity-enhancing vehicle as well as a name-awareness tool. Risks are introduced if a firm selects an inappropriate sponsorship. Risks may not only be financial (in the form of wasted dollars on a sport/event that is a poor fit) but, and perhaps more importantly, perceptual (in the threat of diluting brand image). If a firm selects a sponsorship based solely on demographic fit and disregards personality, the image-association messages are still pervasive. Thus, regardless of the sponsorship objective, since the potential for image by association is present, a firm should not ignore the perceived image of the event/sport. We do not argue that all sponsorship opportunities need to be evaluated based solely on goodness of personality fit; however, we would suggest that when assessing these opportunities, personality fit should always be taken into consideration to some degree.

Limitations

The obvious limitation in Study 1 was that it employed a student sample of limited size. A second major limitation of Study 1 was the limited number of brands and sports utilized in the examination. The absence of more brands and sports constrained our ability to conduct a more detailed analysis. Additionally, in Study 1 perceptions of sponsorship fit were asked following a series of questions pertaining to personality; hence the potential for bias towards personality-driven assessments of fit may have been present. In Study 2, we addressed the shortcomings of Study 1 by utilizing a nonstudent population and extending the number of brands examined to 10. However, the use of a more extensive brand list could offer even greater insight. The Jam Session event was a unique opportunity for data collection, as some of the brands evaluated were Jam Session sponsors. It is difficult, however, to assess if sponsorship of the event biased personality evaluations.

Future Research

Study 2 established the theoretical foundation for a follow-up study to test empirically the ability of sport sponsorship to position a brand. Specifically, the goal of the next examination should be a comprehensive analysis to assess the ability of sponsorship to define or change a brand image.

While Study 2 was able to establish the validity of personality matching, exploring personality matching on a broader scale should follow. The current examination was limited by the number of brands and sports. Thus, a future personality-matching examination with additional sports as well as brands representing numerous product categories could contribute additional insights.

Finally, it is important to examine whether sponsorship fit plays a role in sponsor recall. Postevent testing has indicated that sponsor recall at major sporting events is not impressive. For example, previous proprietary research indicates that recall of a title sponsor hovers around 40%. It would be interesting to explore whether a brand/sport sponsorship with high image congruency produces better recall than others with low congruency. Theory does suggest that information that is consistent in meaning with existing brand associations should be more easily learned and remembered. This would favor the hypothesis that a sponsorship with a high personality match would result in greater recall.

References

Aaker, Jennifer L. (1995). Conceptualizing and measuring brand personality: A brand personality scale. *Working Paper*, Stanford University.

Aaker, David A. (1996). *Building strong brands*. New York: The Free Press.

Brooks, Christine (1994). *Sports marketing: Competitive business strategies for sports*. Englewood Cliffs, NJ: Prentice-Hall.

Cannon, Hugh (1985). Evaluating the profile-distance approach to media selection. *Journal of Advertising*, 14 (March): 4–9.

Carter, David M. (1996). *Keeping score: An inside look at sports marketing*. Grants Pass, OR: The Oasis Press.

Cornwell, T. B. (1995). Sponsorship-linked marketing development. *Sport Marketing Quarterly*, 4 (4): 13–23.

Ferrand, Alain, and Monique Paages (1996). Image sponsoring: A methodology to match event and sponsor. *Journal of Sport Management*, 10: 278–291.

Fiske, Susan T. (1982). Schema-triggered affect: Applications to social perception. *Affect and Social Cognition: The 17th Annual Carnegie Symposium on Cognition*. Hillside, NJ: Erlbaum, 55–78.

Fiske, Susan T. and S. E. Taylor (1991). *Social cognition*. Reading, MA: Addison-Wesley.

Gardner, Meryl P., and Philip J. Shuman (1987). Sponsorship: An important component of the promotions mix. *Journal of Advertising*, 16 (1): 11–17.

——— (1988). Sponsorship and small business. *Journal of Small Business Management*, (October): 44–52.

Gladden, Jay, George Milne, and William Sutton (1998). A conceptual framework for assessing brand equity in Division I college athletics. *Journal of Sport Management*, 12 (1): 1–19.

Hair, J. F., R. E. Anderson, R. L. Tatham, and W. C. Black (1995). *Multivariate data analysis with readings*. Englewood Cliffs, NJ: Prentice-Hall.

IEG Sponsorship Report (1994). 1994 sponsorship spending will exceed $4 billion, 1–2.

Irwin, R. L., and M. Assimakopoulas (1992). An approach to the evaluation and selection of sport sponsorship proposals. *Sport Marketing Quarterly*, 1 (2): 43–51.

Irwin, R. L., and W. A. Sutton (1994). Sport sponsorship objectives: An analysis of their relative importance for major corporate sponsors. *European Journal for Sport Management*, 1 (2): 93–101.

Irwin, R. L., M. Assimakopoulas, and W. A. Sutton (1994). A model for screening sport sponsorship opportunities. *Journal of Promotion Management*, 2 (3/4): 53–69.

Javalgi, Rajshekhar, Mark Traylor, Andrew Gross, and Edward Lampman (1994). Awareness of sponsorship and corporate image: An empirical investigation. *Journal of Advertising*, 23 (4): 47–58.

Joachimstaler, Erick, and David A. Aaker (1997). Building brands without mass media. *Harvard Business Review*, January–February, 39–50.

Kamins, M. (1990). An investigation into the match-up hypothesis in celebrity advertising: When beauty may be only skin deep. *Journal of Advertising*, 19 (1):4–13.

Keller, Kevin L. (1993). Conceptualizing, measuring, and managing customer-based brand equity. *Journal of Marketing*, 57 (January): 1–22.

Kuzma, John R., William L. Shanklin, and John F. McCally (1993). Number one principle for sporting events seeking corporate sponsors: Meet benefactor's objectives. *Sport Marketing Quarterly*, 2 (3): 27–32.

Lough, Nancy L. (1996). Factors affecting corporate sponsorship of women's sport. *Sport Marketing Quarterly*, 5 (2): 11–19.

Marshall, D. W., and G. Cook (1992). The corporate sports sponsor. *International Journal of Advertising*, 11: 307–324.

Martin, James H. (1994). Using a perceptual map of the consumer's sport schema to help make sponsorship decisions. *Sport Marketing Quarterly*, 3: 27–31.

Martin, James H. (1996). Is the athlete's sport important when picking an athlete to endorse a non-sport product? *Journal of Consumer Marketing*, 13 (6): 28–43.

McCarville, R. E., and R. P. Copeland (1994). Understanding sport sponsorship through exchange theory. *Journal of Sport Management*, 8: 102–114.

McCracken, G. (1989). Who is the celebrity endorser? Cultural foundations of the endorsement process. *Journal of Consumer Research*, 16: 310–321.

Meenaghan, J. A. (1983). Commercial sponsorship. *European Journal of Marketing*, 17 (7): 5–73.

Meenaghan, Tony (1991). The role of sponsorship in the marketing communications mix. *International Journal of Advertising*, 10: 35–47.

Milne, George R. (1994). A magazine taxonomy based on customer overlap. *Journal of the Academy of Marketing Science,* 22 (Spring): 170–179.

Park, C., Bernard Whan, J. Jaworski, and Deborah J. MacInnis (1986). Strategic brand concept-image management. *Journal of Marketing,* 50 (October): 135–145.

Sirgy, Joseph M., J. S. Johar, A. C. Samli, and C. B. Claiborne (1991). Self-congruity versus functional congruity: Predictors of consumer behavior. *Journal of the Academy of Marketing Science,* 19 (Fall): 363–375.

Sissors, Jack Z. (1971). Matching media with markets. *Journal of Advertising Research,* 11 (October): 39–43.

Sleight, S. (1989). *Sponsorship: What it is and how to use it.* Maidenhead, Berkshire, England: McGraw-Hill.

Stipp, Horst, and Nicholas P. Schiavone (1996). Modeling the impact of Olympic sponsorship on corporate image. *Journal of Advertising Research*, July/August: 22–28.

Sujan, Mita, and James Bettman (1989). The effects of brand positioning strategies on consumers' brand and category perceptions: Some insights from schema research. *Journal of Marketing Research*, 26 (4): 454–467.

Thwaites, Des (1995). Professional football sponsorship—profitable or profligate? *International Journal of Advertising*, 14: 149–164.

Turco, Douglas M. (1994). Event sponsorship: Effects on consumer brand loyalty and consumption. *Sport Marketing Quarterly*, 3 (3): 35–37.

Winter, Frederick W. (1980). Match target markets to media audiences. *Journal of Advertising Research,* 20 (February): 61–65.

CHAPTER 10

Sport Marketing and the Internet

Introduction

The next frontier for sport marketers to approach in building strong relationships with consumers is the Internet. With its "virtual" communities, the Internet is a natural extension of the "communities" that form around sport organizations and teams. As the Internet becomes mainstream and the number of its users escalates, so will the importance of this interactive medium increase. The Internet appears to offer companies an efficient way to interact with their customers. Firms using this resource are building brand equity and increasing brand loyalty through this new medium. There are, however, a myriad of challenges confronting marketers who test these new and largely unfamiliar waters.

This chapter is divided into three parts. Part I will profile Internet users and explore how the Internet is utilized by sport marketers. Part II provides the results of an empirical study evaluating the features comprising major professional sport team websites. The final section, Part III, will review the challenges and opportunities inherent in conducting market research on the Internet.

Part I: The Role of the Internet

Dramatic growth in personal and commercial Internet usage has brought the usefulness of this interactive medium to the forefront for marketers. The number of World Wide Web (web) sites is doubling every two months. As with site generation, usage of the Internet is doubling every year. There are currently over 30 million users, with estimated worldwide usage expected to reach 150 million by the year 2000 (Comley, 1997). In this fluid medium, user profiles are also evolving. The Graphics, Visualization and Usability Center (GVU) at the Georgia Tech College of Computing has conducted web user surveys every six months since January of 1994. The results of a recent GVU survey (October 1996) provide a useful profile of web users:

- Approximately 30% of users were female, up from 5% in 1994.
- Over 1/3 of users have accessed the Internet for less than 1 year.
- 70.9% list PCs as their primary computing platform, up from 5.1% in 1994.
- 63.8% use the web for entertainment; 53.3% for education; and 50.5% for work.
- 15% report having used the web to shop, up 50% in a year.

- More than 1/3 thought censorship was the most important issue facing the Internet today, followed by 26.3% concerned about privacy issues.
- Nearly half (46.1%) of the users felt more connected since getting online.

Since its development in the 1960s, the Internet has undergone a radical transformation. Initially the exclusive domain of scientists, the Net (as it is commonly known) is now open and easily accessible to all computer-using individuals. This evolution presents tremendous opportunities for marketers. Mass media (e.g., television, print, and radio) offers one-way communication, but the Internet allows for two-way interactive communication. Interactive communication involves two (or more) communicants responding to each other. Thus, at a minimum, A communicates to B, B responds to A, and A reacts to B (Bretz and Schmidbauer, 1983).

Interactive communication with consumers opens entirely new avenues for connecting with customers. According to Rust and Varki (1996):

> By marrying the power of computers with telecommunication technology through digitization, interactive media makes it possible for people to communicate with one another (service-providers included) in multimedia format, i.e., via a combination of graphical, textual, audio, and video information. By empowering individuals thus, interactive media has brought us that much closer to the electronic marketplace by enabling marketers and individuals to conduct virtual "face-to-face" dialogues in cyberspace—a stark contrast to the mass-communication model wherein marketers conduct "monologues" with nameless, faceless individuals (p. 173).

Advances in hardware and software have afforded new opportunities for companies to build relationships with current and potential customers. However, "technology only determines possibility, whereas audience behavior determines actuality" (Comstock, 1989, p. 93). The key to maximizing this technology is understanding what consumer needs are being satisfied through this form of interactive communication.

Prior research indicates that consumers utilize technology to satisfy their affective and cognitive needs (cf. McQuail, 1984). For simplicity, Rust and Varki (1996) have categorized these needs as follows: (1) information needs, (2) entertainment needs, and (3) socialization needs. These needs are described below.

1. *Information Needs.* While mass media is one voice speaking to many, with very general information, interactive media provides individuals easy access to information that is tailored to their specific needs. User-friendly software affords consumers the opportunity to explore large databases of information, accessing only that which is of interest to them.

2. *Entertainment Needs.* Interactive media provides individuals with a great variety of entertaining activities. These include, but are not limited to, playing interactive games with others, participating in chat rooms and/or bulletin boards, and taking "virtual" visits to places like museums or sport facilities. These "virtual" trips are enhanced by the integration of graphical, textual, audio, and video information.

3. *Socialization Needs.* One way in which people satisfy their socialization needs is through talking with friends and community members. Although cyberspace is often thought of as impersonal, it is actually a haven for interactive "chat rooms." Internet "chat rooms" provide a forum for individuals to conduct conversations with several other users in real-time (Rust and Varki, 1996).

These three needs are particularly salient for sport fans. Part of the enjoyment of following sport is the vast amount of available information, ranging from player, team, and league statistics to editorial commentary. As reported in Chapter 2, one study found that among hard-core fans, 88.2% read the newspaper sports pages and 94.7% watched or listened to sports news on the television or radio.

Satisfying entertainment needs also motivates sport consumers. Participating and watching sport provides an escape from the realities of everyday life. Constant action and activity serves to stimulate the senses and evoke pleasurable sensations. For sport consumers, it is difficult to replicate the excitement of a close contest between fierce competitors.

Socialization needs are also primary for these consumers. Sport fans socialize before games (tailgating), during games (talking in the stands), after games (victory party), and even after the season is over. For instance, focus groups for the Orlando Magic basketball team revealed that ticket holders often have social gatherings during the off-season with others from their stadium seating section.

Given that individuals access the Internet to satisfy their needs for information, entertainment, and socialization, how can companies utilize this phenomenon to strengthen relationships with customers and, in the long term, increase profitability? Just as people form meaningful relationships with other members of a community and with the organizers and leaders of that community in the real world, the Internet is no different. The web provides opportunities for people with similar interests to form small, homogeneous communities. These "virtual" communities share the same space in "cyberworld."

The communal nature of the web provides an opportunity for sport marketers to extend the communities that form naturally around sport teams and organizations. Although in general people are becoming disconnected from a sense of community due to changing lifestyles and societal interests, just the opposite is true of sport spectators. Sport builds a collective identity by promoting communication, involving people in group activities, and providing common rituals and symbols. Successfully extending these sport communities to the Internet, however, presents unique challenges. These "virtual" communities have distinguishable characteristics that should be noted by sport marketers attempting to reach these consumers. Primarily, these communities differ in the types of needs they meet. Armstrong and Hagel (1996) classified electronic communities according to four types of consumer needs:

1. *Communities of Transaction:* These communities facilitate the buying and selling of products and services. Participants interact with each other to exchange useful product information. Communities of transaction can be managed by either vendors or community organizers and might offer electronic classified ads or a "marketspace" for transactions.

2. *Communities of Interest:* These communities serve as gathering places for people to interact with each other on specific topics. Interaction is highly interpersonal in these communities, with members sharing information, trading goods, and posting bulletin board queries. These communities, serving as topic resources, often provide links to other related Internet sites and resources.

3. *Communities of Fantasy:* These communities provide members with an arena in which to create new environments, personalities, or stories. Users are able to play out their fantasies in a safe environment without the need for personal identification.

4. *Communities of Relationship:* These communities provide an opportunity for people to come together and share personal experiences. This sharing often leads to the formation of deep personal connections. In sport, for example, the 1996 departure of the Browns football team from Cleveland resulted in depression and grieving behavior among hard-core fans. Communities of relationship evolved on the web to provide support as these fans impatiently wait for the NFL to award an expansion franchise to Cleveland.

Internet communities have the potential to fulfill all four needs simultaneously (transactions, interest, fantasy, and relationship), but most are currently targeting only one need. By addressing all needs in one community, companies can more fully take advantage of the media and build stronger ties with participants (Armstrong and Hagel, 1996). A sports franchise, for example, could maximize the power of the Internet by

- providing information about the players, with links to opponents and the league (community of information);
- giving participants an opportunity to locate another fan to copurchase season tickets (community of relationships);
- offering a game with a chance to travel with the team to an away competition (community of fantasy); or,
- allowing participants to purchase team and league merchandise (community of transaction).

One sport company that is maximizing the potential of this interactive media is ESPN. The ESPN website (http://espnet.sportszone.com) is the most frequently visited site on the web. Their success is partially due to the tremendous popularity of sport worldwide but also attests to ESPN's ability to simultaneously serve all four types of communities described above. Their site serves the community of information by providing exhaustive statistics on athletes, teams, and leagues from around the world. Additional depth is provided through player profiles, breaking news coverage, and the use of expert columnists covering every major team and sport. ESPN's ZoneStore sells sports apparel (e.g., hats, caps, and jerseys) from a variety of major and minor league sports teams. Orders can be placed online by phone or fax (community of transaction). Fans also have the opportunity to compete against other users in fantasy baseball, basketball, and football leagues. These fantasies are tied to reality, since winning depends on the performance of real players during the season. The fantasy is the illusion of running a sports team, which is a dream of many fans (community of fantasy). Lastly, the ESPN site provides opportunities for fans to interact with each other and sport celebrities via chat rooms (community of relationship).

The site is designed to satisfy all the major needs of sport fans and fully takes advantage of the Internet's attributes. This degree of coverage (all four types of communities) is probably rare, but it is difficult to draw this conclusion with any certainty given the lack of systematic research to evaluate the effectiveness of Internet marketing and websites. The next section of this chapter will begin to address this shortcoming by presenting the results of an empirical study evaluating and comparing the features of major professional sport team Websites.

Part II: Study of Professional Team Websites

Two exploratory studies were conducted during January and April 1997 to evaluate the web pages of professional sport teams in the National Football League (NFL), National Basketball League (NBA), National Hockey League (NHL), and Major League Baseball (MLB). Based on a series of interviews with web users at a major northeastern university, a survey instrument consisting of 10 items was developed to evaluate web pages. The survey instrument was peer reviewed and pilot tested on websites to ensure that it covered the domain of the web experience.

The instrument items consisted of a five-point Likert scale, anchored by 1 = strongly disagree and 5 = strongly agree. The instrument contained the following 10 characteristics: graphics/visuals, information, interaction, ease of exploration, links to other sites, games/activities, on-line questions, speed, organizational structure, and overall experience.

In Study 1, the instrument was used to rate 118 professional teams. The evaluator was a trained research assistant who assisted in the development of the instrument. The web addresses for the teams, called Uniform Record Locations (URLs), were found by first going to the league websites or using Internet search engines based on the team names. To find the NFL teams, the NFL home page (www.nfl.com) was first examined to find links to many teams. In some instances, the teams had other official sites that were not associated with the NFL. The URLs for the NBA official websites were found through the NBA official home page (www.nba.com). To locate NHL web pages, a hockey site (www.hockeyguide.com) was reviewed. This site listed the team names and was used to find the home pages of individual teams. For some of the hockey teams, this site was used to link to the URLs; however, not all teams had official sites. MLB teams were located from the MLB home page (www.majorleaguebaseball.com). The majority of teams had official home pages.

In Spring 1997, a second exploratory study was conducted. In Study 2, the URLs for 113 teams located for Study 1 were subsequently evaluated using the same 10-item scale. However, to ensure that more variance was captured, the scale increased from a five-point scale to a seven-point scale. The evaluators doing the second study were 22 Masters-degree candidates in sport management. Each student evaluated 10 of the websites for class credit. In total, 107 of the websites were independently evaluated by two people; six were evaluated by a single individual.

The scores for the multiple raters from Study 2 were averaged. (The scores from single evaluators were used in cases where there were not multiple raters.)

The averages across the leagues for the 10 questions are shown in Table 10–1. In terms of overall

TABLE 10–1. Comparison of websites by professional league on ten dimensions

	NFL [A] $N = 31$	NBA [B] $N = 29$	NHL [C] $N = 27$	MLB [D] $N = 26$	F-value (prob)	Significant contrasts*
Overall experience	5.0	5.8	3.7	4.7	15.28 (0.00)	B > A, B > D , B > C, A > C, D > C
Graphics/Visuals	5.5	5.8	4.0	4.9	12.2 (0.00)	A > C, B > C, D > C
Informative	5.4	6.1	5.3	5.3	3.55 (0.02)	B > C
Interactive	4.5	5.4	3.3	4.4	10.8 (0.00)	B > C, A > C, D > C
Ease of use	5.5	6.3	4.9	5.1	8.77 (0.00)	B > A, B > D, B > C
Site links	5.4	5.5	5.3	4.8	2.48 (0.06)	
Games	3.7	3.8	2.9	4.0	3.26 (0.00)	D > C
Online questions	4.1	5.2	2.9	4.3	16.7 (0.00)	B > A, B > C, D > C, A > C
Speed	5.1	6.0	4.5	4.5	18.64 (0.00)	B > A, B > C, B > D
Structure	5.3	6.3	5.4	4.6	16.11 (0.00)	B > C, B > A, B > D, C > D

*Significant pairwise contrasts are reported at the 0.05 level.

1 = low, 7 = high.

experience, there was a statistically significant difference across the four leagues ($F_{3109} = 15.21$, $p < 0.01$). Statistically significant differences among leagues at the 0.05 level were found for all dimensions, except for site links. The dimensions that had the largest differences among leagues were speed ($F_{3109} = 18.64$, $p < 0.01$), structure ($F_{3109} = 16.11$, $p < 0.01$), graphics/visuals ($F_{3109} = 12.2$, $p < 0.01$), and interaction ($F_{3109} = 10.8$, $p < 0.01$). The significant pairwise Bonferroni contrasts among leagues are also noted in Table 10–1.

The NBA teams were rated most favorably for overall experience (5.8), followed by the NFL (5.0), MLB (4.7), and NHL (3.7). In fact, the NBA sites were rated highest on all dimensions. The highest-rated dimensions within the NBA included structure (6.3), ease of use (6.3), and information (6.1). The highest ratings for the NFL were based on graphics/visuals (5.5) and ease of use (5.5). MLB was seen as strong on the information (5.3) and ease of use (5.1) dimensions. Finally, the NHL, while averaging below average on games (2.9) and online questions (2.9), was relatively strong on the structure (5.4) and information (5.3) dimensions.

To better understand the dimensionality of evaluating web pages, the nine specific dimensions were

factor analyzed. Two factors with eigenvalues > 1 were extracted. The rotated factor pattern for these two factors is shown in Table 10–2. The two factors combined accounted for 68.1% of the variance. Loadings greater than 0.5 are in bold. For this criterion, there were no mixed loadings. The pattern of the item loadings suggest that the first factor captures an interactivity dimension and the second factor captures a functionality dimension. Factor scores were calculated by averaging the values for the significant items. The coefficient alphas for these multiple-item measures were 0.89 for interactivity and 0.83 for functionality.

As shown in Table 10–3, both interactivity and functionality were statistically significant across leagues. Overall, the interactivity dimension was not rated as high as the functionality dimension. The NBA was the highest rated in both of these dimensions. The NHL was the lowest-rated league due especially to its below-average rating on interactivity (3.3).

To learn which factor contributed most to the overall impression of the league's web page, the two factor scores were regressed on the overall impression of the web page. The results of the OLS regression show that these two factors accounted for 79%

TABLE 10–2. Rotated factor analysis results

	Interactivity	Functionality
Graphics/Visuals	**0.81**	0.24
Interactive features	**0.90**	0.20
Games/Activities	**0.82**	0.12
Online questions	**0.85**	0.25
Informative	0.46	**0.69**
Ease of exploration	0.29	**0.82**
Links to other sites	−0.01	**0.68**
Speed	0.16	**0.66**
Organizational structure	0.26	**0.81**
Percentage variance explained	36.2%	31.9%
Coefficient alpha[a]	0.89	0.83

[a] Coefficient alpha was calculated for the items that significantly loaded on each factor. These items are indicated by bold font.

TABLE 10–3. Comparison of websites by professional league on factor scores

	NFL [A] N = 31	NBA [B] N = 29	NHL [C] N = 27	MLB [D] N = 26	F-value (prob)	Significant contrasts*
Interactivity	4.5	5.0	3.3	4.4	12.8 (0.00)	B > C, A > C, D > C
Functionality	5.3	6.0	5.1	4.9	13.4 (0.00)	B > A, B > C, B > D

*Significant pairwise contrasts are reported at the 0.05 level.

TABLE 10–4. Regression of overall impression of web page

	Beta	T-value
Interactivity	0.76	13.9
Functionality	0.49	5.9
F-value	216.8	
Prob > F	0.0001	
Adjusted R-square	0.79	

of the variance (see Table 10-4). The parameters for both interactivity and functionality were highly significant. Interestingly, interactivity explained the most variance.

Certainly, evaluation of the strength of a web page is very subjective, which is all the more obvious when one realizes that good web pages are constantly in transition. Furthermore, two evaluators can have very different experiences, depending on which hypertext links they happen to select as they go through the page. To examine the consistency of the rating scales, we correlated the results from Study 1 with Study 2. While the rank order of the results was the same, there were some fluctuations. In comparing the studies, we found a significant correlation of 0.51 for the overall impression variable.

Despite the inherent limitations of evaluating web pages, we have presented an exploratory study that shows there are differences in the overall quality of the league web pages. Moreover, this research identified the dimensions of interactivity and functionality as being two important factors in the evaluation of web pages. Both of these dimensions are key to creating a favorable impression. In the next section of the chapter, we will focus on how a website can be used to conduct market research.

Part III: Market Research on the Internet—Challenges and Opportunities

Relationship Marketing

The advantage of using the Internet to support marketing efforts is that it allows a sport organization to have a one-to-one relationship with its customer base. Marketers who want to be successful in the future must constantly be listening to their customers, gathering information on the types of products they want and services they desire, and seeking to understand what they do and don't like about current operations. One-to-one marketing requires marketers to treat customers as valuable assets and to encourage open dialogue with the company. A web page can serve as a powerful dialogue tool. In particular, questionnaires can be be used to gain feedback about the organization and the website. Further, website questionnaires can also be used to establish demographic profiles of customers and initiate data-based marketing efforts.

Gaining Feedback on Websites.

Websites are a valuable communication and service vehicle, linking sport organizations to their customers. As sport organizations are in the entertainment industry, visitors will likely have high expectations regarding the entertainment value of the site. Thus, especially for sport teams, it is important to have an exciting, informative website. The website can at some level be considered the customer's opportunity to interact and play with the organization. Because of their importance, websites need to be evaluated, and this can be done with a survey.

New Balance is an example of a company that has placed a survey on its web page to get feedback. Their site has shoe information, retailer locations, race listings, training and health tips, workouts, and company information, among other topics. In its questionnaire, the company begins by asking visitors to provide feedback on their New Balance Cyberpark USA site. They ask respondents to rate each section of the site and offer suggestions on improving the cyberpark.

Gathering Demographic Profiles.

The New Balance site also gathers relevant demographic information, including birthday, sex, marital status, education, income, and occupation. To round out the visitor profile, the company also asks respondents how many times they work out in a week, what they do for exercise/fun, and how often. Customers can not only provide information about which of the site owner's products they buy but they can also report about the competition. New Balance asks respondents to reveal which brands of athletic shoes they have in their closets, the brands they last bought, and where they buy their shoes.

Gathering Data to Initiate Database Marketing Efforts.

Much of the demographic data gathered from the website can be used to build a database and develop a database program. Based on the different backgrounds and activities recorded, many of the database principles suggested in Chapter 5 can be implemented. New Balance, in addition to gathering standard demographics, also collected information about the respondents relationship with the company. Specifically, the company inquired about such items as whether respondents wore New Balance shoes, which brand they wore most often, whether they recently switched to New Balance, whether they had never worn but would consider wearing New Balance shoes, and whether the respondent had any interest in ever buying a New Balance product. Clearly, information from these questions can be used to send different types of communication packages to the self-selected groups.

Another piece of data that is important to collect from visitors is the person's electronic mail (e-mail) address. When gathering this piece of data, as with all data, respondents should receive a guarantee that the data will only be used by the organization to better serve the customer. With this guarantee, and the e-mail address, it is possible to establish a dialogue that goes back and forth between the sport organization and the individual consumers. Taken to the next level, the organization can use the e-mail address to send out targeted surveys.

Web-Based Versus Traditional Paper Surveys

Web-based surveys have been used successfully by researchers and organizations. Perhaps the most ambitious efforts have been those of Georgia Tech's Graphic, Visualization and Usability (GVU) Center. This group was a pioneer in the field of web-based surveying and has made its results publically accessible (GVU 1997). Beginning in January of 1994, the GVU has conducted web-based surveys every six months about topics of interest to the web community. The GVU survey uses nonprobability sampling. Participants are informed of the survey through announcements on Internet-related newsgroups, banners placed on specific pages of high-exposure sites, banners randomly rotated through high-exposure sites, announcements made to the web survey mailing list (maintained by GVU), and announcements made to the traditional media.

There are several advantages in using web surveys over traditional paper surveys. Surveys conducted over the Internet generate much faster response than paper-based surveys. If an organization wants quick feedback from its customers, an Internet survey can get the job done in a couple of days. In addition, it is generally cheaper to conduct an Internet survey, and it is possible to span distance and time. Thus, international surveys are very possible using this medium.

One of the biggest criticisms of surveys placed on web pages is that there is a self-select bias. Clearly, surveys of this nature are not random. A purely random sample may not be probable because there is no complete list of all web users. If there were, the list would always be out of date due to the increase in the number of users every day. However, this does not mean that the results of self-selected surveys are not worthwhile. Research has demonstrated that compared to random samples, self-selected respondents gave higher-quality results, provided longer open-ended questions, and had fewer missing values on responses (Walsh, Kiesler, Sproull, and Hesse, 1992). Further, organizations often want to get feedback from their customers and so are not necessarily looking for a random sample. Rather, a quick response from individuals who are interested in the survey topic may be more meaningful and provide qualitatively more important results.

The format of the questionnaire is an important issue to be considered. The researcher should consider whether the questionnaire should be posted on a web page that allows anyone access, or if access to the questionnaire should be based on prior contact. The first type of questionnaire is similar to the New Balance questionnaire discussed previously. The second type of questionnaire (access based on prior contact) could be implemented if New Balance asked only those customers who had previously provided e-mail addresses to answer a questionnaire. Access to the questionnaire could be controlled by a password, which could be each respondent's e-mail address.

Some surveys have been conducted using e-mail (Strauss, 1996). Although this does produce fast results, the issue of response accuracy should be considered. In constrast to web-page surveys, which have a nice graphical interface, e-mail surveys are not as clean. E-mail survey results are often difficult to bring into a text editor and tabulate. Tabulation error is high, since respondents can place their responses in any location near the question (Strauss, 1996).

Using e-mail to contact customers is an inexpensive approach to maintaining a customer dialogue. However, prior to using this form of communication, it is important to ensure customers that e-mail addresses will not be provided to other organizations. Privacy is a very sensitive topic that concerns a large percentage of web users. Using e-mail lists to reach prospects is not advised. Many web users find this junk e-mail to be quite offensive and are increasingly upset by "spamming" (the practice of sending junk e-mail).

Summary

This chapter has presented a brief overview of using the Internet in the world of sport marketing. It has explained why sport organizations can benefit from this type of marketing, reviewed the websites of major professional teams, and discussed issues related to conducting surveys over the web.

The technology of the Internet is changing the way marketing is being practiced, completing the shift from mass marketing to a one-to-one, relationship marketing paradigm. With consumers of the sport product already forming communities around sport organizations and teams, encouraging sport fans to form "virtual" communities on the web is a natural next step for innovative sport marketers. The Internet provides a great platform to satisfy the informational, social, and entertainment needs that are so central to sport consumers.

References

Armstrong, Arthur, and John Hagel III (1996). The real value of on-line communities. *Harvard Business Review*, May–June, 134–141.

Bretz, Rudy, and Michael Schmidbauer (1983). *Media for interactive communication*. Beverly Hills, CA: Sage Publications.

Comley, Pete (1996). The use of the internet as a data collection method. Paper presented to the ESOMAR/ EMAC Symposium. *Research methodologies for the new marketing*, November.

Comstock, George (1989). *The evolution of American television*. Newbury Park, CA: Sage Publications.

GVU (1997). *GVU's 7th WWW user survey*. GVU Webpage (www.gatech.edu/gvu).

McQuail, D. (1984). With the benefit of hindsight: Reflections on uses and gratifications research. *Critical Studies in Mass Communication*, 1: 177–193.

Rust, Roland, and Sajeev Varki (1996). Rising from the ashes of advertising. *Journal of Business Research*, 37–181.

Sterne, Jim (1995). *World wide web marketing: Integrating the internet into your marketing strategy*. New York: John Wiley and Sons.

Strauss, Judy (1996). Early survey research on the internet: Review, illustration and evaluation. In Edward A. Blair and Wagner A. Kamakura (eds.), *1996 AMA winter educators' conference: Marketing theory and applications*, Vol. 7. Chicago, IL: American Marketing Association.

Walsh, John P, Sara Kiesler, Lee Sproull, and Bradford W. Hesse (1992). Self-selected and randomly selected respondents in a computer network survey. *Public Opinion Quarterly*, 56: 241–244.

Survey Instruments from Empirical Studies

Study of Sport Consumers

The purpose of this study was to collect information on sport participation and spectating behavior. The results of this study have been reported in Chapters 2, 3, 6, and 7. This section provides background about this study and reports the summary findings.

Section 1

How often do you do the following?

	N	Percent				
		Every day or almost every day	About once or twice a week	About once or twice a month	Less than once a month	Never
2. Watch sports events on television	1601	29.7	59.7	7.1	3.0	0.4
3. Listen to sports on the radio	1586	10.5	22.3	21.4	26.1	19.8
4. Read the sports pages of your newspaper	1592	65.9	17.5	6.9	4.8	4.9
5. Watch or listen to sports news on TV or radio	1563	71.3	18.6	3.9	3.6	2.6
6. Read books on sports and athletes	1552	3.5	9.0	17.6	37.5	32.3
7. Read magazines on sports and athletes	1525	6.4	23.3	25.4	28.9	16.1
8. Talk about sports with your friends	1566	37.8	39.3	12.8	7.0	3.0
9. Purchase sports merchandise with a team or brand logo	1569	1.3	2.0	11.5	56.0	29.3
10. Purchase sports equipment (i.e., balls, shoes, racquets, etc.)	1602	0.9	1.8	17.7	62.9	16.7

Section 2

11. What is your favorite sport to participate in? _____

	N	%		N	%		N	%
Aerobics	13	0.9	Swimming	17	1.2	Frisbee	2	0.1
Archery	2	0.1	Table tennis	3	0.2	Squash	1	0.1
Badminton	4	0.3	Tennis	95	6.7	Paddleball	1	0.1
Baseball (hardball)	72	5.1	Volleyball (hard surface)	42	3.0	Handball	1	0.1
Basketball	145	10.2	Volleyball (sand)	1	0.1	Surfing	1	0.1
Bicycle riding	24	1.7	Water skiing	6	0.4	Floor hockey	1	0.1
Billiards/Pool	9	0.6	Weight lifting	10	0.7	Field hockey	1	0.1
Bowling	85	6.0	Walking	15	1.1	Whitewater rafting	1	0.1
Boxing	5	0.4	Auto racing	15	1.1	Power lifting	1	0.1
Bungee jumping	1	0.1	Horseshoes	1	0.1	Combinations	71	5.0
Canoeing/Kayaking	1	0.1	Snowboarding	1	0.1			
Distance running	4	0.3	Dancing	1	0.1			
Fishing (freshwater)	47	3.3	Darts	1	0.1			
Fishing (saltwater)	1	0.1	Hiking	5	0.4			
Football (tackle)	47	3.3	Wrestling	4	0.3			
Football (touch)	22	1.5	Martial arts	6	0.4			
Golf	351	24.7	Plane flying	2	0.1			
Hunting	19	1.3	Pigeon racing	1	0.1			
Ice hockey	14	1.0	Rugby	3	0.2			
Ice skating	1	0.1	Gymnastics	1	0.1			
Mountain biking	1	0.1	Croquet	2	0.1			
Roller skating (in-line)	4	0.3	Lacrosse	3	0.2			
Running/Jogging	15	1.1	Motocross	3	0.2			
Sailing	4	0.3	Racquet ball	15	1.1			
Scuba diving	5	0.4	Boating	2	0.1			
Skiing (cross-country)	13	0.9	Exercising	2	0.1			
Skiing (downhill)	18	1.3	Horse racing	2	0.1			
Soccer	22	1.5	Bocce	1	0.1			
Softball	99	7.0	Horseback riding	1	0.1			

Below are some statements about how people feel about participating in their favorite sport. Think only about the favorite sport you indicated above. Please read each statement, then circle the appropriate number printed below to indicate your agreement or disagreement with the statements.

	N	Mean	S.D.	Percent		
				Disagree	Neutral	Agree
12. I do not have a strong desire to be a success in my favorite sport.	1510	3.3	2.1	55.8	13.5	30.7
13. I would be willing to work all year round in order to be a success in my favorite sport.	1508	4.0	2.2	43.3	13.4	43.3
14. My goal is to become outstanding in my favorite sport.	1509	3.9	2.1	43.9	16.5	39.6
15. My favorite sport helps me develop a competitive work ethic.	1505	4.3	2.0	33.4	18.3	48.4
16. Competition is the best part of participating in my favorite sport.	1512	4.2	2.1	36.8	15.5	47.6

	N	Mean	S.D.	Percent		
				Disagree	Neutral	Agree
17. The better the opposition, the more I enjoy playing my favorite sport.	1513	4.5	2.0	29.2	15.5	55.3
18. I enjoy playing my favorite sport because it gives me a chance to meet new people.	1511	4.4	1.8	28.8	21.2	50
19. Participation in my favorite sport with a group does not lead to improved social relationships.	1512	2.8	1.8	69.2	13	17.8
20. Participation in my favorite sport gives me a chance to spend time with my friends.	1509	5.5	1.6	12.3	10.7	77
21. My enjoyment of my favorite sport is based on having other people to share the experience with.	1505	4.8	1.8	21.7	16.7	61.6
22. I play my favorite sport to stay physically fit.	1513	4.7	1.8	24.7	19.2	56.1
23. I play my favorite sport mainly because I feel it keeps me healthy.	1508	4.5	1.8	28	21.4	50.7
24. I play my favorite sport because it develops physical fitness.	1504	4.5	1.8	28.5	19.4	52.1
25. I enjoy playing my favorite sport because it is not a difficult sport to master.	1511	3.0	1.9	64.5	11.6	23.9
26. Playing my favorite sport is constantly challenging because it is a difficult sport to master.	1511	4.8	2.0	27.5	13.8	58.7
27. It takes a high degree of skill on my part to attain the results I expect when playing my favorite sport.	1510	5.0	1.8	21.5	13.5	65
28. Playing my favorite sport does not involve a high risk of being injured.	1501	4.5	2.1	34.1	13.1	52.8
29. Part of the fun of my favorite sport is the danger involved.	1508	2.1	1.7	82.7	6.6	10.7
30. If I have to sacrifice my body when playing my favorite sport, so be it.	1509	2.6	2.0	71.1	8.4	20.5
31. I put my entire self on the line when I play my favorite sport.	1513	3.4	2.1	53.4	14.9	31.7
32. Participation in my favorite sport makes me feel like I belong to a special group.	1513	4.2	1.8	33.6	20	46.4
33. There is a certain camaraderie among the people who play my favorite sport.	1512	5.3	1.6	12.4	12.5	75.1
34. I feel a bond with the people I play my favorite sport with.	1513	5.0	1.7	16.9	15.7	67.4
35. Participating in my favorite sport can be beautiful.	1504	4.9	1.8	18.7	20.3	61
36. I enjoy the artistry of playing my favorite sport.	1505	4.8	1.7	20.2	20.7	59.1
37. Participating in my favorite sport is one way in which I express myself.	1511	4.7	1.8	22.9	19	58.1
38. I put a bit of my own personality into my performance in my favorite sport.	1510	5.0	1.7	17.6	14.9	67.5
39. Participating in my favorite sport can bring out my aggressive nature.	1514	4.8	1.9	24.7	10.8	64.5
40. Much of my enjoyment of my favorite sport comes from the aggressive aspects of participating.	1508	4.2	2.0	36.1	16	47.8
41. I feel less aggressive after participating in my favorite sport.	1509	3.7	1.8	44.3	25.3	30.4
42. I am free to express my aggressive feelings while participating in my favorite sport.	1511	4.2	1.9	35.1	17.6	47.3

	N	Mean	S.D.	Percent		
				Disagree	Neutral	Agree
43. Playing my favorite sport has helped me understand the value of hard work and dedication.	1510	5.0	1.7	18.7	16.8	64.4
44. Playing my favorite sport teaches me lessons that I may not learn anywhere else.	1511	4.4	1.8	29.2	23.1	47.7
45. Playing my favorite sport has helped make me the kind of person I am.	1512	4.0	1.9	37.2	23.6	39.2

Below are some statements about how people feel about participating in their favorite sport. Please read each statement, then circle the appropriate number printed below to indicate your agreement or disagreement with the statements. Again, please think about only the favorite sport you indicated above. Each statement begins with the phrase "participating in my favorite sport . . . ."

Participating in my favorite sport . . .	N	Mean	S.D.	Percent		
				Disagree	Neutral	Agree
46. makes me feel that I am a successful person.	1511	4.3	1.7	28.5	24.8	46.7
47. makes me feel confident about my abilities.	1509	4.9	1.5	16.3	17.4	66.3
48. gives me a feeling of self-assurance.	1505	4.9	1.5	17.2	17.1	65.7
49. helps me to grow as a person.	1509	4.4	1.6	25.3	24.3	50.4
50. helps me to accomplish things I never thought possible.	1503	4.0	1.7	36.9	23.1	40
51. helps me to reach my potential as an individual.	1509	4.1	1.7	33.9	24.3	41.8
52. is an excellent remedy for me if I am tense, irritable, and anxious.	1510	5.4	1.6	13.4	9.7	77
53. helps me to get away from daily pressures.	1509	5.7	1.5	8.2	8.3	83.4
54. makes me feel less stressed than I did before I started.	1511	5.6	1.5	9.5	10	80.5

Section 3

What is your favorite sport to watch? _____

	N	%		N	%		N	%
Drag racing	5	0.3	Rodeo	2	0.1	Body building	1	0.1
Sports car racing	40	2.6	Skiing	2	0.1	Rugby	1	0.1
Baseball—college	87	5.7	Soccer—professional	21	1.4	Boating	1	0.1
Baseball—professional	59	3.9	Tennis	23	1.5	College soccer	2	0.1
Basketball—college	155	10.2	Track & field	1	0.1	Horse jumping	1	0.1
Basketball—professional	64	4.2	Truck pulling	2	0.1	Motorcycle racing	2	0.1
Bowling	13	0.9	Volleyball (hard surface)	5	0.3	Lacrosse	1	0.1
Boxing	13	0.9	Volleyball (sand)	1	0.1	Diving	1	0.1
Football—college	524	34.4	Wrestling—pro	4	0.3	Triathlon	1	0.1
Football—professional	272	17.8	Softball	1	0.1	Bike racing	1	0.1
Fishing	2	0.1	Martial arts	1	0.1	Combinations	99	4.7
Golf	65	4.3	Gymnastics	6	0.4			

	N	%		N	%		N	%
Horse racing	4	0.3	Biking	1	0.1			
Ice hockey	52	3.4	Swimming	1	0.1			
Ice skating	14	0.9	Field hockey	1	0.1			

Below are some statements about how people feel about watching their favorite sport. Think only about the favorite sport you indicated above. Please read each statement, then circle the appropriate number printed below to indicate your agreement or disagreement with the statements.

	N	Mean	S.D.	Percent Disagree	Percent Neutral	Percent Agree
56. If my favorite team/athlete performs poorly, I feel tense.	1595	4.5	1.9	30.1	13.8	56.1
57. The success of my favorite team/athlete is important to me.	1593	5.0	1.7	18.6	13.5	67.9
58. I feel elated for hours after a victory by my favorite team/athlete.	1595	4.7	1.8	25	17.7	57.3
59. Watching my favorite sport helps me develop a competitive ethic.	1588	4.1	1.8	33.7	22.5	43.8
60. The main reason I watch my favorite sport is for the competition.	1595	4.4	1.8	30.7	17.8	51.5
61. The more intense the rivalry, the more I enjoy watching my favorite sport.	1595	5.4	1.7	14.9	10	75.2
62. I enjoy watching my favorite sport because it gives me a chance to meet new people.	1591	2.8	1.7	68.4	16.6	15
63. Watching my favorite sport with a group leads to improved social relationships.	1591	3.8	1.8	42.9	19.9	37.2
64. Watching my favorite sport gives me a chance to spend time with my friends.	1593	4.2	1.9	33.3	19.8	46.8
65. My enjoyment of watching my favorite sport is based on having other people to share the experience with.	1591	3.5	1.9	51.1	16.5	32.4
66. My enjoyment of my favorite sport is enhanced knowing the high degree of skill required by the players to attain positive results.	1592	5.4	1.5	11.7	10.9	77.4
67. I enjoy watching a highly skilled player perform.	1594	6.2	1.1	3.5	3.3	93.2
68. I enjoy watching my favorite sport because it is a difficult sport to master.	1594	5.2	1.6	13.7	16.9	69.4
69. I enjoy watching my favorite sport because it involves a good deal of risk to the athletes.	1597	3.2	1.9	57.7	16.2	26.1
70. My favorite sport is exciting because the athletes are always in danger of being injured.	1597	2.6	1.9	72.4	10.1	17.4
71. Part of the fun of watching my favorite sport is the danger involved to the athletes.	1589	2.3	1.7	79	9.4	11.5
72. I feel connected to the people with whom I watch my favorite sport.	1595	3.8	1.8	40	23.4	36.6
73. Watching my favorite sport makes me feel like I belong to a special group.	1596	3.2	1.8	56.2	19.5	24.2

	N	Mean	S.D.	Percent		
				Disagree	Neutral	Agree
74. There is a certain comaraderie among the people I watch my favorite sport with.	1590	4.1	1.8	33.8	19.9	46.3
75. My favorite sport can be a beautiful sport to watch.	1589	5.1	1.7	15.9	15.7	68.3
76. I enjoy watching the artistry of my favorite sport.	1592	5.2	1.6	14.9	15	70.1
77. My favorite sport should be considered an art form.	1590	3.6	2.0	48.2	19.9	31.8
78. Watching my favorite sport can bring out my aggressive nature.	1592	3.9	2.0	39.8	16.2	44
79. I enjoy watching my favorite sport when it reflects an aggressive style.	1593	4.1	1.9	36.4	15.6	48
80. I am free to express my aggressive feelings while watching my favorite sport.	1592	4.0	2.0	38.5	18.5	43
81. Watching my favorite sport can help me develop values that will help me in life.	1595	3.2	1.7	56.2	22.4	21.3
82. Watching my favorite sport has helped teach me the value of hard work and dedication.	1597	4.1	1.9	36.8	18.7	44.6
83. Watching my favorite sport teaches me lessons that I may not learn anywhere else.	1596	3.2	1.8	54.7	22.3	23

Below are some statements about how people feel about watching their favorite sport. Read each statement, then circle the appropriate number printed below to indicate your agreement or disagreement with the statements. Each statement begins with the phrase "being a spectator of my favorite sport . . . ."

Being a spectator of my favorite sport . . .	N	Mean	S.D.	Percent		
				Disagree	Neutral	Agree
84. makes me feel that I am a successful person.	1597	2.5	1.6	71.4	17.4	11.2
85. gives me a feeling of self-assurance.	1594	2.7	1.6	68.9	17	14.1
86. increases my feelings of personal pride.	1594	3.2	1.8	55.8	18.4	25.8
87. helps me to develop and grow as a person.	1597	2.8	1.6	66.5	18.7	14.8
88. helps me to accomplish things I never thought I could accomplish.	1593	2.3	1.5	78.0	14.2	7.8
89. helps me to reach my potential as an individual.	1592	2.4	1.5	75.9	13.8	10.2
90. is an excellent remedy for me if I am tense, irritable, and anxious.	1589	4.3	1.8	31.3	20.5	48.3
91. helps me to get away from daily pressures.	1590	4.9	1.7	19.2	15.2	65.6
92. makes me feel less stressed than I did before I watched.	1590	4.4	1.8	28.1	22.1	49.7

Section 4

In general, how would you classify your interest in sports? _____

	Percent					
	Very low	Somewhat low	Medium	Somewhat high	Very high	Don't know
93. As a participant?	13.1	11.5	27.0	22.2	24.5	0.6
94. As a spectator?	2.6	5.1	19.8	31.7	40.5	0.3

How important are the following reasons to you for participating in/being a spectator of sport? _____

As a participant?	N	Mean	S.D.	Percent		
				Disagree	Neutral	Agree
95. Enjoyment of the game	1518	5.8	1.6	9.0	6.9	84.2
96. Sport competition	1513	4.9	1.8	19.5	17.7	62.8
97. Time spent with close friends/family	1510	4.8	1.7	19.0	18.9	62.1
98. Release of tension/relaxation	1514	5.2	1.7	13.8	13.6	72.6
99. Sense of accomplishment	1512	5.0	1.8	18.5	12.8	68.7
100. Skill mastery	1512	5.0	1.8	17	14.3	68.7
101. Sense of being a member of a group	1513	4.3	1.8	31.1	19.9	49
102. Enjoyment of the beauty of the game	1505	4.8	1.8	21.1	16.8	62.1
103. Thrill of victory	1512	5.3	1.8	14.6	12.7	72.7
104. Improved fitness/health	1509	5.1	1.8	16.4	15	68.6
105. Other people's respect for my athletic skill	1592	4.2	1.9	32.0	18.0	50.1
106. Release of aggression	1503	4.1	1.9	35.5	19.0	45.4
107. Enjoyment of risk-taking	1502	3.1	1.8	57.7	18.6	23.7
108. Helps me grow as a person	1508	3.9	1.8	38.1	22.4	39.5
109. Helps me develop positive values	1507	4.2	1.8	30.9	20.1	49
110. Sense of personal pride	1513	5.1	1.8	15.9	12.9	71.2

As a spectator?	N	Mean	S.D.	Percent		
				Disagree	Neutral	Agree
111. Enjoyment of the game	1524	6.0	1.2	3.3	9.0	87.7
112. Sport competition	1515	5.4	1.5	9.0	14.6	76.4
113. Time spent with close friends/family	1510	4.5	1.7	24.4	23.0	52.6
114. Release of tension/relaxation	1509	4.6	1.7	21.2	22.4	56.4
115. Sense of accomplishment	1506	3.3	1.7	51.5	25.4	23.0
116. Skill mastery	1507	3.9	1.9	40.4	22.6	37.0
117. Sense of being a member of a group	1508	3.5	1.8	46.7	23.5	29.8
118. Enjoyment of the beauty of the game	1508	5.0	1.8	18.0	16.8	65.2
119. Thrill of victory	1504	5.5	1.6	10.2	12.0	77.8
120. Improved fitness/health	1591	2.8	1.8	64.6	17.6	17.8
121. Other people's respect for my athletic skill	1569	2.7	1.8	64.9	19.5	15.6
122. Release of aggression	1598	3.3	1.9	52.4	21.0	26.6
123. Enjoyment of risk-taking	1592	2.7	1.8	66.2	17.3	16.6
124. Helps me grow as a person	1500	2.8	1.7	63.8	20.9	15.3
125. Helps me develop positive values	1501	3.2	1.8	54.8	21.5	23.7
126. Sense of personal pride	1505	3.5	2.0	47.0	19.3	33.7

Section 5: Survey Demographics

	Percent		Percent
127. Gender (*n* = 1588)		133. Household income? (*n* = 1528)	
Male	75.3	Under $20,000	6.9
Female	24.7	$20,000–$29,999	12.6
128. Zip code?		$30,000–$39,999	16.4
129. [+4]		$40,000–$49,999	17.6
130. Educational level? (*n* = 1585)		$50,000–$59,999	12.4
Did not graduate high school	3.3	$60,000–$74,999	13.7
Graduated high school	22.2	$75,000–$89,999	6.9
Attended college	29.1	$90,000 or more	13.4
Graduated college	30.7	134. Children living at home (*n* = 1418)	
Graduated graduate school	14.7	None	31.0
131. Age? (*n* = 1585)		Some	69.0
18–34	26.2	135. Marital status? (*n* = 1578)	
35–44	19.3	Single	12.4
45–54	19.0	Married/Co-habitating	80.7
55–64	16.8	Divorced/Widowed	6.8
65 +	18.7	136. Highest level of athletics? (*n* = 1592)	
132. Race? (*n* = 1567)		Never played organized athletics	10.3
Asian	1.7	Intramurals/Recreational	42.5
Black	2.7	High school athletics	55.3
Hispanic	2.0	Intercollegiate athletics	18.3
White	92.6	Semiprofessional	6.6
Other	1.0	Professional	1.5

Section 6

Below is a list of different sports and physical activities. Please indicate your level of participation in each of these sports while they are in season.

		Percent				
	N	**Every day or almost every day**	**About once or twice a week**	**About once or twice a month**	**Less than once a month**	**Never**
137. Aerobics	1579	6.1	9.1	5.3	13.9	65.7
138. Archery	1579	0.8	1.6	1.3	13.7	82.6
139. Badminton	1571	0.1	1.0	2.3	33.1	63.5
140. Baseball (hardball)	1563	2.4	5.6	5.5	28.9	57.6
141. Basketball	1565	3.3	11.2	12.7	31.5	41.3
142. Bicycle riding	1573	6.1	13.0	17.3	30.1	33.4
143. Billiards/Pool	1577	1.7	6.5	11.4	41.3	39.1
144. Board sailing	1579	0.1	0.2	0.7	3.8	95.3
145. Bowling	1575	0.8	11.8	7.5	41.6	38.3
146. Boxing	1576	0.1	0.8	1.2	4.8	93.1
147. Bungee jumping	1583	0.0	0.1	0.0	1.6	98.3
148. Canoeing/Kayaking	1580	0.0	0.6	2.5	21.7	75.2
149. Distance running	1572	2.1	3.6	2.3	11.5	80.6

		Percent				
	N	Every day or almost every day	About once or twice a week	About once or twice a month	Less than once a month	Never
150. Fishing (freshwater)	1579	1.6	6.6	12.3	34.5	45.0
151. Fishing (saltwater)	1571	0.4	2.4	4.3	24.8	68.2
152. Football (tackle)	1570	2.4	3.2	3.8	16.9	73.7
153. Football (touch)	1573	0.8	3.9	6.3	25.2	63.8
154. Golf	1579	4.4	18.6	12.0	22.9	42.1
155. Hunting	1575	2.2	5.4	5.0	16.4	71.1
156. Ice hockey	1583	0.3	1.3	1.1	5.8	91.5
157. Ice skating	1582	0.2	1.6	2.7	20.0	75.4
158. Mountain biking	1585	0.8	2.1	2.8	9.0	85.4
159. Roller skating (in-line)	1577	0.9	1.8	3.1	8.6	85.6
160. Running/Jogging	1579	6.5	8.5	6.2	22.0	56.8
161. Sailing	1581	0.3	0.6	2.2	11.8	85.1
162. Scuba diving	1582	0.1	0.2	0.8	7.5	91.4
163. Skateboarding	1584	0.1	0.0	0.4	5.1	94.4
164. Skiing (cross-country)	1580	0.5	0.9	1.8	8.6	88.2
165. Skiing (downhill)	1578	0.4	2.2	5.3	15.5	76.6
166. Snowboarding	1582	0.1	0.4	0.4	2.4	96.6
167. Soccer	1577	0.4	2.8	2.0	12.0	82.8
168. Softball	1577	2.3	12.8	8.3	29.9	46.7
169. Swimming	1577	4.8	11.7	17.1	42.3	24.0
170. Table tennis	1576	0.8	2.0	6.6	35.9	54.8
171. Tennis	1579	1.4	5.3	8.4	25.8	59.1
172. Ultimate frisbee	1575	0.1	0.9	1.5	10.9	86.7
173. Volleyball (hard surface)	1568	0.6	3.3	4.5	24.9	66.8
174. Volleyball (sand/beach)	1572	0.4	2.2	4.6	23.1	69.8
175. Water skiing	1575	0.7	1.8	4.1	19.7	73.7
176. Weight lifting	1567	6.5	9.6	4.8	12.3	66.9

For those sports/physical activities in which you have participated, please indicate the degree to which each sport is one of your favorites (1, 2 = Not a favorite; 3 = Neutral; 4, 5 = Favorite).

				Percent		
	N	Mean	S.D.	Not a favorite	Neutral	Favorite
179. Aerobics	530	3.0	1.4	38.3	26.8	34.9
180. Archery	276	2.9	1.3	42.4	26.1	31.5
181. Badminton	567	2.6	1.1	48.5	33.2	18.3
182. Baseball (hardball)	659	3.6	1.2	19.6	27.5	53.0
183. Basketball	894	3.8	1.2	15.5	23.6	60.9
184. Bicycle riding	1011	3.4	1.1	18.8	33.6	47.6
185. Billiards/Pool	919	3.2	1.1	23.7	36.5	39.8
186. Board sailing	72	2.6	1.3	47.2	26.4	26.4
187. Bowling	929	3.3	1.2	24.0	32.2	43.8
188. Boxing	112	3.0	1.4	37.5	25.9	36.6

	N	Mean	S.D.	Percent		
				Not a favorite	Neutral	Favorite
189. Bungee jumping	29	2.7	1.5	44.8	24.1	31.0
190. Canoeing/Kayaking	380	3.1	1.0	26.6	38.7	34.7
191. Distance running	298	3.0	1.2	35.9	30.2	33.9
192. Fishing (freshwater)	841	3.6	1.2	19.6	26.3	54.1
193. Fishing (saltwater)	485	3.4	1.2	25.2	26.2	48.7
194. Football (tackle)	413	3.8	1.2	16.0	23.0	61.0
195. Football (touch)	553	3.5	1.1	18.1	30.7	51.2
196. Golf	883	4.0	1.2	13.1	14.6	72.3
197. Hunting	444	3.7	1.3	20.7	19.4	59.9
198. Ice hockey	129	3.5	1.3	23.3	25.6	51.2
199. Ice skating	377	3.0	1.1	33.4	32.4	34.2
200. Mountain biking	228	3.4	1.2	20.6	34.6	44.7
201. Roller skating (in-line)	224	3.3	1.2	29.0	26.3	44.6
202. Running/Jogging	656	3.1	1.2	30.6	33.5	35.8
203. Sailing	233	3.2	1.2	26.6	30.0	43.3
204. Scuba diving	134	3.6	1.1	14.9	28.4	56.7
205. Skateboarding	86	2.4	1.1	57.0	29.1	14.0
206. Skiing (cross-country)	187	3.4	1.1	18.7	34.2	47.1
207. Skiing (downhill)	362	3.8	1.2	15.7	21.5	62.7
208. Snowboarding	55	3.3	1.4	34.5	16.4	49.1
209. Soccer	268	3.3	1.2	25.4	31.3	43.3
210. Softball	827	3.7	1.0	11.5	29.7	58.8
211. Swimming	1172	3.4	1.1	17.3	35.9	46.8
212. Table tennis	697	3.2	1.0	23.2	37.0	39.7
213. Tennis	630	3.5	1.1	20.6	30.2	49.2
214. Ultimate frisbee	208	2.9	1.1	33.7	39.4	26.9
215. Volleyball (hard surface)	519	3.4	1.1	20.0	33.1	46.8
216. Volleyball (sand/beach)	471	3.4	1.1	19.7	32.5	47.8
217. Water skiing	407	3.4	1.1	19.2	31.9	48.9
218. Weight lifting	504	3.4	1.1	22.8	29.2	48.0

Section 7

Below is a list of different sports and physical activities. Please indicate your level of spectatorship of these sports while they are in season.

	N	Percent				
		Every day or almost every day	About once or twice a week	About once or twice a month	Less than once a month	Never
221. Drag racing	1577	0.9	4.3	6.0	25.2	63.6
222. Sports car racing	1577	1.3	8.6	10.1	30.2	49.8
223. Baseball—college	1566	1.1	4.3	9.3	27.1	58.2
224. Baseball—professional	1572	13.3	24.9	20.6	21.8	19.4
225. Basketball—college	1572	8.3	28.4	18.0	17.8	27.5

		Percent				
	N	Every day or almost every day	About once or twice a week	About once or twice a month	Less than once a month	Never
226. Basketball—professional	1576	7.7	26.6	21.4	21.7	22.5
227. Bowling	1576	1.0	6.7	10.7	27.3	54.3
228. Boxing	1564	1.2	6.8	12.0	28.1	51.9
229. Football—college	1571	7.2	45.8	19.3	12.3	15.3
230. Football—professional	1577	10.1	61.0	12.4	6.7	9.8
231. Fishing	1571	1.8	6.6	10.7	23.9	57.0
232. Golf	1579	3.2	19.2	16.4	21.0	40.2
233. Horse racing	1579	1.2	2.8	6.8	30.6	58.6
234. Ice hockey	1577	1.8	11.4	13.7	23.2	49.9
235. Ice skating	1579	1.1	3.9	11.5	30.3	53.1
236. Rodeo	1581	0.8	2.4	5.3	24.1	67.4
237. Skiing	1577	0.6	2.7	8.4	32.3	56.1
238. Soccer—professional	1578	0.7	2.3	5.4	23.3	68.3
239. Tennis	1577	1.5	6.1	14.2	30.3	47.9
240. Track & field	1578	0.4	3.4	8.5	31.4	56.3
241. Truck racing/pulls	1576	0.6	2.6	4.3	14.9	77.6
242. Ultimate frisbee	1578	0.0	0.3	0.8	4.8	94.1
243. Volleyball (hard surface)	1580	0.6	1.8	5.8	23.3	68.4
244. Volleyball (sand/beach)	1571	0.6	2.6	7.8	26.4	62.6
245. Wrestling—professional	1569	0.9	2.9	4.8	14.4	77.0

For those sports/physical activities in which you have been a spectator, please indicate the degree to which each sport is one of your favorites (1, 2 = Not a favorite; 3 = Neutral; 4, 5 = Favorite).

				Percent		
	N	Mean	S.D.	Not a favorite	Neutral	Favorite
249. Drag racing	569	2.9	1.3	42.7	26.0	31.3
250. Sports car racing	778	3.1	1.2	34.6	27.8	37.7
251. Baseball—college	641	3.0	1.1	31.2	38.4	30.4
252. Baseball—professional	1234	3.6	1.2	18.6	26.0	55.3
253. Basketball—college	1110	3.9	1.1	11.5	26.4	62.1
254. Basketball—professional	1180	3.6	1.2	19.7	25.8	54.5
255. Bowling	693	3.1	1.2	34.8	29.3	35.9
256. Boxing	728	3.0	1.2	35.2	29.0	35.9
257. Football—college	1302	4.1	1.0	9.0	17.1	74.0
258. Football—professional	1387	4.4	1.0	5.7	10.4	83.9
259. Fishing	650	3.4	1.2	25.5	29.4	45.1
260. Golf	911	3.7	1.2	19.2	24.0	56.8
261. Horse racing	640	2.8	1.0	38.4	39.5	22.0
262. Ice hockey	763	3.3	1.2	25.8	32.8	41.4
263. Ice skating	719	3.1	1.2	35.2	29.1	35.7
264. Rodeo	504	2.9	1.1	35.5	37.5	27.0
265. Skiing	679	2.9	1.1	38.0	34.2	27.8
266. Soccer—professional	490	2.8	1.2	41.0	31.6	27.3

	N	Mean	S.D.	Percent		
				Not a favorite	Neutral	Favorite
267. Tennis	794	3.1	1.1	29.1	36.0	34.9
268. Track & field	677	2.9	1.0	38.3	35.3	26.4
269. Truck racing/pulls	352	3.0	1.2	37.5	29.3	33.2
270. Ultimate frisbee	90	2.5	1.0	50.0	33.3	16.7
271. Volleyball (hard surface)	492	3.1	1.1	30.7	38.4	30.9
272. Volleyball (sand/beach)	572	3.1	1.1	28.3	38.5	33.2
273. Wrestling—professional	352	2.7	1.2	48.6	29.8	21.6

SERVQUAL Survey

Expectations Section

Directions.

Based on your experiences as a customer of XYZ services, please think about the kind of XYZ company that would deliver excellent quality of service. Think about the kind of XYZ company with which you would be pleased to do business. Please show the extent to which you think such an XYZ company would possess the feature described by each statement. If you feel a feature is not at all essential for excellent XYZ companies such as the one you have in mind, circle the number 1. If you feel a feature is absolutely essential for excellent XYZ companies, circle 7. If your feelings are less strong, circle one of the numbers in the middle. There are no right or wrong answers—all we are interested in is a number that truly reflects your feelings regarding XYZ companies that would deliver an excellent quality of service.

	Strongly disagree					Strongly agree
1. Excellent XYZ companies will have modern-looking equipment.	1	2	3	4	5	6	7
2. The physical facilities at excellent XYZ companies will be visually appealing.	1	2	3	4	5	6	7
3. Employees of excellent XYZ companies will be neat-appearing.	1	2	3	4	5	6	7
4. Materials associated with the service (such as pamphlets or statements) will be visually appealing in an excellent XYZ company.	1	2	3	4	5	6	7
5. When excellent XYZ companies promise to do something by a certain time, they will do so.	1	2	3	4	5	6	7
6. When customers have a problem, excellent XYZ companies will show a sincere interest in solving it.	1	2	3	4	5	6	7
7. Excellent XYZ companies will perform the service right the first time.	1	2	3	4	5	6	7
8. Excellent XYZ companies will provide their services at the time they promise to do so.	1	2	3	4	5	6	7
9. Excellent XYZ companies will insist on error-free records.	1	2	3	4	5	6	7
10. Employees of excellent XYZ companies will tell customers exactly when services will be performed.	1	2	3	4	5	6	7
11. Employees of excellent XYZ companies will give prompt service to customers.	1	2	3	4	5	6	7
12. Employees of excellent XYZ companies will always be willing to help customers.	1	2	3	4	5	6	7
13. Employees of excellent XYZ companies will never be too busy to respond to customer requests.	1	2	3	4	5	6	7
14. The behavior of employees of excellent XYZ companies will instill confidence in customers.	1	2	3	4	5	6	7
15. Customers of excellent XYZ companies will feel safe in their transactions.	1	2	3	4	5	6	7
16. Employees of excellent XYZ companies will be consistently courteous with customers.	1	2	3	4	5	6	7

	Strongly disagree				Strongly agree		
17. Employees of excellent XYZ companies will have the knowledge to answer customer questions.	1	2	3	4	5	6	7
18. Excellent XYZ companies will give customers individual attention.	1	2	3	4	5	6	7
19. Excellent XYZ companies will have operating hours convenient to all their customers.	1	2	3	4	5	6	7
20. Excellent XYZ companies will have employees who give customers personal attention.	1	2	3	4	5	6	7
21. Excellent XYZ companies will have the customers' best interests at heart.	1	2	3	4	5	6	7
22. The employees of excellent XYZ companies will understand the specific needs of their customers.	1	2	3	4	5	6	7

Perceptions Section

Directions.

The following set of statements relate to your feelings about XYZ Telephone Company's repair service. For each statement, please show the extent to which you believe XYZ has the feature described by the statement. Once again, circling a 1 means that you strongly disagree that XYZ has that feature and circling a 7 means that you strongly agree. You may circle any of the numbers in the middle that show how strong your feelings are. There are no right or wrong answers—all we are interested in is a number that best shows your perceptions about XYZ's repair service.

	Strongly disagree				Strongly agree		
1. XYZ has modern-looking equipment.	1	2	3	4	5	6	7
2. XYZ's physical facilities are visually appealing.	1	2	3	4	5	6	7
3. XYZ's employees are neat-appearing.	1	2	3	4	5	6	7
4. Materials associated with the service (such as pamphlets or statements) are visually appealing at XYZ.	1	2	3	4	5	6	7
5. When XYZ promises to do something by a certain time, it does so.	1	2	3	4	5	6	7
6. When you have a problem, XYZ shows a sincere interest in solving it.	1	2	3	4	5	6	7
7. XYZ performs the service right the first time.	1	2	3	4	5	6	7
8. XYZ provides its services at the time it promises to do so.	1	2	3	4	5	6	7
9. XYZ insists on error-free records.	1	2	3	4	5	6	7
10. Employees of XYZ tell you exactly when services will be performed.	1	2	3	4	5	6	7
11. Employees of XYZ give you prompt service.	1	2	3	4	5	6	7
12. Employees of XYZ are always willing to help you.	1	2	3	4	5	6	7
13. Employees of XYZ are never too busy to respond to your requests.	1	2	3	4	5	6	7
14. The behavior of employees of XYZ instills confidence in customers.	1	2	3	4	5	6	7
15. You feel safe in your transactions with XYZ.	1	2	3	4	5	6	7
16. Employees of XYZ are consistently courteous with you.	1	2	3	4	5	6	7
17. Employees of XYZ have the knowledge to answer your questions.	1	2	3	4	5	6	7
18. XYZ gives you individual attention.	1	2	3	4	5	6	7
19. XYZ has operating hours convenient to all its customers.	1	2	3	4	5	6	7
20. XYZ has employees who give you personal attention.	1	2	3	4	5	6	7
21. XYZ has your best interests at heart.	1	2	3	4	5	6	7
22. Employees of XYZ understand your specific needs.	1	2	3	4	5	6	7

Point-Allocation Question

Directions.

Listed below are five features pertaining to telephone companies and the repair services they offer. We would like to know how important each of these features is to you when you evaluate a telephone company's quality of repair service. Please allocate a total of 100 points among the five features according to how important each feature is to you—the more important a feature is to you, the more points you should allocate to it. Please ensure that the points you allocate to the five features add up to 100.

1. The appearance of the telephone company's physical facilities, equipment, personnel, and communications materials.

   _____ points

2. The ability of the telephone company to perform the promised service dependably and accurately.

   _____ points

3. The willingness of the telephone company to help customers and provide prompt service.

   _____ points

4. The knowledge and courtesy of the telephone company's employees and their ability to convey trust and confidence.

   _____ points

5. The caring, individualized attention the telephone company provides its customers.

   _____ points

   TOTAL POINTS ALLOCATED   100 points

Adapted SERVQUAL Instrument

Directions.

Based on your experiences as a customer of professional sport team services, please think about the kind of pro sport franchise that would deliver excellent quality of service. Think about the kind of pro sport franchise with which you would be pleased to do business. Please show the extent to which you think such a pro sport franchise would possess the feature described by each statement. If you feel a feature is not at all essential for excellent pro sport franchises such as the one you have in mind, circle the number 1. If you feel a feature is absolutely essential for excellent pro sport franchises, circle 7. If your feelings are less strong, circle one of the numbers in the middle. There are no right or wrong answers—all we are interested in is a number that truly reflects your feelings regarding pro sport franchises that would deliver an excellent quality of service.

	Mean	Std. dev.
1. Excellent pro sport arenas will have modern-looking equipment.	5.97	1.20
2. The physical facilities at excellent pro sport arenas will be visually appealing.	6.04	1.11
3. Employees of excellent pro sport franchises will be neat in appearance.	6.22	1.00
4. Materials associated with the service (such as pamphlets or statements) will be visually appealing in an excellent pro sport franchise.	5.84	1.20
5. When excellent pro sport franchises promise to do something by a certain time, they will do so.	6.48	0.89
6. When customers have a problem, excellent pro sport franchises will show a sincere interest in solving it.	6.57	0.83
7. Excellent pro sport franchises will perform the service right the first time.	6.30	0.91

	Mean	Std. dev.
8. Excellent pro sport franchises will provide their services at the time they promise to do so.	6.49	0.79
9. Excellent pro sport franchises will insist on error-free records.	6.17	1.05
10. Employees of excellent pro sport franchises will tell customers exactly when services will be performed.	6.29	0.94
11. Employees of excellent pro sport franchises will give prompt service to customers.	6.46	0.81
12. Ticket ushers of excellent pro sport franchises will give prompt service to customers.	6.38	0.88
13. Concessions personnel of excellent pro sport franchises will give prompt service to customers.	6.32	0.93
14. Merchandise salespersons of excellent pro sport franchises will give prompt service to customers.	6.22	1.03
15. Employees of excellent pro sport franchises will always be willing to help customers.	6.48	0.84
16. Employees of excellent pro sport franchises will never be too busy to respond to customer requests.	6.30	0.96
17. Ticket ushers of excellent pro sport franchises will never be too busy to respond to customer requests.	6.26	0.97
18. The behavior of employees of excellent pro sport franchises will instill confidence in customers.	6.18	1.03
19. Customers of excellent pro sport franchises will feel safe in their transactions.	6.41	0.92
20. Customers of excellent pro sport franchises will feel safe in the arena while attending games.	6.60	0.80
21. Customers of excellent pro sport franchises will feel safe when traveling to and from games.	6.31	1.08
22. Employees of excellent pro sport franchises will be consistently courteous with customers.	6.48	0.83
23. Ticket ushers of excellent pro sport franchises will be consistently courteous with customers.	6.44	0.87
24. Concessions personnel of excellent pro sport franchises will be consistently courteous with customers.	6.39	0.93
25. Merchandise salespersons of excellent pro sport franchises will be consistently courteous with customers.	6.34	1.00
26. Merchandise salespersons of excellent pro sport franchises will be knowledgeable about various product lines and product utilization.	6.14	1.04
27. Employees of excellent pro sport franchises will have the knowledge to answer customer questions.	6.27	0.92
28. Ticket ushers of excellent pro sport franchises will have the knowledge to answer customer questions.	6.13	1.06
29. Excellent pro sport franchises will give customers individual attention.	6.04	1.13
30. Excellent pro sport franchises will have operating hours convenient to all their customers.	6.15	1.00
31. Excellent pro sport franchises will have employees who give customers personal attention.	6.15	1.05
32. Excellent pro sport franchises will have the customers' best interests at heart.	6.38	0.99
33. The employees of excellent pro sport franchises will understand the specific needs of their customers.	6.20	0.97
34. Ticket ushers of excellent pro sport franchises will understand the specific needs of their customers.	6.07	1.09
35. Excellent pro sport franchises will provide customers with convenient parking at their arenas.	6.40	0.94
36. The employees of excellent pro sport franchises will have good telephone manners.	6.43	0.88
37. The invoicing and billing services of excellent pro sport franchises will be performed correctly the first time.	6.46	0.82
38. Financial transactions with excellent pro sport franchises will be carried out in an efficient and courteous manner.	6.49	0.82
39. Excellent pro sport franchise payment plans will be flexible enough to meet the needs of its customers.	6.38	0.95
40. Financial records of excellent pro sport franchises will be accurate and up-to-date.	6.47	0.88

Directions.

The following set of statements relate to your feelings about the Orlando Magic's service. For each statement, please show the extent to which you believe the Magic has the feature described by the statement. Once again, indicate your level of agreement (1 = strongly disagree to 7 = strongly agree).

	Mean	Std. dev.
1. Orlando Arena has modern-looking equipment.	6.20	0.95
2. The Orlando Arena's physical facilities are visually appealing.	6.30	0.90
3. The Orlando Magic's employees are neat in appearance.	6.14	0.93
4. Materials associated with the service (such as pamphlets or statements) are visually appealing at the Orlando Magic.	5.97	1.03
5. When the Orlando Magic promises to do something by a certain time, it will do so.	5.88	1.08
6. When you have a problem, the Orlando Magic shows a sincere interest in solving it.	5.79	1.27
7. The Orlando Magic performs the service right the first time.	5.81	1.15
8. The Orlando Magic provides its services at the time it promises to do so.	5.92	1.07
9. The Orlando Magic insists on error-free records.	5.91	1.16
10. Employees of the Orlando Magic tell you exactly when services will be performed.	5.75	1.15
11. Employees of the Orlando Magic give you prompt service.	5.93	1.07
12. Ticket ushers of the Orlando Magic give you prompt service.	5.93	1.16
13. Concessions personnel of the Orlando Magic give you prompt service.	5.47	1.41
14. Merchandise salespersons of the Orlando Magic give you prompt service.	5.70	1.18
15. Employees of the Orlando Magic are always willing to help you.	5.80	1.21
16. Employees of the Orlando Magic are never too busy to respond to your requests.	5.58	1.29
17. Ticket ushers of the Orlando Magic are never too busy to respond to your requests.	5.77	1.20
18. The behavior of employees of the Orlando Magic instills confidence in customers.	5.85	1.09
19. You feel safe in your transactions with the Orlando Magic.	6.17	0.94
20. You feel safe in the arena while attending Orlando Magic games.	6.13	1.08
21. You feel safe traveling to and from Orlando Magic games.	5.37	1.37
22. Employees of the Orlando Magic are consistently courteous with you.	5.95	1.10
23. Ticket ushers of the Orlando Magic are consistently courteous with you.	5.92	1.21
24. Concessions personnel of the Orlando Magic are consistently courteous with you.	5.59	1.26
25. Merchandise salespersons of the Orlando Magic are consistently courteous with you.	5.77	1.13
26. Merchandise salespersons of the Orlando Magic are knowledgeable about various product lines and product utilization.	5.68	1.18
27. Employees of the Orlando Magic have the knowledge to answer your questions.	5.82	1.03
28. Ticket ushers of the Orlando Magic have the knowledge to answer your questions.	5.78	1.19
29. The Orlando Magic gives you individual attention.	5.38	1.43
30. The Orlando Magic has operating hours convenient to all its customers.	5.55	1.24
31. The Orlando Magic has employees who give you personal attention.	5.44	1.41
32. The Orlando Magic has your best interests at heart.	5.09	1.60
33. Employees of the Orlando Magic understand your specific needs.	5.29	1.38
34. Ticket ushers of the Orlando Magic understand your specific needs.	5.45	1.33
35. The Orlando Magic provides you with convenient parking at its arena.	5.02	1.71
36. Employees of the Orlando Magic have good telephone manners.	5.91	1.08
37. Orlando Magic invoicing and billing services are performed correctly the first time.	6.13	1.02
38. Financial transactions with the Orlando Magic are carried out in an efficient and courteous manner.	6.12	1.02
39. Orlando Magic payment plans are flexible enough to meet your needs.	5.22	1.72
40. Financial records of the Orlando Magic are accurate and up-to-date.	6.04	1.10

Service Quality Gap Scores Table

This table presents the gap scores for each of the forty questions on the Adapted SERVQUAL Survey. Gap scores are calculated by taking the difference between the score on the preceptions questions and the expectation question.

	Mean	Std. dev.
Gap 1 = Expectations 1 − Perceptions 1	−0.21	1.26
Gap 2 = Expectations 2 − Perceptions 2	−0.25	1.14
Gap 3 = Expectations 3 − Perceptions 3	0.10	1.04
Gap 4 = Expectations 4 − Perceptions 4	−0.11	1.15
Gap 5 = Expectations 5 − Perceptions 5	0.63	1.12
Gap 6 = Expectations 6 − Perceptions 6	0.78	1.31
Gap 7 = Expectations 7 − Perceptions 7	0.49	1.17
Gap 8 = Expectations 8 − Perceptions 8	0.59	1.04
Gap 9 = Expectations 9 − Perceptions 9	0.29	1.14
Gap 10 = Expectations 10 − Perceptions 10	0.54	1.12
Gap 11 = Expectations 11 − Perceptions 11	0.55	1.06
Gap 12 = Expectations 12 − Perceptions 12	0.46	1.14
Gap 13 = Expectations 13 − Perceptions 13	0.87	1.45
Gap 14 = Expectations 14 − Perceptions 14	0.57	1.21
Gap 15 = Expectations 15 − Perceptions 15	0.69	1.22
Gap 16 = Expectations 16 − Perceptions 16	0.74	1.43
Gap 17 = Expectations 17 − Perceptions 17	0.52	1.26
Gap 18 = Expectations 18 − Perceptions 18	0.34	1.16
Gap 19 = Expectations 19 − Perceptions 19	0.25	1.00
Gap 20 = Expectations 20 − Perceptions 20	0.49	1.10
Gap 21 = Expectations 21 − Perceptions 21	0.95	1.57
Gap 22 = Expectations 22 − Perceptions 22	0.53	1.04
Gap 23 = Expectations 23 − Perceptions 23	0.54	1.21
Gap 24 = Expectations 24 − Perceptions 24	0.81	1.29
Gap 25 = Expectations 25 − Perceptions 25	0.57	1.10
Gap 26 = Expectations 26 − Perceptions 26	0.46	1.14
Gap 27 = Expectations 27 − Perceptions 27	0.45	1.05
Gap 28 = Expectations 28 − Perceptions 28	0.34	1.23
Gap 29 = Expectations 29 − Perceptions 29	0.65	1.45
Gap 30 = Expectations 30 − Perceptions 30	0.58	1.29
Gap 31 = Expectations 31 − Perceptions 31	0.68	1.40
Gap 32 = Expectations 32 − Perceptions 32	1.28	1.60
Gap 33 = Expectations 33 − Perceptions 33	0.89	1.39
Gap 34 = Expectations 34 − Perceptions 34	0.59	1.31
Gap 35 = Expectations 35 − Perceptions 35	1.38	1.81
Gap 36 = Expectations 36 − Perceptions 36	0.51	1.05
Gap 37 = Expectations 37 − Perceptions 37	0.33	1.01
Gap 38 = Expectations 38 − Perceptions 38	0.36	0.94
Gap 39 = Expectations 39 − Perceptions 39	1.15	1.79
Gap 40 = Expectations 40 − Perceptions 40	0.44	1.02

Index

Note: Page numbers followed by f indicate figures; those followed by t indicate tables.